Tony Chapman

Mental Health Law

MAJOR ISSUES

Perspectives in

Law &
Psychology

Series Editor: **BRUCE DENNIS SALES,** *University of Nebraska, Lincoln*

Mental Health Law

MAJOR ISSUES

David B. Wexler

University of Arizona
Tucson, Arizona

PLENUM PRESS · NEW YORK AND LONDON

Library of Congress Cataloging in Publication Data

Wexler, David B
  Mental health law.

  (Perspectives in law and psychology; v. 4)
  Includes index.
  1. Mental health laws—United States. 2. Insane—Commitment and de-
tention—United States. I. Title. II. Series.
KF3828.W49   344.73′044   80-20523
ISBN 0-306-40538-5

© 1981 Plenum Press, New York
A Division of Plenum Publishing Corporation
227 West 17th Street, New York, N.Y. 10011

Printed in the United States of America

For Brenda

Acknowledgments

The following works of mine have, in some form or another, found their way into the present volume, and I am grateful to have been able to draw on them: "The Administration of Psychiatric Justice: Theory and Practice in Arizona," 13 *Arizona Law Review* 1 (1971) (with S. Scoville *et al.*); "Therapeutic Justice," 57 *Minnesota Law Review* 289 (1972); "A Definite Maybe: Proof and Probability in Civil Commitment," 2 *Law and Human Behavior* 37 (1978) (with J. Monahan); *Criminal Commitments and Dangerous Mental Patients* (G.P.O., 1976); "Criminal Commitment Contingency Structures," in B. Sales (Ed.), *Perspectives in Law and Psychology, Vol. 1: The Criminal Justice System* 121 (Plenum, 1977); "Foreword: Current Currents in Institutionalization," 14 *San Diego Law Review* 979 (1977); "Patients, Therapists, and Third Parties: The Victimological Virtues of *Tarasoff*," 2 *International Journal of Law and Psychiatry* 1 (1979); "Book Review," 85 *Harvard Law Review* 1489 (1972); "Mental Health Law and the Movement Toward Voluntary Treatment," 62 *California Law Review* 671 (1974); "Of Rights and Reinforcers," 11 *San Diego Law Review* 957 (1974); "Token and Taboo: Behavior Modification, Token Economies, and the Law," 61 *California Law Review* 81 (1973); "Behavior Modification and Other Behavior Change Procedures: The Emerging Law and the Proposed Florida Guidelines," 11 *Criminal Law Bulletin* 600 (1975). The publications were copyrighted, in the years specified, by the law reviews (or their respective law review associations) and are used here with permission.

For seeing this book to fruition, I owe thanks to a number of persons. Thanks are due first to my wife, Brenda, to whom the book is dedicated, and to Nancy and Douglas, my children, for the feat, I am repeatedly reminded, of simply living with me. My mother has been a motivating influence by persistently pushing for a hardbound book, rather than a collection of untidy reprints, to grace her coffee table. On a more substantive level, I am grateful to Jeffrie Murphy, of the Department of Philosophy, University of Arizona (who contributed greatly by suggesting a format for the book), to Roy Spece, of the University of Arizona law faculty, Bruce Winick, of the University of Miami Law School, and Saleem Shah of the National Institute of Mental Health, for serving as substantive sounding boards, and to Bruce Dennis Sales, of the University of Nebraska, for serving as a superb editor and for guiding me through each and every step of the process. Terry Dalke, Lawrence Raifman, and Robin Perin, law students at the University of Arizona, have provided important research assistance, and Rosemary Emery, formerly of the law school staff, has performed invaluable administrative and secretarial tasks.

Finally, perhaps not surprisingly, given the average tenure of deans in modern legal education, my thinking relating to the development of this work occurred over a period during which three persons served as dean of the University of Arizona College of Law: Charles E. Ares, Joseph M. Livermore, and Roger C. Henderson. I am indebted to each of them.

Chuck Ares hired me, gave up the Law and Psychiatry Seminar so that I might try my hand at it, and encouraged my early efforts at legal scholarship. Joe Livermore, whose substantive interests are rather close to mine, has been a constant source of intellectual stimulation. (When I reach the point of intellectual satiation, which I am able to do with remarkable rapidity, he is also a ready source of unmatched wit.) Roger Henderson has worked to create a genuine, and very helpful, atmosphere of scholarship at the College of Law. He has also taken the step of explicitly tying merit salary increases to scholarly productivity. As much as anything, this book is a test of his good word.

DAVID B. WEXLER

Contents

1

Introduction

THE CORE OF MENTAL HEALTH LAW

A musty file in Arizona's Greenlee County Courthouse reveals that on January 22, 1912, shortly before Arizona became a state, a 19-year-old Mexican-American woman residing in Morenci was taken into custody and placed in the county jail by a deputy sheriff who, that same day, filed with the Greenlee County Probate Court the following commitment petition:

> Have known girl about one year. Last summer—July or Aug. 1911— commenced to act irrational. Has been under treatment of physicians past 4 months. They called me this A.M. and told me they were unable to treat her successfully—that she is crazy and I must arrest her.

The proposed patient was apparently examined the next day by two physicians, who duly completed the required medical questionnaire. In addition to mentioning that the patient's physical health was good, that she was "cleanly" in her personal habits, that she did not use liquor, tobacco, or drugs, and that neither she nor any of her relatives had ever been mentally ill or hospitalized in the past, the doctors listed the following information on those portions of the form devoted to mental illness and dangerousness:

> Dangerousness:
> No threats or attempts to commit suicide or murder. Is of a very happy temperament. Has a tendency to laugh and sing.
> Facts indicating insanity:
> She wanted to dance. Most of conversation was fairly rational.
> Appearance and Activity of patient:
> Was in constant motion. Could not sit or stand still. Laughs at anything said or done.

1

Other facts:
The patient formerly was very quiet and retiring. Is now very voluble and
will talk with anyone.

Diagnosing her mental problems as being supposedly caused by
"bathing in cold water at menstrual period" and as probably being "only
temporary" in nature, the physicians nevertheless concluded that in
their judgment, "the accused is insane, and it is dangerous to the accused and to the person and property of others by reason of such insanity that the accused go at large." On January 23, 1912, after a judicial
hearing, the probate judge signed an order committing the patient to the
"Territorial Asylum for the Insane, at Phoenix, Arizona, until sufficiently restored to reason, or otherwise discharged according to law."

But the 1912 commitment order does not complete the court file. It is
followed by another order, requested by the hospital, permitting the
institution to apply some of the patient's personal funds to pay the
maintenance cost of her involuntary confinement. That order, however,
was dated May 26, 1969. An investigation conducted during the 1970-71
academic year by the author and his students confirmed the frightening
fact that the patient, then 78 years of age, was, at least as of 1971, still a
resident at the hospital, the great bulk of her life reflected well by two
drab documents resting back-to-back in a court file.

As stories such as this one began to accumulate, mental health law
rather abruptly burst into its own as an area of scholarly inquiry and of
practical concern. Give or take a year or two, the birth of mental health
law as a discrete discipline probably occurred about 1970. Thus, the
Mental Health Law Project, a public interest law firm that has been
involved in much of the principal litigation in the field, was formed in
1972, and individual attorneys who organized the Project had, by then,
already been toiling in the area. Other organizations interested in law
and psychology or law and psychiatry—the American Psychology–Law
Society, the American Academy of Psychiatry and Law, the Law and
Psychiatry Section of the Association of American Law Schools—also
sprang up in the late 1960s or early 1970s.

In any event, since its conception, interest in the field has been
unflagging and scholarship has flourished. Moreover, mental health law
is fully multidisciplinary. It is of interest to—and has been contributed to
by—scholars and professionals in the fields of law, psychology,
psychiatry, sociology, philosophy, criminal justice, and other related
fields. Indeed, the present volume refers generously, as it must, to
works in each of the above fields, and is addressed to students, researchers, and practitioners in those disciplines.

This book should serve several functions for those audiences. First, it is hoped that, as a scholarly work, it will encourage thought and research in this important field. Second, as a quasi-treatise, it can provide professionals with an appreciation of the complexity of the issues that many of them must confront on a daily basis. Third, as a text, it should serve to introduce graduate and undergraduate students in a number of disciplines to the basic legal problems and therapeutic and ethical dilemmas posed by the influence of law on the practice of mental health.

During the past decade, the core developments in mental health law have fallen principally into two major categories: (1) the commitment system and (2) the impact of law on therapy. This book follows that two-part organizational framework. This introductory chapter is meant to explain the workings—and interrelationships—of the book as a whole. For example, the commitment system itself contains many components and can be viewed from several different perspectives. The "ordinary" process of commitment, unconnected with a person's involvement in the criminal justice or correctional system, is "civil" commitment. On the other hand, commitment which occurs as an offshoot of one's involvement in the criminal justice system—such as a defendant committed as incompetent to stand criminal trial or committed following a "successful" invocation of the insanity defense—is known as "criminal" commitment.

The book deals with both categories of commitment, but begins with a discussion of civil commitment. Moreover, since civil commitment is, to be sure, one area of the law where practice often departs sharply from theory, the civil commitment section seeks to explore the fundamental theoretical questions before it introduces the reader to a comparison between the theoretical structure and the system in actual operation.

Chapter 2, then, will explain in detail the major theoretical problems, tensions, and value conflicts confronting a system of civil commitment. The chapter describes the gradual societal shift from a criminal justice model to a model of "therapeutic justice," the costs and benefits of such a shift, and some reasons why there has been, and continues to be, an ebb and flow in our feelings toward the often competing systems of social control. Chapter 2 will differentiate the paternalistic basis for civil commitment from the public protection ("dangerousness") basis for commitment and will thus explore the various substantive standards of committability. It will also pay considerable attention to the sorts of due process procedures that have been recommended—or opposed—for the resolving of commitment cases in court.

To provide a broad perspective, many of the major problems discussed in Chapter 2 will be examined not only in the context of mental illness, but also in the interesting comparative context of addiction. Because of its breadth, Chapter 2 serves in large part the additional function of introducing the reader to many of the issues addressed in the remainder of the volume (even to some of the law and therapy issues of Part Two). Its principal value, however, is its exploration, from a broad perspective, of the traditional substantive standards employed for civil commitment and of the procedures used in adjudicating commitment cases.

Chapter 3 then seeks to expand the reader's understanding of these standards and procedures by exploring briefly their theoretical relationship. The relationship focuses on the procedural problem of the quantum of proof (preponderance of the evidence, clear and convincing evidence, or beyond a reasonable doubt) in civil commitment. (Technically, though somewhat confusingly, the "quantum of proof" is referred to by the law as the "standard of proof," and I will accordingly use that phraseology within this book. The standard of proof is, however, a procedural matter and should not be confused with substantive standards of commitment, i.e., the commitment criteria.) Chapter 3 will make the point that, in theory at least, the procedural "proof" problem should not be resolved in isolation from a jurisdiction's governing "substantive standard" of commitment. Yet, in *Addington* v. *Texas*,[1] the Supreme Court resolved the required standard of proof—it settled on the "clear and convincing" standard—in clear isolation from the substantive standard of commitment. The chapter closes by suggesting certain practical reasons, relating principally to the easy and orderly administration of justice, why the *Addington* Court took the route it did.

The practical reasons for departing from theory at the close of Chapter 3 serve well as a springboard for Chapter 4, which deals with civil commitment in practice. Against the background of the theory of civil commitment, with its concepts, terminology, standards, and procedures, that chapter will present the results of a detailed empirical examination of a state civil commitment system conducted by the author and his students, the very examination which uncovered the incident with which this chapter opened—the lifelong commitment of the "laughing lady" from Arizona.

By contrasting the theory of civil commitment with its practice, Chapter 4 should illustrate vividly why mental health law and its reform have become so important. That chapter will describe the commitment system, as it operated under a typical state system, from the stage of apprehension through the stage of judicial hearing. Close attention will be paid to the roles of attorneys and mental health professionals in the administration of therapeutic justice. Though it is clear that theory and practice are often far apart in civil commitment, there is nonetheless an interactive effect between the two: sometimes, theory bends to accommodate practice (as discussed in Chapter 3 regarding *Addington*), and sometimes the discovery of practice departing so far from theory (as in Chapter 4) leads to efforts to reform the practice by clarifying and reformulating the theory.

After this rather complete coverage of the civil commitment system, Chapter 5 proceeds to examine the system of criminal commitment. Since entry into the mental health system from the criminal justice system may occur at various points and by various mechanisms, the criminal commitment system actually contains several component systems: commitment of those who are incompetent to stand criminal trial, commitment of those who stand trial but are found not guilty by reason of insanity, commitment of those who are convicted but who need to be transferred from prison to a mental health hospital, and commitment of "special" varieties of offenders such as so-called sexual psychopaths. Chapter 5 will explain those categories and also, theoretically and strategically, why certain paths of entry are preferred, by the defendant or by the state, over other ones.

Concluding the discussion of the commitment process, Chapter 6 explores problems of civil and criminal commitment through an actual case example. The account of an actual incident provides a pedagogical stepping stone for exploring the difficulties in, and the relationship between, the civil and criminal commitment systems. The case will be set forth and the various issues and strategies raised by it (or by slight variants of it) will be rather exhaustively examined. This chapter should serve to bring the previously discussed material very much to life, should integrate much of the material, and, one hopes, should serve incidentally as a potent and painless tool for review.

After commitment, of course, the major legal issues center on the relationship between law and therapy; law–therapy issues therefore provide the foundation for the second part of the book. Actually, although the bulk of the law–therapy controversy arises in the postcommitment context, one terribly touchy issue surfaces in the treatment of outpatients, and Part Two therefore focuses first, in Chapter 7, on that problem—the so-called *Tarasoff*[2] problem. *Tarasoff* is one of the most celebrated and controversial court decisions in mental health law. The case required the therapist of an outpatient to breach confidentiality and to protect an endangered third person from the patient's potential dangerousness. *Tarasoff* has been condemned as an unwanted, and unwarranted, legal intrusion that will deal a devastating blow to therapy.

On the other hand, given the fact that a potential victim is typically a family member who may well play a role in inciting (or in calming) a patient's violent tendencies, the decision has also been applauded as one which will properly prompt mental health practitioners to move, in this area, from an *intrapsychic* to an *interpersonal* model of treating patients who utter violent threats. Though it comes down on the latter side, Chapter 7 discusses both sides of the debate and, in so doing, reviews the pertinent legal and therapeutic literature.

The remainder of Part Two deals with law–therapy issues regarding institutionalized mental patient populations. Chapter 8 discusses psychosurgery—clearly the most controversial of all the therapies. This chapter will lay the factual foundation for psychosurgery and will discuss, analyze, and criticize the conceptual underpinnings of the *Kaimowitz* case,[3] the major legal decision concerning psychosurgery. The case is an excellent vehicle for confronting the conflicting values of personal autonomy and state paternalism and for probing the underlying legal elements for informed consent: competence, knowledge, and voluntariness.

Although psychosurgery is the most dramatic of the therapies performed on institutionalized patients and, therefore, starkly raises the relevant issues, it is not at all a common procedure. Far more common is the use of behavior modification, particularly in the form of "token economies," where patients receive "reinforcers" for engaging in appropriate "target behaviors." Legal and ethical questions often arise, however, over the sorts of reinforcers sometimes used (food, beds, privacy, etc.). Chapter 9 sets forth the behavioral principles underlying token economies, reviews the literature regarding the sorts of reinforcers actually in use, and, from a legal and constitutional perspective, scrutinizes the activities of the behavior modifiers.

Because of the dangers and infringements of rights that have been documented in situations where therapists' behavior control activities are wholly unscrutinized, members of the legal and mental health professions have increasingly been brought together—as adversaries or as collaborators—to argue about or to develop protective, yet therapeutically workable, mechanisms for regulating behavior control. Many models, varying widely in scope and structure, have been and are being considered for adoption. Chapter 10, which closes the book's law–therapy portion, discusses the need for a model of regulation and explains the history, development, and content of one model proposed by the author and other members of a multidisciplinary team brought together to draft protective guidelines for institutional use after a crisis situation developed in a Florida mental retardation facility.

Finally, in Chapter 11 we look briefly toward the future. Certain "second generation" mental health law issues—principally related to deinstitutionalization and community living—are now emerging and are accordingly noted in this chapter. Principally, however, the chapter looks at changing judicial perspectives, necessary changes in the role of advocacy, and, most important for our purposes, the crucial interrelationship between the future of mental health law development and the future of multidisciplinary mental health law scholarship.[4]

NOTES

[1]99 S.Ct. 1804 (1979).

[2]17 Cal.3d 425, 551 P.2d 334, 131 Cal.Rptr. 14 (1976).

[3]Kaimowitz v. Dept. of Mental Health, Civ. No. 73-19434-AW (Cir. Ct. of Wayne County, Mich., July 10, 1973), reprinted in A. BROOKS, LAW, PSYCHIATRY AND THE MENTAL HEALTH SYSTEM 902 (1974).

[4]An excellent bibliographic source of books, articles, and cases in mental health law appears in A. BROOKS, LAW, PSYCHIATRY AND THE MENTAL HEALTH SYSTEM (Supp. 1980).

Part One
THE COMMITMENT SYSTEM

A. Civil Commitment
I. In Theory

2

Therapeutic Justice

AN OVERVIEW AND A DISCUSSION OF CIVIL COMMITMENT STANDARDS AND PROCEDURES

INTRODUCTION

The criminal justice system and related mechanisms of social and legal control are today experiencing a period of marked doctrinal and philosophical tension. Actually, the tension is not new, and the current conflict simply marks the latest phase—with a somewhat modern twist—of the tug-of-war between the "classical criminology" (a blending of Kantian retributive justice and the utilitarianism of Cesare di Beccaria and Jeremy Bentham) and the "deterministic criminology" of Enrico Ferri.

The classical scheme was postulated on a psychology of free will, from which flowed a series of consequences: that persons who willingly flout legal commands are morally blameworthy and are properly candidates for the infliction of society's retributive wrath, which should be meted out by punishments proportionate to the crimes committed, but sufficient also to serve a deterrent function.[1]

While the classical model may seem terribly wanting according to modern philosophical and behavioral perspectives, it was actually far superior to its predecessor, which was primarily a "Hobbesian, selfish, individualistic, cruel, law-and-order-oriented institution,"[2] reflecting a naked exercise of the police power through repression. Thus, according to a recent comprehensive study of the changing conceptions of criminal law, it was Beccaria who proposed certain notions now regarded as fundamental to our criminal jurisprudence: that only overt acts be

11

punishable, that crimes and sentences not be applied ex post facto, that sentences not be excessive, and that the state bear the burden of proving criminal guilt.[3]

Despite its advances, however, the classical approach was soon the subject of severe criticism. The principal objection, of course, was that classical criminology contained simply a series of mechanistically imposed penalties that ignored important distinctions among individual offenders. Developments in biology, sociology, and psychology began to chip away at the underpinnings of the free will doctrine—and a fortiori at the correlative concepts of individual responsibility and moral blameworthiness—and began to challenge head-on the classical justification of achieving deterrence in part through retributive punishment. If environmental or biological factors played important, even determinative, roles in human behavior, then it made little sense indeed to think that retribution itself could offset or correct those causal influences. Instead, advocates of a deterministic criminology, like Enrico Ferri, a law professor in late nineteenth century Italy, called for the abolition of criminal responsibility and moral guilt as essential ingredients of the criminal law, and proposed that "when an individual has been found to have committed an act harmful to society, the law should not be concerned with questions of guilt and its degrees nor with measuring a fit punishment, but should humanely apply whatever measures are necessary to protect society from further transgressions by the same individual."[4]

Ferri's influence in modern criminal law can be felt as strongly as can Beccaria's. His notion that punishment should be tailored to fit the criminal rather than the crime is reflected in large part in modern indeterminate sentence statutes; his deemphasis of criminal responsibility is reflected in the trend of expanding the insanity defense beyond its origin in the limited M'Naghten rule, together with schemes for committing for indefinite treatment those persons acquitted on grounds of insanity; finally, Ferri's concern for counterbalancing adverse environmental influences is reflected in the importance modern penology attaches, at least in theory, to considerations of rehabilitation and vocational training of offenders.

But Ferri's influence cannot be confined simply to reforms made within the criminal system itself. Indeed, an application of Ferri's model to many deviant actors suggests the sheer futility, for them, of the entire penal framework. Professor Nicholas Kittrie provides an apt example:

> [T]he severity of the crime provides no meaningful measure for the time or methods required to deal with a particular offender. The conduct of an alcoholic charged with disturbing the peace is not extremely offensive and,

consequently, the penalties prescribed for him are not severe. Yet, the reformation of a chronic alcoholic may require more time and facilities than the rehabilitation of the one-time passion murderer whose conduct (arousing a greater urge for social condemnation) traditionally results in more severe criminal sanctions. As long as the emphasis was upon the retributive punishment of the offender and the deterrence of others, a punishment fitting the crime was logically sound. Once the emphasis shifted to the rehabilitation of the offender and his return to society, the traditional system of penalties appeared totally inappropriate.[5]

In other words, the very application of the criminal justice system to certain types of deviants—to chronic alcoholics, to narcotics addicts, to sexual deviates, to the mentally ill—seems in many instances senseless and unproductive. In many such cases, no combination of traditional criminal penalties could serve as an effective response. Accordingly, there has been mounting pressure to divest the criminal law of jurisdiction over certain actors and activities that can assumedly be better handled under a different legal framework. The new framework is designated as civil commitment, and its announced aim is therapeutic. Deviants who are committed civilly are, under this model, turned over to a body of behavioral experts for treatment.

This development, which Kittrie terms "the divestment of criminal justice and the coming of the therapeutic state,"[6] received its modern-day momentum in 1962 from the United States Supreme Court in *Robinson* v. *California*.[7] In *Robinson*, the Court held it violative of the cruel and unusual punishment clause of the Constitution to punish a person criminally for the illness of addiction, but in dictum the Court suggested it would be constitutionally proper to confine addicts involuntarily for the express purpose of treatment.

But the constitutional go-ahead provided by *Robinson* and the consequent increased reliance on the therapeutic model may have been but a beginning of the modern impact of Enrico Ferri. Recent advances (or claims of advances) in the behavioral and biological sciences have been so rapid and so far-reaching that there will be enormous pressure, some of it already evident, to transfer control of such persons to therapeutic experts. For instance, B. F. Skinner, the Harvard behavioral psychologist who developed the theory and practice of operant conditioning, has asserted in a best selling book that free will—or "autonomous man"—is an illusion that is simply a shorthand way of attributing to inner forces those patterns of behavior for which we can not yet pinpoint a scientific causal nexus.[8] But Skinner and a host of his followers in the field of applied behavior analysis,[9] together with other specialists in behavior modification,[10] believe that there is already a technology capable of immediate utilization. Moreover, the past decade has witnessed a resurgence of biological explanations of behavioral deviance. Thus, neurological theories are being advanced to the effect that much violent behavior is attributable to pathology of the limbic (emotional) region of the brain, and is subject to improvement or correction by various devices, including psychosurgery—the surgical destruction of the diseased part of the brain[11] (see Chapter 8).

Given the current dissatisfaction with the criminal justice system and the concomitant present and anticipated pressure to extend the therapeutic premise, it seems appropriate at this time to take stock of the promises and problems of a therapeutically oriented legal system, to sketch the various competing considerations, and to offer a backdrop against which to plan for the legal future. As should already be evident, the therapeutic ideal is by no means an unmixed blessing, and the Supreme Court is well aware of that fact. Although, as we have seen, the Court in 1962 opened the therapeutic door in *Robinson*, it recognized as early as five years later that certain legal constraints ought to be clamped on the curative model.[12] And a decade after *Robinson*, the Court, noting the large number of persons processed through various civil commitment schemes, expressed surprise over the fact that the state's coercive curative power had been so seldom the subject of litigation; indeed, the Court seemed to invite litigation to consider the appropriate contours of therapeutic intervention.[13] As yet, however, the Court has not squarely addressed the major issues. Thus, they remain fertile for discussion.

PROBLEMS WITH THE THERAPEUTIC MODEL

Of the multitude of problems associated with the therapeutic model, the great bulk can be summarized under a single unifying theme: that the therapeutic approach knows no bounds. If, through the use of modern scientific techniques, the prevention or cure of deviant behavior is elevated to a superseding status, all other factors that have long been traditionally embedded in our jurisprudence are by definition dwarfed. This section will first consider the problems relating to the absence of limits in the therapeutic model, and will then discuss other problems posed by the therapeutic ideal.

PROBLEMS OF LIMITS

Consider the logical implications of a therapeutic premise to the effect that, with respect to deviants, "the law should not be concerned with questions of guilt and its degrees nor with measuring a fit punishment, but should humanely apply whatever measures are necessary to protect society from further transgressions by the same individual."[14] Actually, the premise is even broader, for it would include therapeutic *prevention* as well as correction, and would apply to the eradication of self-harming as well as society-harming conduct. The ramifications of the limitless premise, and also of the opportunities for abuse, are startling.

Substantive Standards

First of all, the scope of conduct theoretically subject to state control and correction is potentially enormous. It has been demonstrated, for example, that even such standard tests as being "mentally ill and dangerous to oneself or others" or being "mentally ill and in need of care, custody or treatment" are frequently worthless as concrete or even general guidelines. A concept such as "abnormality" has many possible meanings—including statistical deviation, improper biomedical functioning, ideological deviation, and less than optimal psychological adjustment—and "mental abnormality" is, definitionally, no more clear-cut:

> One need only glance at the diagnostic manual of the American Psychiatric Association to learn what an elastic concept mental illness is. It ranges from the massive functional inhibition characteristic of one form of catatonic schizophrenia to those seemingly slight aberrancies associated with an emotionally unstable personality, but which are so close to conduct in which we all engage as to define the entire continuum involved. Obviously, the definition of mental illness is left largely to the user and is dependent upon the norms of adjustment that he employs. Usually the use of the phrase "mental illness" effectively masks the actual norms being applied. And, because of the unavoidably ambiguous generalities in which the American Psychiatric Association describes its diagnostic categories, the diagnostician has the ability to shoehorn into the mentally diseased class almost any person he wishes, for whatever reason, to put there.[15]

Nor is the inherent vagueness of the term "mental illness" saved by the ordinary additional requirement that, to be committed, a person must also be dangerous or in need of care or treatment. Danger-to-others can run the gamut from a serious risk of homicide, through a propensity to drive carelessly, to simply offending the sensibilities of others. Indeed, one court found a probable "check bouncer" dangerous to others.[16] Danger-to-self need by no means be restricted to the risk of suicide, but can easily be broadened to encompass other physical harm, "loss of assets from foolish expenditures, or even loss of social standing or reputation from behaving peculiarly in the presence of others."[17] And the need-for-care-or-treatment test obviously provides no real constraint on the exercise of therapeutic power, for, almost by definition, many experts would hold that all persons who are mentally ill or otherwise deviant are in need of some sort of supervision or treatment.

The essential problem with regard to substantive standards, then, is their inherent elasticity. (Indeed, the elasticity is heightened by the therapeutic model's abandonment of Beccaria's "overt act" requirement. If deviance can be offset by therapy, the argument runs, there is little reason to *await* the commission of a deviant act before intervening, especially if intervention could *prevent* the deviant act. If a manic can be prevented from squandering assets, why allow the person to squander them prior to treatment?) The elasticity of the standards, however, coupled with a pressure to intervene and treat whenever that appears possible, enables the therapeutic state to coerce conformity in many instances where coercion is not essential for societal protection.

The fears of the therapeutic state overstepping its bounds are not simply speculative or academic. In a somewhat different context, Professor John Kaplan has warned us to scrutinize carefully any legal scheme ostensibly designed to protect against self-harming conduct, for those situations are often ones where the self-harming conduct is also regarded as immoral, and the real purpose of the legal control may be to enforce a dominant morality or to stigmatize and control unpopular groups.[18] The most frightening example, uncovered by Dr. Thomas Szasz,[19] is a medical theory published by a Southern doctor in 1851 describing two diseases—"drapetomania" and "dysaesthesia Aethiopis"— peculiar to the Negro race. Stripped of medical rhetoric, drapetomania described a syndrome of a Negro slave escaping from a white master, while dysaesthesia Aethiopis described a slave's behavior in neglecting work!

Modern examples of therapeutic excesses are by no means uncommon. An elderly man who, instead of preserving his estate for his heirs, decides to spend his later years travelling and buying expensive gifts for a young girlfriend, may well find himself under guardianship or commitment as the result of proceedings initiated by his potential heirs alleging his "senility," his "mental incompetence," and his "abnormal spending habits."[20] It is clear, too, that some persons, such as "hippies," have been declared mentally ill and committed because of their unconventional life style or beliefs.[21] Finally, with some psychoanalysts contending that members of the John Birch Society may in fact be paranoid schizophrenics,[22] we may not be as far as we would like to think from the Soviet practice of confining nonconformist intellectuals and political dissidents in mental hospitals.[23] In that connection, it is perhaps not terribly surprising that liberals and extreme conservatives are equally concerned about abuses of the therapeutic state, and that

> [n]ot long after a representative of the New York Civil Liberties Union testified before Congress that involuntary civil commitment should be abolished or at least sharply curtailed, . . . conservative Arizonans, concerned over the possible involuntary commitment of persons for political and religious beliefs, convinced like-minded legislators to call for legislation which, if enacted, "would have required the examination of all persons being committed to the hospital by two physicians, including one who was a member of the American Association for the Abolition of Involuntary Mental Hospitalization."[24]

Treatment

According to the therapeutic premise, once a deviant becomes subject to coercive state control, it is axiomatic that the period of such control or confinement must be *indefinite*—for as long as is necessary to effect a "cure." Moreover, with respect to therapy itself, it follows that the behavioral experts ought to be entitled to employ whatever therapeutic devices are called for in order to alleviate the deviant condition. Interestingly, even within the context of the penal system, Chief Justice Burger has apparently advocated a system in which "the 'guilty' defendant could be committed by the trial judge to the custody of the government for an indeterminate period for such medical treatment, psychiatric therapy, discipline, and vocational training as would help him and rehabilitate and restore him to a useful life."[25]

Importantly, however, modern day treatment is not confined to traditional "talk" psychotherapy, which apparently works well with intelligent and educated neurotics, but is far from fruitful when used with inarticulate, lower class deviants. The newer therapies, which are not dependent on a communicative relationship between the "client" and the therapist, are derived principally from psychological theories of learning and from developments in neurology.

These psychologically derived therapies can take the form of "positive control," where appropriate behaviors are rewarded or "reinforced," often by the use of points or tokens that can later be exchanged for desired objects such as snacks and cigarettes, or they can take the form of "aversive control," where undesirable behavior is associated with or followed by unpleasant conditions, such as the case where "two hospitalized narcotic addicts were made nauseous following a 'fix' with morphine by the administration of apomorphine [an emetic] during thirty-eight treatment sessions conducted over a period of five weeks."[26] The theory underlying the psychological therapies is, of course, that reward-earning behavior will increase and that behavior associated with or producing aversive conditions will be extinguished.[27] The neurological theories, on the other hand, postulate that much deviant and violent behavior is attributable to brain disease, correctable either by antiseizure medication or by brain surgery.[28]

While these therapies offer new hope for reforming deviants who may prove refractory to conventional techniques, there are, of course, serious questions about whether the new methods ought to be inflicted on involuntary patients and, indeed, whether our concerns for matters of dignity, humaneness, and human personality ought not to preclude their use. A discussion of the new techniques in the context of each of the above values should help clarify the issues.

Dignity. It might be thought that schemes of "positive control," insofar as they simply reward appropriate behavior and do not resort to punishments, would pose few problems. Actually, however, even this "mildest" form of modern therapy is open to serious criticism. That is because some such schemes utilize as *rewards,* and require patients to *earn,* items and activities that basic principles of dignity, and of law,[29] would demand as a matter of absolute, noncontingent right (see Chapter 9).

For instance, a system of positive control at Patton State Hospital in San Bernadino, California, starts all its patients in an orientation group, where they are required to exhibit proper behavior (such as efficient work habits) in order to earn tokens which can later be used to purchase wanted items. A patient who successfully adjusts to the orientation group can be elevated to a better environment. A psychiatric technician connected with the program described it as follows:

> This group sleeps in a relatively unattractive dormitory which conforms to bare minimums set by the state department of mental hygiene. There are no draperies at the windows or spreads on the beds, and the beds themselves are of the simplest kind. In the dining room the patient sits with many other patients at a long table, crowded in somewhat uncomfortably. The only eating utensil given him is a large spoon. The food is served in unattractive, sectioned plastic dishes. So long as he is in this group, he is not allowed to wear his own clothes and cannot go to activities which other patients are free to attend off the unit. He may not have permission for off-the-ground visits, and the number of visitors who can see him are [sic] restricted.
>
> During this time, the patient learns that his meals, his bed, his toilet articles, and his clothes no longer are freely given him. He must pay for these with tokens. . . . These tokens pay for all those things normally furnished and often taken for granted. In the orientation group most of the things the

patient wants are cheap; for example, it costs one token to be permitted to go
to bed, one token for a meal. Patients find it easy enough to earn the few
tokens necessary for bare subsistence.[30]

While these systems of "token economies" have been used principally with chronic psychotics,[31] they have been employed also with
populations of narcotic addicts,[32] alcoholics,[33] juvenile delinquents,[34]
and others.[35] Of course, not all of these programs of "positive" control
resort to the type of deprivations used to motivate chronic psychotics at
Patton State Hospital, but there is a real possibility that, if the therapeutic state is not carefully scrutinized, the type of system described above
might be extended even to nonpsychotic clinical populations. Indeed,
one program instituted with nonpsychotic alcoholics closely resembled
the Patton State Hospital model.[36]

Humaneness. If "positive" control is the mildest of the new
therapies, then we can well expect to encounter some serious problems
with techniques that are admittedly "aversive." Under the Eighth
Amendment, cruel and unusual *punishments* are forbidden. Should the
matter stand on a different footing if the motivation for inflicting the
"highly unpleasant" condition is curative rather than retributive? Arguably, according to the orthodox therapeutic model, such techniques
would be permissible notwithstanding their aversive nature and notwithstanding the fact that the aversive condition imposed is out-of-
proportion to the crime or deviant act committed.

To appreciate the fact that therapeutic schemes ought not to be
immune from "cruel and unusual" type restrictions, one need only consider the use of "anectine" or "succinylcholine" therapy. Anectine is a
muscle relaxant drug "that rapidly produces complete paralysis of the
skeletal muscles, including those which control respiration."[37] It has
been used therapeutically in aversion therapy. For example, attempts
have been made to condition alcoholics against drinking by administering the drug just prior to offering the alcoholic a drink; then, "[j]ust as
the patient is about to drink the alcohol, paralysis occurs, producing
great fright about being unable to breathe and a fear of suffocation."[38]
Anectine therapy has also been administered to disruptive inmates in
California institutions, sometimes without their consent. In one such
institution, the practice was

> to administer 20 to 40 mg. of Succinylcholine intravenously with oxygen and
> an airway available, and to counsel the patient while he is under the influ-
> ence of the drug that his behavior is dangerous to others or to himself, that it
> is desirable that he stop the behavior in question, and that subsequent be-
> havior of a nature which may be dangerous to others or to himself will be
> treated with similar aversive treatments.[39]

The procedure is strikingly similar to that portrayed in *A Clockwork Orange*.[40]

Human Personality. Probably the greatest threat to human personality is posed by emerging techniques of psychosurgery—the "new lobotomies" used to rectify violence-producing brain pathology resulting from heredity, birth injuries, head injuries, viral infections, and other causes (see Chapter 8). According to the "new neurology," if brain pathology taking the form of abnormal electrical activity cannot be corrected by anti-seizure medication, surgery may be required.[41]

> The traditional surgical procedure has been lobectomy—the removal of the front portion of the diseased temporal lobe. A more modern technique, however, is stereotactic surgery, which involves, through the use of a surgical drill and other special instruments, implanting electrodes in the brain, determining through stimulation and recording procedures which brain cells are misfiring, and destroying a small number of cells in a precisely determined area by passing a heat-generating current through the appropriate electrode.[42]

While some scientists speak of psychosurgery principally in cases of uncontrollable violence,[43] its potential is by no means that restrictive. Already, it has been reported that the California Department of Corrections toyed with the idea of brain cauterization for inmates who were serious management problems,[44] and elsewhere, "[h]omosexuals have allegedly been turned straight... through destruction of part of the brain called Cajal's nucleus—the supposed 'sexual switchboard.'"[45] In Mississippi, moreover, hyperactive children as young as five years old have been subjected to psychosurgery,[46] and the possibilities seem endless. For example, one explanation of drug addiction is that self-medication is a response to a neurological disorder of the brain's pleasure center, presumably correctable by neurosurgery.[47]

As expected, a therapy as drastic as psychosurgery has produced its share of enraged critics. Probably the most outspoken is Dr. Peter R. Breggin, a psychiatrist who has investigated current psychosurgical practices and who has reviewed the voluminous literature.[48] Breggin is not simply unconvinced about psychosurgery's assumed beneficial effects, but he strongly believes, from his review of the evidence, that "[a]t best, it [psychosurgery] blunts the individual, and at worst, it destroys all his highest capacities."[49] Inevitably, according to Breggin, psychosurgery affects not only the precise area destroyed, but, as even certain neurosurgeons admit, also affects other functions performed by the brain—creativity, introspection, concentration, independence. In short, in destroying the patient's deviance, Breggin claims it also destroys the patient's "identity" and "self."[50]

Control over Nondeviant Actors

Under the retributive theory of criminal law, it will be recalled, individual responsibility and moral blameworthiness were the kingpins of state control and punishment. Ferri's deterministic incursion into the criminal justice system, however, called into question the concept of the deviant actor's culpability and responsibility. Ferri called for dealing with the deviant as the product of deterministic forces, and for treating him accordingly, which has become the foundation for the modern day therapeutic model. But logically, the jurisdiction of the therapeutic state should not be restricted even to the broad limits set by Ferri. If a deviant is not truly responsible for his or her own behavior, it may be that, in many cases, the behavior problem cannot be dealt with effectively by therapy directed solely at the patient. Social science theory recognizes that actors are not behaviorally autonomous, and that an individual's deviant behavior may well be attributable to actions of other parties. If the deviance is to be eradicated, then, some sort of therapeutic control may have to be exercised over those other parties.

Perhaps the clearest example of aberrant behavior resulting from interpersonal interaction can be seen in the area of family relations. Some time ago, for example, Johnson and Szurek postulated that "parents' unwitting sanction or indirect encouragement is a major cause of, and the specific stimulus for, such antisocial behavior as fire-setting, stealing, truancy, and unacceptable sexuality displayed by young delinquents."[51] And in a provocative critique of legal education for, among other things, ignoring the interdisciplinary dimensions of the law, Savoy raises the pertinent question in a somewhat broader context:

> We know, for example, that most homicides do not occur in the street, but in the home, and not between strangers, but between people who are close to each other. This suggests that homicide may be a symptom of dysfunctional patterns of interaction within a family, and that the subject of investigation and treatment ought to be the potentially homicidal family rather than a class of dangerous individual offenders. Similarly, an act of "juvenile delinquency," from an interactional perspective, may be viewed as a situation in which the juvenile is being "scapegoated" and is expressing an upset or disequilibrium within the entire family as a social unit. The delinquent act "can be looked upon as the only 'safe' way of calling attention to an intolerable family situation," or it may ultimately be an effort to preserve self by leaving the family.
>
> What implications would an interactional analysis of mental illness have for a legal order that authorizes the institutionalization of one member of a dysfunctional family on the petition of another? And what new problems are raised for "rehabilitation" models of control over individual conduct if we discover... that efforts to reintegrate the "identified patient" back into the

family, without treating the entire family *as a family* may be disastrous because the family has a vested interest in keeping the patient "sick"?[52]

At this time, the interactional approach to the control of crime and
deviance is virtually foreign to our legal system. Apart from the remotely
related area of criminal liability of parents for failure to control their
children,[53] the one exception, present in some of the juvenile court acts,
empowers a juvenile court, under certain circumstances, to issue an
order regulating a parent or guardian, and requiring him or her to perform, or to refrain from performing, certain acts.[54] Conceivably, such
authority could be invoked to encourage or compel a parent to help
mold appropriate behavior in his or her child by requiring the parent to
dispense certain reinforcers contingent on proper behavior by the
juvenile.[55]

Beyond the issuance to parents of care and protection orders by
some juvenile courts, however, our legal system has not attempted to
control nondeviant actors. Even in the area of mental health law, for
example, where interspouse tensions and frictions frequently lead to
emotional distress or commitment of one of the partners, commitment
courts are not presently authorized to require the nonpatient partner to
submit to counseling or to cooperate in the recovery of the patient.

Conceptually, however, the therapeutic premise might mandate
forcible cooperation of the nonpatient spouse in order to rehabilitate the
deviant actor, and as the interactional perspective of deviance gains
wider acceptance, we can probably expect to see pressure exerted to
enlarge the personal jurisdiction of the therapeutic state. Moreover, logically speaking, the control of nonactors for the purpose of avoiding or
correcting deviance can extend beyond family bounds, and drawing
appropriate limits to restrict the therapeutic state therefore could become a real problem. To what extent, for example, should school
teachers, who are perhaps at the root of a great deal of truancy on the
part of pupils, be susceptible to legal and therapeutic control?

Procedure

Under the model of classical criminal justice, where punishment is
inflicted in part according to a retributive rationale, the accused is
theoretically entitled to every advantage. The deprivation of liberty for
the purpose of punishment is considered so drastic a measure that there
is general agreement that the criminal law ought to be applied sparingly,
and that the criminal penalty ought to be imposed only after an adversary proceeding at which the accused is represented by competent counsel and at which he or she is entitled to a panoply of other protections,

some of which were catalogued by Jeffrie Murphy, a legal philosopher, in reviewing Karl Menninger's therapeutically oriented book, *The Crime of Punishment:*[56]

> Our system of criminal due process involves such guarantees as the following: (1) No man is to be deprived of his liberty for what he is or what he might do, but only because he has in fact violated some legal prohibition. This is the traditional requirement for an overt act. (2) A man is to be presumed innocent. This means that the state must prove its case beyond a reasonable doubt to a jury of the defendant's peers and that the defendant may exploit the adversary system to its full to make such proof impossible. (3) A man is to be responsible only for what he has done as an individual. He is not to be held guilty because others like him often commit crimes. (4) A man is not to be forced to testify against himself, to help the state in its attempt to deprive him of his liberty.[57]

Murphy goes on to note, however, that "such guarantees would have no place in a purely therapeutic or preventive context, and Menninger quite correctly argues that the procedures they involve are not the best way to arrive at truth and thus that they interfere with the efficiency of securing public safety."[58] Indeed, the argument for relaxing procedural safeguards can be made even stronger: Where the state's aim is not to punish but to assist by providing therapy, there is no need for an adversary process because *all* parties have the best interest of the deviant at heart. And, the argument continues, the criminal law safeguards have no place in a therapeutic proceeding, for they serve only to "criminalize" the process and further stigmatize the subject, and they are simply unnecessary impediments to achieving the central goal, which is to help the deviant actor. The most extreme conclusion, of course, is that the entire question is simply a medical or scientific matter, and that the courts have no business at all meddling in these need-for-hospitalization decisions.

By and large, although the winds of change have sometimes stirred, the therapeutic argument has often been accepted with respect to the "civil" commitment of deviants, and thus American law has traditionally had two parallel but very different procedural systems for controlling aberrant behavior—a criminal system with a host of procedural rights and a therapeutic system with rather few.

Although existing narcotic addict commitment schemes have been sharply criticized for their failure to provide sufficient safeguards,[59] legal protections available to addicts far surpass those available to other deviants subject to civil commitment. Until 1967, when the Supreme Court intervened to alter the practice,[60] for example, juveniles in delinquency proceedings were not entitled to counsel or to the privilege against self-incrimination. And even today, mental commitment procedures often follow the therapeutic model, sometimes to the extreme conclusion that the question of hospitalization ought simply to be a medical determination.

In some states, for example, the patient is not entitled to counsel,[61] and even when attorneys are involved, they generally do not properly understand their role,[62] and the hearings, which ordinarily are not transcribed, often consume no more than five minutes,[63] whereupon the patient may be ordered committed for an indefinite period. Moreover, several states follow the purely medical model and permit commitment solely on the basis of medical certificates, without any court intervention at all, even though after being committed the patient will be able to go to court to challenge the confinement, if he or she requests a judicial hearing.[64]

OTHER PROBLEMS

Most of the problems thrust to the surface by the therapeutic model are, as we have seen, problems regarding the "illimitable" therapeutic premise. There are, however, certain other questions raised by the model—most of which are highly conjectural and subject to empirical inquiry—that seem to be worthy of some mention. Chiefly, these are the possible sociological and psychological implications of a societal shift from a punitive to a therapeutic model. In that regard, it is interesting to note that the process of divestment of criminal justice has taken hold at a time when we still know very little about the role played by criminal punishment in satisfying the public's need for retribution and in preventing and correcting crime.

Thus, while it seems that a psychology of determinism undercuts the notion of blameworthiness and accordingly calls into question the propriety of retribution on moral grounds, retributive punishment may nonetheless have utility on sociological grounds. Mr. Justice Stewart, concurring in *Furman* v. *Georgia*,[65] put the matter nicely:

> The instinct for retribution is part of the nature of man, and channeling that instinct in the administration of criminal justice serves an important purpose in promoting the stability of a society governed by law. When people begin to believe that organized society is unwilling or unable to impose upon criminal offenders the punishment they "deserve," then there are sown the seeds of anarchy—of self-help, vigilante justice, and lynch law.

The "urge to punish,"[66] in short, may be an important ingredient of our traditional legal system. Although subject to a variety of possible explanations, a recent study of governmental systems at "Achievement Place," a family-style home for predelinquent boys, may shed some empirical light on the dimensions of the urge to punish (and also to be punished).[67] Achievement Place experimented with various governmental models of peer behavioral control. These included systems where a "peer manager" could dispense only rewards (points convertible into privileges) for conforming conduct, and systems where the manager could not only reward conforming conduct but could also punish (subtract points) for deviant conduct. The research disclosed many interesting findings regarding the punitive process. For instance, when the peer managership position was purchasable, the boys were willing to pay far more points to occupy that position when it carried the authority to punish as well as to reward as opposed to when it carried only the authority to reward. Moreover, although the boys at large preferred an *elected* managership, they most preferred an elected managership system where the manager would have the authority to punish as well as to reward.

However the Achievement Place results are ultimately interpreted, it seems that principles of punishment are now part-and-parcel of our governmental fabric. Leaders expect to be able to punish nonconforming conduct and the public expects and desires that rule-breaking behavior will be punished. It is possible, then, that a shift away from punishment and toward therapy may produce some problematic repercussions. If the therapy administered is not, in a retributive sense, "proportionate" to the crime or act of deviance committed, the urge to punish may find expression in extralegal ways, or perhaps will manifest itself indirectly by resort to cruel therapies such as anectine treatment. It is possible, too, that the public may be offended by criminals receiving less than their "due," and that this may eventually lead to a widespread relaxation of inhibitions and a consequent increase in deviant behavior.[68] Possibly, of course, the existing "urge to punish" may be more cultural than inherent, and it may accordingly be subject to eventual modification or elimination.[69] But even if so, there will surely be a long transitional period during which the problems of dispensing with a retributive outlet may arise, and shapers of the therapeutic state must be sensitive to those issues.

A related problem concerns the concept of deterrence in a changing legal order. Unfortunately, our existing knowledge about deterrence is woefully inadequate.[70] Many proponents of a therapeutic paradigm assert that deterrence obviously does not work, as evidenced by the high rates of crime and recidivism. But that argument misses the mark, for it does not negate the possibility that those rates would be higher still under a therapeutic model.

The therapeutic state is technically unconcerned with matters of general deterrence. Periods of incarceration, for example, are not set according to schedules that will deter others from transgressing. Instead, treatment is theoretically indefinite in length, so that the deviant can be released as soon as he or she responds to therapy. And even when the therapy is unpleasant to the patient, the underlying motivation is not to set an example. As Ralph Schwitzgebel has put it, "aversion therapy is not the same as 'punishment' in the broad sense of social retribution or general deterrence. Although the procedures used are aversive, they are justified only by therapeutic efficacy, not by a theory of retribution or general deterrence."[71]

Conceivably, then, with deterrence and retribution relaxed, the therapeutic arrangement may actually encourage more deviance than the criminal system. On the other hand, precisely the opposite result could obtain. If aversion therapy is widely employed, and especially if it is given wider legal latitude than is given to traditional criminal punishment, deviance may be increasingly deterred. Further, the specter of indefinite confinement and treatment—the "certainty of uncertain severity"—might well be distasteful enough to deter deviants to an extent greater than they would be deterred by the prospect of set sentences, particularly if the average length of therapeutic confinement proves to be substantial. Surely, if the disinclination of defendants to raise the insanity defense (because of the possibility of indefinite institutionalization)[72] or if the dislike by prisoners of indeterminate sentencing[73] are any indication, the prospect of therapeutic commitment may indeed be sufficiently unpleasant so as to operate as a strong deterrent. But while these matters of deterrence are subject to endless speculation, they are, of course, answerable only by research, which ought to be viewed as an ingredient essential to effective therapeutic planning.

A final, closely related question, again answerable definitively only through research, is the extent to which the therapeutic processing of deviants will affect their life-chances, their self-concept, and their subsequent conduct. Comparatively speaking, for example, it may be that the stigma of a therapeutic label is a greater hindrance to the affected deviant than is the stigma of a criminal conviction.

Thus far, we have only assumptions, not facts, about this problem. Consider, for example, the dissenting remarks of Mr. Justice Clark in *Robinson* v. *California*: "Any reliance upon the 'stigma' of a misdemeanor conviction in this context is misplaced, as it would hardly be different from the stigma of a civil commitment for narcotics addiction."[74] But Justice Clark has no factual support for his conclusion, and we simply do not know whether an addict will be stigmatized, and hence hindered in his or her social readjustment, more by a criminal conviction, a commitment as an addict, or, as is still possible in a number of states, a commitment as a person who is mentally ill.[75] Yet, answers to these questions are crucial in charting an appropriate therapeutic course. The little we do know about the area is interesting indeed. We know, for instance, that former mental patients who present themselves to prospective employers as having been hospitalized because of "problems in living" receive a far better response than those who present themselves as having had "mental problems."[76] The two labels, in fact, yield completely different lines of inquiry on the part of the prospective employers.[77] We know, too, that many individuals strenuously resist therapeutic labels. Alcoholics, for example, resist "mental illness" labels,[78] as do many homosexuals. At the annual convention of the American Psychiatric Association held in Dallas, Texas, in May, 1972, activist members of the gay community distributed a sheet entitled "Gay, Proud and Healthy," and protested the then prevailing psychiatric theory that homosexuals are mentally ill:

> Central to the conflict between psychiatry and the homosexual community is the "sickness theory" of homosexuality and the whole related complex of negative attitudes toward homosexuality, which try to make of homosexuality something inferior to and less desirable than heterosexuality. It matters not whether the word used be sickness, disorder, affliction, disturbance, dysfunction, neurosis, immaturity, fixation, character or personality disorder, pathology, or any other—or whether homosexuality be considered as merely symptomatic of these—the effects are the same: (1) To support and buttress the prejudices of society and to assist the bigots in the perpetration and perpetuation of their bigotry; and, at least equally important (2) To destroy the homosexual's self-confidence and self-esteem, impair his or her self-image, degrade his or her basic human dignity.

The quoted homosexual grievance indicates that the particular label attached to a deviant—juvenile delinquent, criminal, addict, mentally ill—is important not only with respect to the procedure it calls for, the treatment it yields, and the stigma it produces, but also with respect to the related question of its influence on the deviant's self-concept and later behavior.[79] It is known, for example, that the very process of societal reaction or the act of labeling a person deviant can operate to alter a person's self-concept and behavior. In that connection, Freedman and Doob[80] demonstrated empirically one impact of a deviant label by conducting a social psychology experiment with normal students solicited ostensibly to submit to a "personality" test. I have summarized their findings as follows:

> Freedman and Doob experimentally induced a feeling of deviance in some of the subjects by informing a random group that they had received personality test scores far from the "average". Then, other experiments were performed

to assess the impact of the deviant label. Interestingly, the investigators learned that when the personality test results were not made public, the "deviants", in an apparent attempt to conceal their deviancy, preferred to work alone. The desire to avoid close contact with others disappeared, however, when the test results were made public, but the deviants then preferred to associate with the other experimentally manufactured deviants rather than with the nondeviant subjects.[81]

Of particular pertinence to the impact of labeling under the therapeutic model is that the therapeutic premise attributes deviancy to causes other than individual responsibility. Consequently, it is not uncommon for deviants, borrowing from the language of psychiatry and related disciplines, to develop a "vocabulary of motives" for lawless behavior that includes a denial of personal responsibility and an attribution of their aberrant behavior to causes beyond their control.[82] More important, perhaps, is the fact that the denial of personal responsibility is accompanied by a self-concept that accepts a lack of self-control, and the altered self-image can in turn lead to *increased deviance.*[83]

Rotter has performed some interesting research on behavioral correlates of "perceptions of causality."[84] He has developed a scheme for classifying individuals as believing in "internal" control or in "external" control. In short, internals believe they control their own destinies, whereas externals attribute causation to outside forces. Rotter notes that views regarding internal and external control can be culturally derived, as evidenced by the Ute Indian tradition of relying heavily on fate as a causal explanation. Most significant, in connection with the emerging therapeutic model, is Rotter's finding that internals really *are* more effective than are externals in altering their environments and in controlling themselves. For instance, "internal inmates in a reformatory learned more than external inmates did about the reformatory rules, parole laws, and the long-range economic facts that would help one get along in the outside world."[85] A related finding—with possible significance for the field of addiction—is that, after the release of the Surgeon General's report regarding the hazards of tobacco, internals were apparently better able than were externals to give up smoking.[86]

It may be, of course, that Rotter's findings are not pertinent to the topic at hand. Conceivably, externals come to believe in external causation *because* they are repeatedly unable to change themselves or their environment, rather than *vice versa.* But, particularly when combined with other findings,[87] such as the culturally induced externality of the Ute Indians, it is perfectly plausible to assume that a *belief* in external causality may, of its own force, create a situation where an individual *becomes* less able to control or change himself.

What all of this suggests for present purposes is that even if individual responsibility is an illusion,[88] it may be dysfunctional for us to "cease to regard people as agents of dignity and responsibility who are capable of being blameworthy for what they do."[89] Glasser views the divestment of responsibility as having already gone too far, and he has developed a "reality therapy" that focuses on *what* the deviant did, without paying attention to *why* he did it.[90] But whether or not the problem is yet out of hand, several writers[91] have expressed concern over the long-range implications of accepting an "illness" or "medical" model of deviance. Professor Kittrie has summed up the point nicely:

> Another potentially undesirable product of the therapeutic state is the hastening of the erosion of society's reliance upon the concept of personal responsibility. While the determinists found no scientific justification for classical criminal law's insistence upon the institution of free will and sought to abolish the concept of personal guilt, the modern engineers of social organization cannot overlook the utility of these concepts—even if recognized to be only fictional and ritualistic—in the promotion of socially desired behavior. Granting that mental patients, juveniles, addicts, and psychopaths (as well as the rest of the populace) may in fact never exercise total free will in their social conduct, cannot society's endorsement of the free-will concept still work toward the enhancement of whatever self-restraint the diverse members of these groups might be able to generate?[92]

TOWARD A PROPER PERSPECTIVE

GENERAL CONSIDERATIONS

As always, it is easier to pose problems than to suggest solutions. To the extent that the process of posing problems sensitizes individuals to the important issues, however, the mere presentation of the issues serves to better the situation. Moreover, at least some of the problems call for rather simple solutions. The possible sociological and psychological problems just mentioned, for example, are admittedly speculative, and a reasonable suggestion for grappling with them would be simply to be cognizant of their possible development, and to focus resources for research around some of the pertinent social and psychological implications of a shift to a therapeutically oriented legal system.

But the other items catalogued above as problems with the therapeutic model—the problems of the "limitless" therapeutic premise—are far more troubling. To solve those problems, boundaries must be established, but, as we have seen, the task of line-drawing, utilizing exclusively a therapeutic model, is virtually impossible. The point, obviously, is that the problems of an *illimitable* therapeutic state arise only under a model where the curative goal is elevated *above all others*. Matters fall better into place, and establishing limits becomes somewhat less difficult, when it is recognized that there are a multitude of values *other* than the prevention and cure of deviant conduct that deserve expression, even in a social and legal scheme relating to the control of deviance.

Actually—and this point is not made often enough in the context of how far we should go to eliminate deviance—some deviance actually *promotes* social organization or serves other positive functions. While a "functional analysis" of deviance[93] is clearly beyond the scope of the present work, it is worth noting that deviant conduct serves, among many other things, to accentuate the conformity and cohesiveness of nondeviants and to provide a warning about strain in the social structure. With respect to the latter, Albert Cohen has written:

> Deviance may also function as a signal light or warning, inviting attention to defects of organization. Increases in absenteeism from work, truancy from school, AWOL's from the army, runaways and other disturbances in correctional institutions, surly and sullen compliance with orders, and deliberate defects of workmanship, may compel re-examination of existing procedures, reveal unsuspected causes of discontent, and lead to changes that enhance efficiency and morale. The deviant may, by sticking his neck out, thereby render a service to reluctant conformers, who may be subject to the same strains but prefer to suffer them than to violate the rules.[94]

In that connection, incidentally, we should scrutinize carefully systems of control and treatment that may alleviate symptoms without correcting underlying causes. If, for example, psychosurgery were performed on violent prison inmates,[95] their violence might be subdued at the expense of exposing and reforming atrocious prison conditions that may have been the root cause of their violence and rebelliousness. Similarly, but less obviously, if heroin were to be legally dispensed to relieve narcotic addicts, we should be careful not to deflect attention from understanding and correcting those socioeconomic conditions that may be a fertile breeding ground for addiction.[96]

But to return to the central point, it should be clear that the eradication of deviance ought not to be society's superseding goal. Some deviance is indeed more functional than dysfunctional, and besides, other values, which compete with the elimination and correction of deviance, are entitled to recognition and are viewed by many as more important than crime control.

Thus, Richard Schwartz[97] has described an Israeli community where deviant behavior is so well controlled by public opinion and informal social pressure that there is not a need for, and there does not exist, a legal mechanism of control resembling a judicial body. But it is highly questionable whether, in our society, many of us would be willing to sacrifice the privacy that must be sacrificed in order to make the informal controls function properly. In the Israeli *kvutza*, for instance, children are sensitized to the force of public opinion by living and playing together, and, even as adults, there is such constant contact with the group—working together, eating meals cafeteria style, showering in common facilities, living in quarters lacking privacy—that the public opinion grapevine is travelled rapidly and informal disapproval of deviance is easily expressed.

Privacy is only one value that most of us would elevate above the eradication of deviance. Humaneness is clearly another. Even under the retributive and deterrence-oriented criminal law system, it is true, as Andenaes has noted, that

> [i]t was never a principle of criminal justice that crime should be prevented at all costs. Ethical and social considerations will always determine which measures are considered "proper." As Ball has expressed it: "[A] penalty may be quite effective as a deterrent, yet undesirable." Even if it were possible to prove that cutting off thieves' hands would effectively prevent theft, proposals for such practice would scarcely win many adherents today.[98]

Surely, the same sort of restraints ought to operate under a therapeutic model: therapeutic efficacy ought not to be the exclusive test of legality. Moreover, legal restrictions will have to be developed with respect to those therapies deemed by the subjects to be unpleasant or aversive. This is a particularly complicated area needing more experience and reflection before concrete recommendations can be made,[99] but certain guidelines come quickly to mind. Aversive therapies should ordinarily require the informed consent of the patient,[100] although it is recognized that the informed consent doctrine will often be difficult to apply with a population of deviants: many of the deviants may be mentally impaired, which can affect their capacity to consent, and even if they have the capacity, some would view the consent to be coerced in the sense that submission to the treatment might realistically constitute the only chance for release from custody; finally, the consent, some would argue, could not be truly "informed" with respect to therapies which are largely experimental in nature[101] (see Chapter 8). Surely, drastic therapies should not be resorted to where less drastic ones would be clinically sufficient.[102] And to the extent that the therapies are in fact experimental, they ought probably to conform to emerging legal and ethical restrictions regarding experimentation with human subjects.[103]

Perhaps even more than all the others, liberty is a value cherished in this society. It, too, must therefore be balanced with the therapeutic premise. In the context of commitment of the mentally ill, this point has been made well in the form of a pertinent question: "[I]s the treatment and cure of the mentally ill individual of more benefit to society than the liberty of which he is deprived and the principle (lost, or tarnished) that no one should assert the right to control another's beliefs and responses absent compelling social danger?"[104] Finally, respect for liberty demands adherence to the principle of "less drastic means"—that commitment and deprivation of liberty not be resorted to if other, less restrictive, treatment alternatives are available, reasonably effective, and more to the liking of the subject.[105]

These and other values, then, will serve as guidelines for curbing therapeutic jurisdiction. Apart from the limitations suggested above, the therapeutic model will also need to be restricted by procedural safeguards given to deviants and by substantive standards defining the appropriate scope of therapeutic involvement. It is, then, to those problems that we will now turn.

PROCEDURAL SAFEGUARDS

Although, in theory, procedural safeguards in a system of therapeutic justice might arguably be described as unnecessary impediments, it is very difficult in practice to justify any substantial relaxation of traditional procedural protections. First of all, as the Supreme Court recognized in *Gault*, the best of benevolent intentions does not always yield an acceptable therapeutic atmosphere, and "unbridled discretion, however benevolently motivated, is frequently a poor substitute for principle and procedure."[106] If commitment can lead to unwanted deprivation of liberty and to aversive and even ineffective therapy, it is difficult to discard procedural protections. Moreover, even if all concerned supposedly have "the best interests" of the deviant at heart, therapeutic proceedings cannot afford to dispense altogether with an adversary framework.

The sciences of behavior, particularly but not exclusively psychiatry, are sufficiently inexact to allow for considerable room in scrutinizing the evaluations of the testifying experts through skillful cross-examination by counsel and by the presentation of independent experts.[107] It is well known, for example, that psychiatric predictions of dangerousness are notoriously inaccurate and are decidedly in the direction of *overpredicting* future dangerous conduct.[108] Moreover, a lawyer-psychologist who has reviewed the pertinent literature has demonstrated that intradisciplinary disputes in psychiatry and clinical psychology are so prevalent, and basic doctrines are so open to question, that few expert assumptions can safely go unchallenged.[109] Indeed, even the "harder" (and presumably more credible) sciences such as neurology are in need of serious ventilation in the commitment context. Thus, some physicians, drawing on neurological knowledge to the effect that violent behavior attributable to brain pathology can often be detected by electroencephalogram (EEG) readings, have recommended that violent offenders with demonstrated abnormal electrical brain activity be removed from society until their EEGs become normal.[110] Only an aggressive adversary proceeding, however, would enable a deviant to demonstrate some of the flaws of EEG interpretation: that, for example, a sizable proportion of the *normal* population has abnormal EEGs, and that an abnormal EEG, instead of being a *cause* of violence, could be the result of a violent episode involving a head injury.[111]

Though counsel and independent experts are obviously required in order to effectively scrutinize medical and behavioral science testimony, counsel is also needed to perform more mundane, but equally important, functions. Counsel, for example, is indispensable in investigating the factual basis for the exercise of therapeutic power, in ascertaining whether any alternatives less restrictive than commitment are suitable in the particular case, and whether those alternatives have been properly explored by the relevant officials.[112]

Although, as we have seen, many therapeutic commitment proceedings today conform to a "medical" model which often does not provide for a court hearing with counsel, independent experts, and the like, the trend of the past decade has been decidedly in favor of providing basic protections, though not of as elaborate a nature as those provided in criminal proceedings. For example, the United States District Court for the Eastern District of Wisconsin rendered in *Lessard* v. *Schmidt*[113] a far-reaching decision dealing with the commitment of the mentally ill, but probably pertinent to the entire ambit of therapeutic justice. The court ruled that a proposed patient was entitled, among other things, to notice of the judicial proceedings, to a privilege against self-incrimination vis-à-vis the examining psychiatrists, to a relatively prompt judicial hearing, to retained or appointed counsel who is to function as an advocate, and to a commitment determination meeting a strict standard of proof. (On the required standard of proof, see Chapter 3).

Beyond those provided boldly in *Lessard*, a handful of additional safeguards are necessary to prevent possible abuse: the right to an independent medical or behavioral science expert, the right to be provided with a transcript of the proceedings, the right to an expedited appellate review of a commitment determination, and the right, following commitment, to a periodic judicial review (with counsel and independent experts, and with the state carrying the burden of proof) of the need for continued commitment or treatment.

Lessard is not simply an isolated example, but is instead reflective of a more general concern for protection even in a therapeutic environment. Legislative enactments and proposals are following a surprisingly similar course. The Uniform Drug Dependence Treatment and Rehabilitation Act, for example, provides for many of the described safeguards, as does the Arizona mental health code and other existing or suggested statutes.[114] But the most encouraging development of all, perhaps, is that the question of the necessity for procedural protections is no longer one that is almost automatically answered along polarized lines, with the legal profession urging protection and the medical and allied professions urging the abandonment of legal apparatus. In that connection, the pertinent portion of the American Psychiatric Association's "Position Statement on Involuntary Hospitalization of the Mentally Ill" is worthy of quotation:

> Any form of involuntary hospitalization should provide full rights of due process; all of these rights should be guaranteed the patient regardless of his ability to pay for the services they may entail. It is suggested that these rights encompass the following provisions:
>
> 1. That a psychiatric examination and evaluation be made by the hospitalizing physician;
>
> 2. That the patient and other parties to the procedure have legal counsel available to them;
>
> 3. That the court *promptly* determine the need for hospitalization, and in making such determination have available to it the results of an examination of the patient by one or more psychiatrists;
>
> 4. That, in addition, examination by one or more independent psychiatrists other than those appointed by the court be allowed the patient if he requests it;
>
> 5. That if, and after, the patient is hospitalized, frequent and periodic reports of his condition, treatment, and progress be made to the committing court or to its agency, to the patient's attorney, and to all of the examining physicians, and further, that the responsibility for follow-up action on these reports be that of an agency attached to the committing court;
>
> 6. That the patient have the right to seek a judicial determination of the need for his continued hospitalization at reasonable intervals of time, and not less than every six months, that in such proceedings the patient be entitled to legal counsel and to examination by one or more *independent* psychiatrists, and that the burden of proof of the need for continued hospitalization rest with the responsible treatment authority or agency; and
>
> 7. That no patient be denied treatment because of administrative, judicial, or institutional delay.[115]

SUBSTANTIVE STANDARDS

General

Although the Supreme Court has never enthusiastically acted on its invitation, it did, in *Jackson* v. *Indiana*, [116] virtually invite reconsideration of the substantive bases for the assertion of therapeutic control:

> The States have traditionally exercised broad power to commit persons found to be mentally ill. The substantive limitations on the exercise of this power and the procedures for invoking it vary drastically among the States. The particular fashion in which the power is exercised—for instance, through various forms of civil commitment, defective delinquency laws, sexual psychopath laws, commitment of persons acquitted by reason of insanity—reflects different combinations of distinct bases for commitment sought to be vindicated. The bases that have been articulated include dangerousness to self, dangerousness to others, and the need for care or treatment or training. Considering the number of persons affected, it is perhaps remarkable that the substantive constitutional limitations on this power have not been more frequently litigated. [117]

The articulated bases of control (danger to others, danger to self, and need for care and treatment) are, as we have already seen, rather imprecise concepts. [118] Furthermore, the concepts, if loosely drawn, actually overlap to a considerable extent. Thus, need for care and treatment can easily be viewed as a subset of a broadly read danger to self test, for the refusal to undergo needed treatment is surely, in a broad sense, damaging to one's self. Also, there is no sharp dividing line between the danger to self test and the danger to others test. Arguably, for example, it is damaging to oneself to engage in conduct which is dangerous to others and which, accordingly, may result in a severe disruption of the deviant's own life, perhaps leading to a prolonged period of punitive or therapeutic confinement. And finally, because of the intricacies of social life, very little if any self-harming conduct affects *only* the actor and not other members of society, and thus, as Kaplan has noted, most conduct which is dangerous to oneself poses at least "secondary" harm to others. [119] A motorcyclist who refuses to wear a helmet and is injured can become an expensive public ward, and, moreover, if he or she has a family, it too could become state-supported. The same can be said for alcoholism and drug dependence:

> As an emotional matter, moreover, nonsupport justifications for laws which attempt to prevent self-harming conduct often command considerably more power than do public ward justifications. Thus, despite the enormous public ward justifications for halting alcohol abuse, one of the most powerful Prohibitionist posters contained a drawing of a saloon with the father drinking at

the bar while his clean, but poorly dressed, little daughter stood in the
doorway saying, "Father, Father, please come home. Mother needs you."[120]

Given the uncertainty of these terms and of their scope, it is probably preferable, for purposes of legal analysis, to look to traditional legal
concepts for asserting state control over individuals and to determine
from them the acceptable boundaries for the exercise of therapeutic
jurisdiction, both for conduct that is dangerous to others and for self-
harming conduct. The traditional doctrines are, of course, the police
power of the State (a protection of society rationale) and the State's role
as *parens patriae* (a paternalistic rationale).

Police Power

Ordinarily, the state's police power is exercised pursuant to the
criminal law process, where punishment and restraint are imposed on a
deviant found, after-the-fact, to have committed a societal harm. But in
the therapeutic arena, commitment of deviants for the protection of
society is often done before-the-fact, in anticipation of future harm. Like
it or not, such a course takes us into the unfamiliar and uncomfortable area
of preventive detention.

Although preventive detention remains unfamiliar to us conceptually, it has actually long been practiced in American law, particularly
with respect to the commitment of the mentally ill.[121] Moreover, some
forms of restraint in order to prevent harm to others, such as imposing
quarantines on persons suffering from serious contagious diseases,
strike us as wholly legitimate.[122]

While the vast topic of preventive detention is obviously beyond the
scope of the present work, it is nonetheless probably safe to assert that
preventive restraint strikes us as legitimate only when we can feel confi-
dent that, if unrestrained, the subject would cause harm to others. Such
would hold true for an individual suffering from a serious contagious
disease as well as for an angry psychotic who believes God has instructed him or her to kill all sinners.[123] Furthermore, so drastic a remedy as substantial deprivation of liberty seems proper only to prevent
serious harms, and not, for example, the "secondary" public ward and
nonsupport type harms discussed by Kaplan.[124] Presumably, coercive
restraint and treatment to offset rather *minor* harms might be permissible only if a brief deprivation of liberty or a rather inoffensive treatment
might, as would a quarantine, assuredly prevent the resulting harms.[125]
It has been said that "[i]f the chronic common cold could be permanently
cured by a week in a solarium, the social benefit would probably be

worth the cost in liberty and sunburn."[126] So might the balance be struck with deviance.

The problem is, however, that predictions of dangerousness are hazardous indeed,[127] and proving contingent harm to a satisfactory degree of confidence is a most difficult task. In the mental health law area, the prediction problem has been in part overcome by requirements of some recent statutes and cases that dangerousness be proven by a recent overt act, attempt, or threat to do substantial harm.[128] That approach, though it is obviously in need of additional refinement, seems to be emerging as a generally acceptable model of preventive restraint.

The applicability of that model to drug dependence poses some interesting questions. It would seem, for instance, that addicts are not per se dangerous. On the contrary, because of the sense of well being that accompanies drug taking, addicts rarely commit violent crimes,[129] although violence can occur when their habit is "down on" them.[130] They commit virtually no sexual crimes,[131] and far fewer aggravated assaults than does the general population. Although their robbery rates somewhat exceed those of the general population, many technically designated robberies are simply purse snatchings.[132] Moreover, reports to the effect that addicts are responsible for half of New York City's crimes have been described as a canard, for such statistics apparently include violations of narcotic prohibition laws, which addicts by definition violate daily.[133] On the other hand, it does seem clear that addicts, even though not all of them, are likely to commit property offenses, such as petty theft, in order to finance their habits.[134]

But committing addicts in order to avert property crimes poses a number of serious issues. In addition to the offensiveness of committing people partially because they are poor (we would not be willing to commit nonaddict poor people simply on a showing that they were likely to steal), we are faced with the argument that

> the virtual certainty that addicts will break the law is in a direct sense the state's own fault. An addict's need for narcotics is by definition beyond his control. By denying him legal access to narcotics, the state makes him *ipso facto* an habitual criminal. By obliging him to obtain his drugs at exorbitant black market prices, the same legislative policy also drives poor addicts inexorably to theft. It flouts fundamental fairness for the state to force a man to commit crimes and at the same time to punish or confine him on grounds of his resultant criminality.[135]

Fundamental fairness or not, current law and practice permits the state *both* to punish and to commit because of the resultant criminality. Yet, the criminality could be virtually eliminated if the law were to sanction drug maintenance systems, for we know that addiction does not per se

lead to crime, as evidenced by the large number of persons at the turn of
the century who became medically addicted to morphine and to heroin
but who, with the drugs legally available, did not engage in criminal
activity.[136] Proposals for maintenance systems, particularly for heroin
maintenance patterned after the British model, have been sharply
criticized not only on moral grounds but on grounds that it will spread
addiction, demoralize and depoliticize the ghettos, and leave addicts at
the mercy of the government.[137] Seemingly, a carefully constructed
maintenance approach could grapple successfully with those issues. But
for preventive detention purposes, whether or not heroin maintenance
is adopted, there is a strong argument that, at the least, "the state
should certainly be estopped from confining addicts for fear of the
crimes it obliges them to commit."[138]

Surely, the state should be so estopped so long as the criminal law
remains available to punish addiction-related theft offenses. It seems
unlikely that the doctrine of *Robinson* v. *California*[139] will in the foreseeable future be extended, along the lines of a notion of "pharmacological
duress," to excuse addiction-produced property offenses. Hence, given
that premise, the danger to property seems an insufficient reason for
preventive detention (unless, of course, we wish to break entirely new
ground and preventively detain addicts to prevent property offenses on
the rationale that addicts will presumably not be criminally apprehended for numerous property offenses that they commit). Only if
we had a sure-fire cure for addiction by brief confinement or by some
miracle drug might we, by analogy to a quarantine, preventively detain
to avoid rather minor offenses such as property crimes.

Of course, the after-the-fact criminal approach is obviously not an
ideal solution any more than is preventive detention. But if we believe in
any case that preventive detention should not be invoked short of a
showing that the deviant recently demonstrated a propensity to do substantial harm by means of a threat, attempt, or overt act,[140] that will
mean, at least in the context of narcotics addiction, that the addict will
probably have committed a crime, such as theft or attempted theft,
cognizable by the criminal law. Instead of preventive detention, however, we could devise an acceptable alternative: the criminal law process
could be used to detect those addicts who commit or attempt property
offenses and, by enabling them to elect treatment in lieu of punishment,
could be used to encourage them to seek treatment for their addiction.[141]

The treatment alternative should be legally structured to provide
sufficient safeguards and to encourage its election. For example, criminal punishment could be held in abeyance for those addict-defendants
who elect treatment. The treatment should be for a period not exceeding

the typical criminal penalty for the offense, and, if an additional "carrot" for the treatment avenue is thought necessary, the therapeutic period could entail a length of time less than the criminal period. Proper completion of treatment should result in vitiating the criminal proceedings, but an uncooperative attitude toward therapy could result in a transfer to the criminal system, with, however, credit toward the criminal sentence for all time spent in the therapeutic process. Interestingly and perhaps significantly for this peno-therapeutic paradigm, a study of the federal Narcotic Addict Rehabilitation Act, which has provision both for pure civil commitment and for the election of treatment while criminal charges remain pending, found the success rate under the latter provision to exceed the success rate under the former, which, according to the authors of the study, "suggests that external legal pressure to comply with the program is a factor in success."[142]

Parens Patriae

General. Although commitments pursuant to the police power may often involve therapeutic elements, the real basis for intervention under the police power is, of course, the protection of society. Accordingly, the true essence of the therapeutic state is its paternalistic or *parens patriae* jurisdiction, whereby state intervention is assumedly exercised to serve the best interests of the deviant subject.

Ordinarily, however, we have rather strong philosophical and legal objections to the exercise of paternalistic power. The guiding premise has been that provided by John Stuart Mill,[143] that society ought to interfere with an individual against his or her will only to protect others, not to protect the individual personally. And a strong case can be made that society should, indeed, refrain from interfering even when there is a possible harm to others, so long as that harm is simply "incidental" or "secondary," such as public ward or nonsupport harm.[144] There are presumably several reasons underlying the general philosophical resistance to paternalistic interferences: the state may not know what is in fact "best" for the individual, it may not have the ability to improve his or her lot even if it properly understands the person's best interest, and perhaps most important, it offends one's dignity to have the state meddling in his or her affairs.[145]

By and large, the antipaternalistic premise has been adhered to in law and practice. Society does not typically intervene to prevent self-harming conduct. The law, of course, does not require that we diet, refrain from smoking, or seek treatment for serious coronary problems. Nor does society intervene to prevent even rather bizarre risk-taking.

News stories have included, for example, reports that one couple, claiming accusations against DDT were false, decided to prove their case by ingesting some daily, and that an ambitious oarsman had just completed a solo rowing trip of 4,400 miles.

The real question, it seems, is not simply whether paternalistic intervention is in the individual's best interests but "whether the state has the right to decide that question for him."[146] Typically, the state is given that right when it can be demonstrated that the individual is mentally incompetent to know, or to make rational decisions regarding, his or her own best interest.

In the area of commitment of the mentally ill, the older view was that mentally ill persons were per se incompetent, enabling society to commit and treat them, even over objection, in order to further their best interests. Recently, however, it has been clearly demonstrated that mental illness does not automatically produce incompetence—"that many persons who are mentally ill are entirely competent to make rational and important decisions concerning their affairs, including the decision to accept or reject hospital treatment."[147] Accordingly, paternalistic intervention with respect to a mentally ill person should now require as a prerequisite a specific showing that the person is incompetent to make responsible decisions regarding his or her treatment.

The difficulty even with the modern test is that too often the mere refusal of a patient to accept hospitalization or treatment is improperly taken to establish his or her mental incompetence. Of course, some refusals to accept treatment may be the result of incompetence, but a refusal, even if wrong, should not itself establish incompetence, for the true test ought to be not whether the patient's particular decision is wise, but whether he or she is mentally capable of competent decision making.[148]

Moreover, a patient's "wrong" decision to refuse treatment may, on close analysis, prove to be *correct*. Ennis makes the point well:

> To begin with, the choice of liberty rather than treatment might not be "wrong." Some types of mental illness are not treatable at all. And even for those types that are treatable, the probability that a given patient will permanently be cured, or even improved, *because of the treatment*, is discouragingly low. Of course, a good number of patients committed to mental hospitals are released "as improved" within a matter of months, but most of them return. Also, there is very little hard evidence that even temporary improvement is the result of the treatment and is not, instead, a spontaneous remission.

> In determining whether it is necessarily "wrong" for a mentally ill person to choose liberty rather than hospitalization, it should also be noted that even short-term hospitalization can, of itself, reinforce and exacerbate some types of mental illness, and that long-term hospitalization is particularly anti-

therapeutic. In that event, the choice is not between liberty and health, but between functioning at an impaired level or getting worse. More precisely, the choice is the risk of getting worse on the outside, compared with the risk of getting worse in the hospital. We must also remember that treatment in a mental hospital is often degrading and occasionally brutal, and . . . even voluntary hospitalization creates a terrible and lasting stigma. Finally, most state hospitals provide only custodial welfare, not treatment.[149]

From the above, we ought to be able to derive some principles for the proper exercise of the *parens patriae* power. First, we must carefully examine the patient to determine whether he or she is in fact incompetent or whether the person is simply making a "wrong" choice regarding treatment. Second, even if the person is incompetent, we must look to see whether, in actuality, forced commitment or treatment is in the patient's best interest. Thus, incompetence may be a necessary condition for the assertion of *parens patriae* jurisdiction, but it alone is not a sufficient condition. In addition to a finding of incompetence, in other words, we must also make a social judgment whether we ought to override the patient's stated desires. To answer the second prong of the test affirmatively, we ought to demand clear proof that, according to some objective consensus, the patient's "best interests" require that he or she submit to the proposed course of hospitalization or therapy. In other words, prior to taking the drastic course of overriding even an irrational will, we should be clearly persuaded that a rational person in the patient's position would opt for the proposed therapeutic course. That question ought to be answered by carefully weighing a multitude of factors, including the patient's prognosis and the likely length of confinement, the treatment available, his or her preference for liberty, the interruption of the person's vocational and family life, the individual's attitude toward mental hospitals, conditions of everyday life at the hospital, the stigma of hospitalization, and related matters.

This analysis may perhaps be enriched by illustrating how the *parens patriae* paradigm might apply outside the realm of mental illness per se. Apt examples may be found in the area of narcotics addiction and abuse.

Narcotics Addiction.   The propriety of exercising paternalistic power in the drug addiction area can be discussed according to analytically identical lines, although the relevant empirical facts may of course differ. The question of the incompetence of drug addicts, for example, seems even more difficult and more subtle than is the question of the incompetence of mental patients. Many mental patients are so psychotic and out of touch with reality that they may not know their own identity or may totally lack orientation regarding time and place. They may easily meet the necessary test of incompetence and irrationality. Drug addicts, on the other hand, are seldom classified as psychotic, and they ordinarily retain contact with reality. If addicts are to be considered incompetent, then, it must be because their overpowering compulsion to consume drugs prevents them from reaching a rational decision regarding treatment.

There seems to be a great deal of dispute regarding the competency of narcotic addicts to rationally choose to forego drugs and seek treatment. Dr. Nils Bejerot, for example, has characterized drug addiction, as opposed to mere drug abuse, as the equivalent of a "basic drive," and one where "the dependence dominates the individual and his way of life."[150] Discussing the overpowering qualities of addiction, Bejerot notes that in the insect world, a certain type of ant becomes spontaneously addicted to a secretion produced by a certain beetle, and that the ants will, in times of danger, protect the beetles before they rescue their own eggs—a situation not unlike that in old China, where opium smokers sometimes sold their wives and children to obtain needed opium. In short, Bejerot concludes that narcotics addiction is a pathological condition so enjoyed by the addict that he or she may be incapable of structuring life in any way other than around the continued satisfaction of his or her habit. If that is so, we might well have a factually and legally acceptable approximation of incompetence. (The incompetence would appear to be "volitional" rather than "cognitive.") But it is also true, of course, that some addicts *do* decide to enter treatment, and that cuts against a blanket notion equating addiction with incompetence. One commentator has argued rather persuasively that addiction should not in itself establish incompetency:

> But if addicts have lost their powers of self-control, so have all chain smokers and compulsive gamblers. They have all lost control over a partial and clearly limited area of conduct, but not over conduct or decision-making capacity generally. They are unable to decide not to smoke or gamble, but they are as competent to decide to attempt a cure of their habit as to decide whether to undergo an operation or to come in out of the rain. Addiction, as a shorthand expression for compulsive psychological dependence, makes no man a ward of the state unless his weakness has some additional effects on his mental processes generally.[151]

From the existing facts, the most that can be said, perhaps, is that the question of the competency of addicts is debatable, but even if they are deemed incompetent it is difficult to justify their commitment, at least along traditional lines where abstinence is the goal and where the means include institutionalization, detoxification, counseling, and supervised aftercare. Commitment is not easily justified because the second prong of the requirement for the exercise of paternalistic power—that coerced treatment is in fact clearly in the patient's best interest—is exceedingly difficult to meet in the area of addiction. First of all,

> an addict's refusal to be treated is not necessarily irrational. For one thing, even if the cure were always a lesser evil than the disease, the prospect of cure is uncertain and distant, and the prospects of long confinement and indefinite supervision are correspondingly excellent. Moreover, whatever his failings, the addict has a special competence with regard to assessing the value of treatment for him. He may not know what commitment would be like, but he better than anyone knows the evils of addiction, and he knows what his life was like before addiction. The point is not that addiction is bliss, but rather that for many addicts neither is life without drugs. Even an informed, intelligent, and otherwise sane addict might conceivably prefer not to endure institutional confinement for the privilege of facing the world without a crutch.[152]

Addicts may differ, of course, with respect to their need for crutches in dealing with life, but there is widespread uniformity among evaluators and commentators that the traditional method for dealing with addiction (the abstinence model involving forced detoxification, hospitalization, and aftercare) is an expensive failure. The civil commitment schemes for controlling addiction have simply not worked.[153] The strong consensus is in conformity with the view expressed by Aronowitz that

> there is no evidence that the method of treatment which the addict would be compelled to undergo if he were committed offers any reasonable hope of curing his addiction. At present, proponents of involuntary commitment can offer virtually no empirical data to support the claim that institutionalization in a drug-free environment followed by an intensive aftercare supervision offers even a fair chance of cure for the average narcotic addict.[154]

It is true, of course, that some of the newer methods of addiction control (such as those, like methadone maintenance, which abjure the abstinence model) are quite successful in accomplishing their goals.[155] But coercive treatment of an addict is no less objectionable simply because the therapeutic experts *might*, in their discretion, decide to place the committed addict on a methadone maintenance program: so long as the addict may be physically committed and subjected to the traditional abstinence approaches, the validity of the paternalistic intervention will remain questionable, even though the addict may find himself or herself fortunate enough to be tried on methadone maintenance. That is so, of course, because the paternalistic interference must be judged by its *maximal* control over an addict.

But the legal and philosophical situation might be quite different, therefore, if a court exercising paternalistic jurisdiction were permitted to order therapy short of hospitalization.[156] Such a court, in a narcotics context, might be authorized, for example, to order an addict to participate in a methadone maintenance program. To justify that exercise of paternalistic jurisdiction, the court in each case would have to decide whether, from all the facts about the addict and about methadone programs, it is objectively in the addict's best interests to subject him or her to such a treatment procedure. Even if so, however, the order could legitimately be issued only if the conceptual and empirical questions regarding the competency of addicts were resolved in the negative.

A nutshell summary of the proper exercise of *parens patriae* jurisdiction over narcotic addicts, then, suggests that they should not be subjected to traditional commitment programs, and that they might be subjected to rather effective programs only if we were to conclude that they are incompetent to decide rationally whether they are better off in or out of treatment. It should be noted, however, that this approach permits us to reach addicts under the *parens patriae* power only after they have already become addicts, and hence when they are most difficult to treat successfully. Prior to their becoming actual addicts, even repeated abusers would be difficult to reach under the traditional paternalistic model because they have not yet lost control over their drug taking and hence seem perfectly competent to decide their own fate. The traditional position has been expressed as follows:

> Addiction itself, then, is not grounds for benevolent commitment. Nor, *a fortiori*, is an imminent danger of addiction resulting from the repeated use of narcotics. Repeated use without addiction is not itself a mental disability of any sort, nor is there here even that limited loss of self-control which some courts have in other contexts mistakenly thought to be sufficient for commitment.[157]

Narcotics Abuse.   It is arguable, however, along two related but distinct lines of thought, both of which are admittedly somewhat unconventional, that the *parens patriae* power could legitimately be extended to reach the earlier stage of narcotics abuse and that paternalistic jurisdiction could more appropriately be exercised then, rather than after addiction has taken hold. But justified paternalistic intervention at that early stage must be viewed as speculative, for it requires the acceptance of a somewhat novel conceptual framework, the proper resolution of several empirical questions, and perhaps a level of scientific knowledge which we have not yet reached.

The first theory is based on an extension of the concept of consent. Obviously, paternalistic measures taken on behalf of a person *with* his or her consent are ordinarily unobjectionable. Furthermore, as the contemporary philosopher Gerald Dworkin has demonstrated in his essay "Paternalism,"[158] there are instances where paternalistic interference can be justified by the doctrine of consent even though, at the precise time of the paternalistic intervention, the affected individual might object to the action:

> Under certain conditions it is rational for an individual to agree that others should force him to act in ways which, at the time of action, the individual may not see as desirable. If, for example, a man knows that he is subject to breaking his resolves when temptation is present, he may ask a friend to refuse to entertain his requests at some later stage.[159]

True, he may later assert that he has changed his mind, but "since it is *just* such changes that he wished to guard against we are entitled to ignore them."[160]

That type of consensual theory is employed today to justify various therapeutic measures. Applied behavioral psychologists have, for example, devised schemes of "behavioral contracting" or "contingency contracting," where the subject may agree that certain benefits should be given him or her contingent on certain appropriate behavior.[161] For instance, Mann[162] used a contingency contract procedure to encourage weight loss in overweight adults. Persons desiring to lose weight could voluntarily surrender various meaningful items to the therapist and enter into a contract whereby various items would be returned or forfeited (donated to charities) contingent on weight loss or weight gain. The contract was actually a "behavior trap" since, after it was voluntarily entered into, it would have a lasting influence on behavior, and a later change of heart on the part of the client would be to no avail. A similar behavior trap, now given legal blessing, is operative in the institutional treatment of narcotics addiction. An addict who voluntarily seeks treatment for his or her addiction in a federal facility and who pursues the proper legal channels can be accepted for treatment on the condition that he or she remain for a specific period of time. Although early cases went the other way,[163] recent cases hold that the addict is bound by his or her agreement and cannot legally leave the hospital at will. The addict's voluntary application is technically converted into a commitment, and in the words of *Ortega* v. *Rasor*,[164] "The Court will not permit the petitioner to terminate his treatment simply because the road to recovery is bumpy."[165]

But the consent concept can be stretched even further than in the above examples. Dworkin again gives an example:

> [I]t is very difficult for a child to defer gratification for any considerable period of time.... [G]iven the very real and permanent dangers that may befall the child it becomes not only permissible but even a duty of the parent

to restrict the child's freedom in various ways. There is however an important moral limitation on the exercise of such parental power which is provided by the notion of the child eventually coming to see the correctness of his parent's interventions. Parental paternalism may be thought of as a wager by the parent on the child's subsequent recognition of the wisdom of the restrictions. There is an emphasis on what could be called future-oriented consent—on what the child will come to welcome, rather than on what he does welcome.[166]

"Future-oriented" consent, while used in the above example to justify interference with a legally incompetent subject, need not necessarily be restricted to instances of incompetency. Persons who attempt suicide are by no means always mentally incompetent at the time of the attempt. Of the competent ones, some may have rationally wanted to die, while others, though perhaps sincere in their desire to die, may have been "wrong." If all persons who attempted suicide were somehow saved by society's suicide prevention efforts, the saved persons would presumably have differing reactions concerning society's paternalistic efforts. The incompetent ones, if and when they regained competency, might well appreciate society's efforts, as might those who were competent but "wrong" about their decision to die. Only those who were competent and arguably rational about their attempted suicide (for instance, terminally ill persons, etc.) might strongly object to society's "benevolent" action in saving them.

If we wanted to be philosophically pure in our paternalistic suicide prevention efforts—and if we were practically equipped to make the necessary subtle distinctions—we might well let the competent but "correct" persons die,[167] but might save the others in the expectation of receiving their future consent. Surely, if future consent were to be actually given, we would doubtless feel justified in our earlier paternalistic invasions. And because we cannot in practice determine at the critical time of rescue which persons would give future consent to the rescue efforts and which would not, we feel justified in saving them all, presumably on the assumption—and this is an empirical matter—that not an insubstantial number would be belatedly appreciative.

The future consent analysis regarding suicide prevention is suggestive of an approach for paternalistically acceptable intervention in the area of narcotics *abuse*. Interestingly, the same approach generally cuts *against* paternalistic intervention in the area of narcotics *addiction*.

It is probably true that most addicts would be unwilling to submit to conventional abstinence treatment. Indeed, Dr. Alan Stone reports that

in New York a heroin addict may be arrested for stealing to support his habit, and if convicted for stealing will serve a brief sentence as a criminal and be back out on the street. If, however, he is discovered to be an addict, he may not be punished; instead, he may spend up to three years civilly confined for treatment as a patient. Many addicts prefer brief criminal punishment to prolonged treatment, given these alternatives. In fact, some observers report that the recent spate of suicides in the Tombs (as the New York jail is appropriately called) is the result of this cruel choice—attempting to conceal their addiction, prisoners withdraw without medical assistance and some, it is said, commit suicide in the throes of their withdrawal. [168]

Not only would most addicts be initially opposed to the traditional treatment, but it is likely that, were they forcibly subjected to it, they would *withhold* their future consent. But that by no means suggests that addicts do not wish to be cured. Instead, it probably means simply that, as we have seen, traditional treatment techniques are therapeutically ineffective.

It may well be that most addicts, though unwilling to submit to traditional treatment, *do* wish they were not addicted, and would submit to therapy if it were truly effective and not terribly burdensome. That, however, is an empirical question, for some addicts, desirous of a social crutch to offset an oppressive environment, might opt for continued addiction rather than cure. It would, indeed, be interesting (and presumably important in terms of defining appropriate paternalistic power) to ascertain the proportion of addicts who in fact strongly wish they were not addicted.

Even assuming, however, that the number of addicts seriously unhappy with their condition were overwhelmingly high, the exercise of paternalistic jurisdiction over them would, as we have seen, be highly questionable, for once they are addicted they will prove refractory to conventional treatment and probably can, at best, find relief through some sort of maintenance program. But a finding that addicts overwhelmingly deplore their condition should, under an application of a future-consent rationale, enable us to intervene paternalistically and *preventively* with narcotic abusers in order to offset the possibility that the abusers will become addicted.

Therapeutic intervention could, for example, require preaddicts ("snorters," "joy-poppers," and the like) to submit to counseling and to compulsory drug education focusing on the facts of addiction. Furthermore, if some sort of narcotic antagonist could be developed which countered the euphoric and other effects of narcotics without producing undesirable side effects, a nonaddict narcotics abuser could be required periodically to take the antagonist, which should preclude his becoming an addict. And interestingly, since by definition nonaddict abusers have not yet lost control over their drug taking behavior, traditional criminal penalties inflicted at the narcotics abuse stage might serve as general and specific deterrents to drug abuse. Ironically, this may be an area where the criminal law may actually have a *paternalistic* function by deterring persons from engaging in conduct which, if they engaged in it continually, they would come to realize was against their best interests. A judicious blending of therapeutic and perhaps penal measures at the abuse stage might operate to reduce drastically the problem of narcotics addiction.

Accordingly, the ancitipated future-consent doctrine might be read to permit paternalistic intervention with narcotic abusers more so than with full-fledged addicts. Even though some addicts may prefer addiction to nonaddiction in order better to cope with a stressful environment, if the factual evidence demonstrates that addicts overwhelmingly regret having become addicted, policy considerations would probably permit across-the-board efforts to prevent addiction, on the proper assumption that, much like the suicide prevention example, we would be unable to predict which abusers would ultimately come to appreciate the paternalistic intervention and which would not.

There are, of course, several problems with the future-consent model, some of which are not directly relevant to the present discussion. For example, it is clear that not all interventions can be legitimated by future consent. Psychosurgery, for instance, may be ratified by the patient after the fact, but therapy that drastic may well have so altered the personality that the consent may actually be coming from an "identity" different from the presurgical personality. But even with the drug abuse situation, the model is not a perfect fit. Note, for example, that in the suicide prevention illustration, the rescued persons, highly cognizant of their new leases on life, would surely be able to appreciate the paternalistic intervention and to give it their belated consent. With the drug abusers, however, successful preventive efforts will operate to foreclose the subjects from ever becoming addicts and experiencing the presumed agony of addiction. Accordingly, while they may later come to appreciate the paternalistic prevention, they also may *not* come to do so. They might, for example, feel later just as they did at the time of the intervention: that they would never have become "hooked" and that the state simply acted to prevent them from engaging in a pleasurable activity. This problem, and others like it, must be handled by appropriate balancing efforts.

The appropriate balancing test seems rather easy to formulate: the state should not act to prevent self-harming activities on a future-consent basis unless the resentment it engenders from the subject population is clearly outweighed either by the consent eventually given by that population or by the agony endured by a similar population that has not been prevented from engaging in the self-injurious behavior. According to the suggested test, then, marijuana use, even if somewhat harmful to repeated users, ought not to be paternalistically prohibited, for the affront to dignity and the resentment caused by paternalistic efforts—efforts which are not likely to eventuate in future consent—cannot comfortably be outweighed by the known harm done to some by prolonged use. On the other hand, if narcotic addiction is shown to be absolutely tormenting to the great bulk of addicts, the anguish of that population ought to be sufficient, under a "would-be-future-consent" approach, to prevent abusers from developing a full-blown habit, whether or not the abusers ultimately come to appreciate fully the paternalistic efforts taken on their behalf.

The second theory that may enable paternalistic power to be exercised at the stage of narcotics abuse seems to come to the same result as the future-consent theory, but by a somewhat different line of reasoning. Even the antipaternalistic position of John Stuart Mill did not state absolutely that the will of competent persons could never be paternalistically overridden. Mill, for example, would impose the following paternalistic limitation:

> In this and most other civilized countries, for example, an engagement by which a person should sell himself, or allow himself to be sold, as a slave, would be null and void; neither enforced by law nor by opinion. The ground for thus limiting his power of voluntarily disposing of his own lot in life, is apparent, and is very clearly seen in this extreme case. The reason for not interfering, unless for the sake of others, with a person's voluntary acts, is consideration for his liberty. His voluntary choice is evidence that what he so chooses is desirable, or at the least endurable, to him, and his good is on the whole best provided for by allowing him to take his own means of pursuing it. But by selling himself for a slave, he abdicates his liberty; he foregoes any future use of it, beyond that single act. He therefore defeats, in his own case, the very purpose which is the justification of allowing him to dispose of himself. He is no longer free; but is thenceforth in a position which has no longer the presumption in its favor, that would be afforded by his voluntarily remaining in it. The principle of freedom cannot require that he should be free not to be free. It is not freedom, to be allowed to alienate his freedom. [169]

Mill's slavery example may be illustrative of a paternalistic principle. It seems that "the main consideration for not allowing such a contract is the need to preserve the liberty of the person to make future choices,"[170] and that paternalism may be permissible to prevent actions which, once taken, would lead irreversibly to a far-reaching constriction of future freedom.[171]

Without attempting at this point to define the necessarily vague contours of that principle, we could nonetheless easily conclude that narcotics addiction is quite clearly equivalent to a condition of bondage.

We have already seen, for example, that narcotics addiction has been characterized as a "basic drive," and one where "[t]he individual loses the power to master his craving for the drug: the dependence dominates the individual and his way of life."[172]

Surely, then, at least within the context of our current legal structure which prohibits heroin maintenance, narcotics addiction could be treated as a form of physiological and psychological bondage. A more troubling empirical question is whether addiction would also constitute slavery in the context of a system authorizing heroin maintenance. To date, for example, no study has satisfactorily measured the impact of heroin euphoria on the mental functioning and social productivity of addicts.[173] On the one hand, the heroin high is said to produce a sense of security and self-confidence, traits which of course are highly consistent with productivity. But the high has also been described as a feeling of aloofness, creating a tendency to postpone decisions and urgencies traits which are clearly counter-productive.[174] Whatever the specific effect of the high, however, heroin maintenance might have to be structured so that the addict would have to make several trips daily to obtain a needed supply of drugs,[175] and, no matter how much better a situation that may be than alternate solutions to the narcotics problem, the complete dependence of the addict on obtaining a needed dose may so restrict his or her freedom of action that the condition may still resemble slavery.

If, of course, heroin maintenance proves in fact not to resemble slavery, and if maintenance systems are given the legal go-ahead and come into widespread existence, there may be less justification, under this "renounced freedom" philosophical theory, to try paternalistically to forcibly cure or prevent addiction. (Note, however, that even if heroin maintenance is not deemed to be slavery, its effects or its inconvenience might be such that addicts might still regret having become addicted, thus perhaps opening the door to a future-consent justification for paternalistic preventive efforts.) But there are, as we have seen, several serious objections to heroin maintenance systems,[176] or at least to heroin maintenance systems that are not rigidly restricted in operation.[177] Hence, if heroin maintenance does not come into existence, or if it does come into existence but is nevertheless found empirically to constitute a form of bondage, the renounced-freedom paternalistic rationale might be available for purposes of intervention, and therapeutic measures could arguably be mandated if they held real promise for breaking the bonds of addiction. Once again, however, paternalistic intervention after the onset of addiction would be difficult to justify in light of our therapeutic impotence at that stage. But mandatory counseling, required attendance at addiction education programs, and the required consumption of "ideal" narcotic antagonists, perhaps combined with the possibility of criminal penalties, might be paternalistically ordered for nonaddict narcotics abusers in order to effectively prevent them from donning the shackles of addiction.

CONCLUSION

The emergence of the therapeutic orientation in our legal system for dealing with deviant behavior is at once an exciting and a troubling development. Many of the sociological and psychological implications of the gradual shift in orientation will not be determined without further research. It is already known, however, that an unbridled therapeutic premise threatens many other values cherished by society, and that legal constraints must accordingly be carefully placed on the exercise of therapeutic jurisdiction. In particular, certain important procedural safeguards must not be sacrificed, and the substantive standards for the exercise of the state's police power and *parens patriae* jurisdiction must be clearly defined. It is even possible, in theory at least, that civil commitment procedural safeguards should to some extent vary according to the operative substantive standard for commitment. The potential theoretical relationship between civil commitment substantive standards and procedural protections can perhaps best be illustrated by examining the procedural "standard of proof" required to commit an individual. That is the subject matter of the brief chapter that follows.

NOTES

[1] N. KITTRIE, THE RIGHT TO BE DIFFERENT: DEVIANCE AND ENFORCED THERAPY 20-21 (1971).
[2] *Id.* at 8.
[3] *Id.* at 20-21.
[4] *Id.* at 29.
[5] *Id.* at 37.
[6] *Id.* at 1.
[7] 370 U.S. 660 (1962).
[8] B. F. SKINNER, BEYOND FREEDOM AND DIGNITY (1971).
[9] *See generally* Goodall, *Shapers at Work*, 6 PSYCHOLOGY TODAY, 53 (Nov., 1972).
[10] A. BANDURA, PRINCIPLES OF BEHAVIOR MODIFICATION (1969).
[11] V. MARK & F. ERVIN, VIOLENCE AND THE BRAIN (1970). *See* NATIONAL COMMISSION FOR THE PROTECTION OF HUMAN SUBJECTS OF BIOMEDICAL AND BEHAVIORAL RESEARCH, REPORT AND RECOMMENDATIONS : PSYCHOSURGERY (1977).
[12] *In re* Gault, 387 U.S. 1 (1967).

[13]Jackson v. Indiana, 406 U.S. 715 (1972). The invitation was, however, rather rudely retracted in some later cases. Perhaps struck by the difficulty of the issues, the Court has often ducked the difficult questions and has decided cases on narrow grounds. *See, e.g.,* O'Connor v. Donaldson, 422 U.S. 563 (1976).

[14]KITTRIE, *supra* note 1, at 29.

[15]Livermore, Malmquist, & Meehl, *On the Justifications for Civil Commitment,* 117 U. PA. L. REV. 75, 80 (1968). For an excellent recent analysis of this and related problems, *see* Morse, *Crazy Behavior, Morals and Science: An Analysis of Mental Health Law,* 51 So. CALIF. L. REV. 527 (1978).

[16]United States v. Charnizon, 232 A.2d 586 (D.C. Ct. App. 1967).

[17]Livermore, Malmquist, & Meehl, *supra* note 15, at 83.

[18]Kaplan, *The Role of the Law in Drug Control,* 1971 DUKE L. J. 1065, 1071–72.

[19]Szasz, *The Sane Slave: An Historical Note on the Use of Medical Diagnosis as Justificatory Rhetoric,* 25 AM. J. PSYCHOTHERAPY 228 (1971).

[20]Note, *The Disguised Oppression of Involuntary Guardianship: Have the Elderly Freedom to Spend?,* 73 YALE L. J. 676 (1964). *Cf. In re* Strittmater's Estate, 53 A.2d 205, 206 (N.J. 1947) ("I think it was her paranoic condition, especially her insane delusions about the male, that led her to leave her estate to the National Women's Party. The result is that the probate should be set aside").

[21]*In re* Sealy, 218 So. 2d 765 (Fla. App. 1969); Wexler, Scoville *et al., The Administration of Psychiatric Justice: Theory and Practice in Arizona,* 13 ARIZ. L. REV. 1, 20 (1971).

[22]Dallas Morning News, May 1, 1972, at 2D, col. 1.

[23]S. BLOCH & P. REDDAWAY, RUSSIA'S POLITICAL HOSPITALS: THE ABUSE OF PSYCHIATRY IN THE SOVIET UNION (1977).

[24]Wexler, Scoville *et al., supra* note 21, at 242.

[25]Note, *Conditioning and Other Technologies Used to "Treat?" "Rehabilitate?" "Demolish?" Prisoners and Mental Patients,* 45 S. CAL. L. REV. 616, 617 (1972). For an extensive bibliography on the growing right to refuse treatment, *see* A. BROOKS, LAW, PSYCHIATRY AND THE MENTAL HEALTH SYSTEM 258–264 (Supp. 1980).

[26]Schwitzgebel, *Limitations on the Coercive Treatment of Offenders,* 8 CRIM. L. BULL. 267, 286 (1972).

[27]*See generally* BANDURA, *supra* note 10.

[28]*See generally* MARK & ERVIN, *supra* note 11.

[29]Wexler, *Of Rights and Reinforcers,* 11 SAN DIEGO L. REV. 957 (1974).

[30]Bruce, *Tokens for Recovery,* 66 AM. J. NURSING 1799, 1800–01 (1966).

[31]T. AYLLON & N. AZRIN, THE TOKEN ECONOMY: A MOTIVATIONAL SYSTEM FOR THERAPY AND REHABILITATION (1968).

[32]Glicksman, Ottomanelli, & Cutler, *The Earn-Your-Way Credit System: Use of a Token Economy in Narcotic Rehabilitation,* 6 INT'L J. OF THE ADDICTIONS 525 (1971).

[33]Narrol, *Experimental Application of Reinforcement Principles to the Analysis and Treatment of Hospitalized Alcoholics,* 28 Q. J. STUDIES ON ALCOHOL 105 (1967).

[34]Schwitzgebel, *Limitations on the Coercive Treatment of Offenders,* 8 CRIM L. BULL. 267 (1972).

[35]KAZDIN & BOOTZIN, *The Token Economy: An Evaluative Review,* 5 J. APPLIED BEHAVIOR ANALYSIS 343 (1972). *See generally* Kazdin, *Recent Advances in Token Economy Research,* in PROGRESS IN BEHAVIOR MODIFICATION (M. Hersen & R. Eisler eds. 1975); Agras, *The Token Economy,* in BEHAVIOR MODIFICATION: PRINCIPLES AND CLINICAL APPLICATIONS 64 (W. S. Agras ed. 1978).

[36]*See generally* Narrol, *supra* note 33.

[37]Schwitzgebel, *Limitations on the Coercive Treatment of Offenders*, 8 CRIM. L. BULL. 267, 279 (1972).

[38]*Id.*

[39]Note, *supra* note 25, at 635–36.

[40]A. BURGESS, A CLOCKWORK ORANGE (1962).

[41]*See generally* V. MARK & F. ERVIN, *supra* note 11.

[42]Chapter 8, this volume.

[43]Weiner, *The Clockwork Cure*, THE NATION, April 3, 1972, at 433.

[44]*See generally* V. MARK & F. ERVIN, *supra* note 11.

[45]Note, *supra* note 25, at 633.

[46]Breggin, *The Return of Lobotomy and Psychosurgery*, 118 CONG. REC. E.1601 (daily ed. Feb. 24, 1972).

[47]*Id.*

[48]*Id. See also* Breggin, *Psychosurgery for Control of Violence*, 118 CONG. REC. E3380 (daily ed. March 30, 1972).

[49]Breggin, *supra* note 46, at E1602, E1610.

[50]*Id.*

[51]Johnson & Szurek, *Etiology of Antisocial Behavior in Delinquents and Psychopaths*, 154 J.A.M.A. 814 (1954).

[52]Savoy, *Towards a New Politics of Legal Education*, 79 YALE L. J. 444, 497–99 (1970). On a somewhat related inquiry, *see* Chapter 7 of the present volume.

[53]Note, *Criminal Liability of Parents for Failure to Control Their Children*, 6 VALPARAISO L. REV. 332 (1972).

[54]S. FOX, THE LAW OF JUVENILE COURTS IN A NUTSHELL 223–25 (1971).

[55]R. THARP & R. WETZEL, BEHAVIOR MODIFICATION IN THE NATURAL ENVIRONMENT (1969); Thorne, Tharp, & Wetzel, *Behavior Modification Techniques: New Tools for Probation Officers*, 31 FED. PROB. 21 (June, 1967).

[56]K. MENNINGER, THE CRIME OF PUNISHMENT (1968).

[57]Murphy, *Criminal Punishment and Psychiatric Fallacies*, 4 LAW & SOC. REV. 111, 115 (1969).

[58]*Id.*

[59]Note, *Due Process for the Narcotic Addict? The New York Compulsory Commitment Procedures*, 43 N.Y.U.L. REV. 1172 (1968).

[60]*In re* Gault, 387 U.S. 1 (1967).

[61]THE MENTALLY DISABLED AND THE LAW 125–27 (2d ed. S. Brakel & R. Rock eds. 1971).

[62]*See generally* Poythress, *Psychiatric Expertise in Civil Commitment—Training Attorneys to Cope with Expert Testimony*, 2 L. & HUMAN BEH. 1 (1978). *See also* Cohen, *The Functioning of the Attorney and the Commitment of the Mentally Ill*, 44 TEXAS L. REV. 424 (1968).

[63]*See* Chapter 4, this volume.

[64]KITTRIE, *supra* note 1, at 73. In Parham v. J. R., 99 S. Ct. 2493 (1979), the Supreme Court upheld a medical model commitment procedure for the admission of minors. Although the case was confined to the question of minors, some observers believe the Court may be willing to extend the minimal due process procedures of *Parham* to the context of adult commitments as well.

[65]408 U.S. 238, 308 (1972).

[66]H. WEIHOFEN, THE URGE TO PUNISH (1956).

[67]Fixsen, Phillips, & Wolf, *Achievement Place: Experiments in Self-Government with Pre-Delinquents*, 6 J. APPLIED BEHAVIOR ANALYSIS 31 (1973). *See also* Wolf, Phillips, Fixsen *et al.*, *Achievement Place: The Teaching-Family Model*, 5 CHILD CARE QUARTERLY 92 (1976).

[68]Andenaes, *The General Preventive Effects of Punishment*, 114 U. PA. L. REV. 949 (1966).

[69]*See* H. Weihofen, *supra* note 66.

[70]*See* Andenaes, *supra* note 68; Chappel, Geis, & Hardt, *Explorations in Deterrence and Criminal Justice*, 8 Crim. L. Bull. 514 (1972). On deterrence and the difficulties of performing deterrence research, *see* J. Gibbs, Crime, Punishment, and Deterrence (1975).

[71]Schwitzgebel, *Book Review*, 36 Fed. Prob. 66 (March, 1972).

[72]A. Goldstein, The Insanity Defense 24 (1967). *See generally* Chapter 5, this volume.

[73]Larsen, *A Prisoner Looks at Writ-Writing*, 56 Calif. Law Rev. 343 (1968). *See* Chapter 5, this volume.

[74]370 U.S. 660, 683 n.1 (1962).

[75]Kittrie, *supra* note 1, at 236.

[76]Rothaus, Hanson, Cleveland, & Johnson, *Describing Psychiatric Hospitalization: A Dilemma*, 18 Am. Psychologist 85 (1963).

[77]Rothaus & Hanson, *The Path of Inquiry in Mental Illness and Problem Centered Self-Description*, 1 Commun. Ment. Health J. 29 (1965).

[78]Kittrie, *supra* note 1, at xvii.

[79]E. Schur, Labelling Deviant Behavior : Its Sociological Implications (1971). *See* Chapter 8, this volume.

[80]J. Freedman & A. Doob, Deviancy: The Psychology of Being Different (1968).

[81]See Chapter 8, note 7, this volume.

[82]F. Hartung, Crime, Law and Society (1965); Sykes & Matza, *Techniques of Neutralization: A Theory of Delinquency*, 22 Am. Sociol. Rev. 664 (1957).

[83]*See* W. Glasser, Reality Therapy (1965); Hartung, *supra* note 82. *See also* A. Ellis, A Guide to Rational Living (1975).

[84]Rotter, *External Control and Internal Control*, 5 Psychology Today 37 (June, 1971).

[85]*Id.* at 58.

[86]*Id. See also* Brice & Sassenrath, *Effects of Locus of Control, Task Instructions, and Belief on Expectancy of Success*, 104 J. Social Psychology 97 (1978).

[87]*See generally* Glasser, *supra* note 83; Hartung, *supra* note 82.

[88]*See* B. F. Skinner, *supra* note 8.

[89]Murphy, *supra* note 57, at 121 n. 8.

[90]*See* Glasser, *supra* note 83.

[91]Kittrie, *supra* note 1, at 46; Schur, *supra* note 79, at 165.

[92]Kittrie, *supra* note 1, at 46.

[93]A. Cohen, Deviance and Control 6–11 (1966); Schur, *supra* note 79, at 140–47.

[94]Cohen, *supra* note 93, at 10.

[95]*See* Note, *supra* note 25.

[96]*See* Markham, *What's All This Talk of Heroin Maintenance?*, New York Times Magazine, July 2, 1972, at 6. *See also* Rosenthal, *Partial Prohibition of Nonmedical Use of Mind-Altering Drugs: Proposals for Change*, 16 Houston L. Rev. 603 (1979).

[97]Schwartz, *Social Factors in the Development of Legal Control: A Case Study of Two Israeli Settlements*, 63 Yale L. J. 471 (1954).

[98]Andenaes, *supra* note 68, at 957.

[99]*See* Chapters 9 and 10, this volume.

[100]Wyatt v. Stickney, 344 F. Supp. 373 (M.D. Ala. 1972).

[101]Note, *supra* note 25, at 670–73. For an excellent recent general discussion of informed consent, *see* Meisel, *The Exceptions to the Informed Consent Doctrine: Striking a Balance between Competing Values in Medical Decision Making*, 1979 Wis. L. Rev. 413.

[102]*See* Chapters 9 & 10, this volume; *see also* Bandura, *supra* note 10.

[103]Experimentation with Human Subjects (P. Freund ed. 1970); J. Katz, Experimenta-

TION WITH HUMAN BEINGS (1972); DEVIANCE AND DECENCY: THE ETHICS OF RESEARCH WITH HUMAN SUBJECTS (C. Klockars & F. O'Connor eds. 1979); Robertson, *The Law of Institutional Review Boards*, 26 U.C.L.A. L. REV. 484 (1979).

[104]Livermore, Malmquist, & Meehl, *supra* note 15, at 75, 88.

[105]Lake v. Cameron, 364 F.2d 657 (D.C. Cir. 1966); Chambers, *Alternatives to Civil Commitment of the Mentally Ill: Practical Guides and Constitutional Imperatives*, 70 MICH L. REV. 1107 (1972).

[106]*In re* Gault, 387 U.S. 1, 18 (1967).

[107]J. ZISKIN, COPING WITH PSYCHIATRIC AND PSYCHOLOGICAL TESTIMONY (2d ed. 1978); *see also* Cohen, *supra* note 62.

[108]Dershowitz, *The Psychiatrist's Power in Civil Commitment: A Knife That Cuts Both Ways*, 2 PSYCHOLOGY TODAY 43, Feb., 1969; Cocozza & Steadman, *The Failure of Psychiatric Predictions of Dangerousness: Clear and Convincing Evidence*, 29 RUTGERS L. REV. 1084 (1976).

[109]*See* ZISKIN, *supra* note 107. *See also* Ennis & Litwack, *Psychiatry and the Presumption of Expertise: Flipping Coins in the Courtroom*, 63 CALIF. L. REV. 693 (1974). On psychiatric predictions in capital cases, *see* Dix, *Administration of the Texas Death Penalty Statutes: Constitutional Infirmities Related to the Prediction of Dangerousness*, 55 TEXAS L. REV. 1343 (1977).

[110]*See* Chapter 8, this volume.

[111]*See* MARK & ERVIN, *supra* note 11; Chapter 8, this volume.

[112]*See* Cohen, *supra* note 62.

[113]349 F. Supp. 1078 (E.D. Wis. 1972). *See also* 413 F. Supp. 1318 (E.D. Wis. 1976) (reinstating, after a convoluted procedural journey, the original judicial order).

[114]National Conference of Commissioners on Uniform State Laws, Uniform Drug Dependence Treatment and Rehabilitation Act; ARIZ. REV. STAT. §§501 *et seq.*; PRESIDENT'S COMMISSION ON MENTAL HEALTH, REPORT TO THE PRESIDENT 70 (1978) (recommendations for model commitment legislation).

[115]American Psychiatric Association, *Position Statement on Involuntary Hospitalization of the Mentally Ill*, 128 AM. J. PSYCHIATRY 1480 (1972). Procedural protections similar to those specified by *Lessard* and by the American Psychiatric Association's position statement have also been endorsed by the PRESIDENT'S COMMISSION ON MENTAL HEALTH, *supra* note 114, at 70.

[116]406 U.S. 715 (1972).

[117]*Id.* at 736–37. On the retraction of the invitation, *see* note 13 *supra*.

[118]Livermore, Malmquist & Meehl, *supra* note 15, at 18 *et seq.*

[119]*See* Kaplan, *supra* note 18, at 1065.

[120]*Id.* at 1066.

[121]Dershowitz, *The Law of Dangerousness: Some Fictions about Predictions*, 23 J. LEGAL EDUC. 24 (1970).

[122]Note, *Civil Commitment of Narcotic Addicts*, 76 YALE L.J. 1160, 1179 (1967).

[123]*Id.* at 1182–83.

[124]*See* Kaplan, *supra* note 18.

[125]*See* Livermore, Malmquist, & Meehl, *supra* note 15.

[126]Note, *supra* note 122, at 1188–89.

[127]Dershowitz, *supra* note 121, at 24.

[128]Lessard v. Schmidt, *supra* note 113; *compare* Mathew v. Nelson, 461 F. Supp. 707 (N.D. Ill. 1978). *See also* Note, *Overt Dangerous Behavior as a Constitutional Requirement for Civil Commitment of the Mentally Ill*, 44 U. CHI. L. REV. 562 (1977).

[129]Aronowitz, *Civil Commitment of Narcotic Addicts*, 67 COLUM. L. REV. 405 (1967); Note, *supra* note 122, at 1183.

[130]AMERICAN BAR ASSOCIATION, NEW PERSPECTIVES ON URBAN CRIME 48–49 (1972) (report of Special Committee on Crime Prevention and Control).

[131]Note, *supra* note 122, at 1183.

[132]Aronowitz, *supra* note 129, at 414.

[133]Note, *supra* note 122, at 1177 n.55.

[134]*Id.* at 1183.

[135]*Id.* at 1185.

[136]AMERICAN BAR ASSOCIATION, *supra* note 130, at 26–27.

[137]*See* Markham, *supra* note 96. For a recent proposal that the United States begin "carefully controlled experimental outpatient programs in which heroin addicts may be lawfully maintained on heroin or injectable methadone," *see* the thorough analysis of Professor Michael Rosenthal, *supra* note 96, at 603.

[138]Note, *supra* note 122, at 1187.

[139]370 U.S. 660 (1962).

[140]Lessard v. Schmidt, No. 71-C-602 (E.D. Wis. filed Oct. 18, 1972).

[141]Robertson, *Pre-trial Diversion of Drug Offenders: A Statutory Approach*, 52 B. U. L. REV. 335 (1972). Note, *Addict Diversion: An Alternative Approach for the Criminal Justice System*, 60 GEO. L.J. 667 (1972). *See also* National Conference of Commissioners on Uniform State Laws, *supra* note 114.

[142]Bowden & Langenauer, *Success and Failure in the NARA Addiction Program*, 128 AM. J. PSYCHIATRY 853, 855 (1972).

[143]Mill, *On Liberty*, in J. S. MILL & T. CARLYLE, HARVARD CLASSICS 203 (1909).

[144]*See* Kaplan, *supra* note 18.

[145]Stone, *Psychiatry and the Law*, PSYCHIATRIC ANNALS 18, 28 (Oct., 1971).

[146]Note, *supra* note 122, at 1168.

[147]Ennis, *Civil Liberties and Mental Illness*, 7 CRIM. L. BULL. 101, 104 (1971).

[148]*Id.*; Note, *supra* note 122, at 1173 and n.44.

[149]Ennis, *supra* note 147, at 105–06.

[150]Bejerot, *A Theory of Addiction as an Artificially Induced Drive*, 128 AM. J. PSYCHIATRY 842, 843 (1972).

[151]Note, *supra* note 122, at 1174.

[152]*Id.* at 1176.

[153]AMERICAN BAR ASSOCIATION, *supra* note 130, at 41; COMM'N OF INQUIRY INTO THE NON-MEDICAL USE OF DRUGS, TREATMENT 10–17 (1972); Aronowitz, *supra* note 129; Kramer, *The State Versus the Addict: Uncivil Commitment*, 50 B. U. L. REV. 1 (1970).

[154]Aronowitz, *supra* note 129, at 417.

[155]AMERICAN BAR ASSOCIATION, *supra* note 130, at 53–54; COMM'N OF INQUIRY INTO THE NON-MEDICAL USE OF DRUGS, *supra* note 153, at 23–31.

[156]*See supra* note 105.

[157]Note, *supra* note 122, at 1176–77.

[158]Dworkin, *Paternalism*, in R. WASSERSTROM, MORALITY AND THE LAW 107 (1971). For more on paternalism, *see* J. MURPHY, RETRIBUTION, JUSTICE, AND THERAPY 165–82 (1979).

[159]Dworkin, *supra* note 158, at 119.

[160]*Id.* at 120 (emphasis in original).

[161]Mann, *The Behavior-Therapeutic Use of Contingency Contracting to Control an Adult Behavior Problem: Weight Control*, 5 J. APPLIED BEHAVIOR ANALYSIS 99 (1972); Thorne, Tharp, & Wetzel, *supra* note 55, at 21.

[162]*See* Mann, *supra* note 161.

[163]*Ex parte* Lloyd, 13 F. Supp. 1005 (E.D. Ky. 1936).

[164]291 F. Supp. 748 (S.D. Fla. 1968).

[165]*Id.* at 752.

[166]Dworkin, *supra* note 158, at 119. In the mental health commitment context, Alan Stone has dubbed this the "Thank You Theory of Civil Commitment." A. STONE, MENTAL HEALTH AND LAW: A SYSTEM IN TRANSITION 70 (1975).

[167]Szasz, *The Ethics of Suicide*, 31 ANTIOCH REV. 7 (1971). *See generally* Greenberg, *Involuntary Psychiatric Commitments to Prevent Suicide*, 49 N.Y.U.L. REV. 227 (1974).

[168]Stone, *supra* note 145, at 29.

[169]Mill, *supra* note 143, at 311–12.

[170]Dworkin, *supra* note 158, at 118.

[171]*Id.* at 123.

[172]Bejerot, *supra* note 150, at 843.

[173]AMERICAN BAR ASSOCIATION, *supra* note 130, at 58. The recent, but highly inconclusive, literature is well presented in Rosenthal, *supra* note 96, at 603, 631–40 (1979). *See also* D. CAPLOVITZ, THE WORKING ADDICT (1978).

[174]AMERICAN BAR ASSOCIATION, *supra* note 130, at 45.

[175]Note, *supra* note 122, at 1186 n.79.

[176]*See* Markham, *supra* note 96, at 6.

[177]*See* AMERICAN BAR ASSOCIATION, *supra* note 130.

3

An Illustration of the Theoretical Relationship between Civil Commitment Standards and Procedures

THE STANDARD OF PROOF PROBLEM

With the United States Supreme Court's decision in *Addington* v. *Texas*,[1] the procedural issue of the required standard of proof in civil commitment cases finally came to the fore. Addington was involuntarily committed by a Texas court for an indefinite period of time. His commitment was upheld by the Texas Supreme Court, which held constitutionally sufficient a "preponderance of the evidence" standard of proof. When his case reached the United States Supreme Court, Addington argued that his committability must be supported by evidence "beyond a reasonable doubt." The Supreme Court settled on an intermediate standard and accordingly required "clear and convincing" proof of committability.

As postured before the Court, *Addington* was not concerned with the proper substantive standard for commitment. Instead, appellant assumed[2] the constitutionality of the Texas test, which authorizes the indefinite commitment of a mentally ill person found to require hospitalization "for his own welfare and protection or the protection of others."[3] When a commitment statute speaks, as does the Texas one, of the "protection of others," it requires mental health and judicial decision makers to assess an individual's potential for future dangerousness. As seen in the preceding chapter, that public protection rationale is part and parcel of modern commitment statutes. The present chapter will briefly explore the criterion of dangerousness and will begin to probe the relationship between procedural standards of proof and the dangerousness substantive standard of commitment.

According to Alan Stone, former President of the American Psychiatric Association, "the predictive success appropriate to a legal decision can be described in three levels of increasing certainty: preponderance of the evidence, 51 percent successful; clear and convincing proof, 75 percent successful; beyond a reasonable doubt, at least 90 percent successful."[4] Based on his review of the research literature, Stone states that mental health professionals have not proven their ability to predict violent behavior by even a preponderance of the evidence. Cocozza and Steadman, accepting Stone's quantification, conclude that "any attempt to commit an individual solely on the basis of dangerousness would be futile if psychiatric testimony were subjected to any of these three standards of proof."[5] In fact, Cocozza and Steadman hold that the research has demonstrated "clear and convincing evidence of the *inability* of psychiatrists or anyone else to predict dangerousness accurately."[6]

Finally, Kahle and Sales, in reporting the results of a national survey of psychiatrists, psychologists, and lawyers regarding civil commitment, state that an "evidentiary paradox" exists. Their respondents endorsed a standard of "clear and convincing proof (approximately 75% or more certainty)," yet estimated the percentage of accurate predictions of dangerousness to others at only 40–46%. "Thus, we can never establish that a person is dangerous with sufficient certainty to comply with evidentiary standards. . . . This paradox will undoubtedly be the focus of considerable controversy concerning involuntary civil commitment in the near future."[7]

It seems, however, that the controversy should lie elsewhere. Ironic as it may seem, mental health professionals (or actuarial tables) may well be able to prove "dangerousness" beyond a reasonable doubt. That is true, however, if and only if "dangerousness" is viewed as a *probability* statement, rather than as an *absolute* claim that violent behavior will occur. And as we shall see, some civil commitment statutes and statutory proposals specifically cast the dangerousness criterion in probabilistic terms.

When a mental health professional makes a prediction of "dangerousness" without further specifications, he or she is making at least three separable assertions:

1. The individual being examined has certain characteristics.
2. Those characteristics are associated with a certain probability of violent behavior.
3. The probability of violent behavior is "sufficiently" great to justify preventive intervention.

The first two of these assertions are subject to various "standards of proof" and the third is essentially a social policy trade-off to be decided in the political process.[8] The social policy assertion is subject to scrutiny on constitutional grounds, but it is technically outside the scope of mental health prediction and of legal and judicial proof. Such confusion as exists in this area resides in the fact that many have construed "standards of proof" as applying to the third assertion, as if one were stating that *the probability of violence* must be .90 (under a "beyond a reasonable doubt" standard) or .75 (under a "clear and convincing evidence" standard) or .51 (under a "preponderance of evidence" standard). The more correct reading of the law, in my view, is that one must prove to a given standard only that a specified probability threshold has been crossed, the threshold being decided on a priori policy grounds.[9]

Take as an illustration the case of a psychiatrist or psychologist who examines a patient and finds him to be, among other things, a young, male paranoid schizophrenic, with several arrests for assault, who is addicted to heroin and who is stating that he intends to kill his wife. The patient is committed as mentally ill and "dangerous to others."

What is being predicted here and how is it to be proven? It seems that the psychologist or psychiatrist is making two classes of assertions that are subject to proof, and one statement of personal values to which the concept of "proof" is inapplicable. The psychologist or psychiatrist is stating:

1. Among the clinically significant characteristics of the patient are (a) his youth, (b) his sex, (c) his diagnosis of paranoid schizophrenia, (d) his history of violence, (e) his state of addiction, and (f) his verbal threat to kill.
2. In past research, or in the clinical experience of the mental health professional, this combination of characteristics has been associated with X probability of violent behavior occurring in a given time period.
3. X is a sufficiently high probablity to justify commitment.

Note that it may well be possible in a given case to prove *even beyond a reasonable doubt* the existence of given characteristics and their probabilistic association with violent behavior. In the example, one can surely ascertain with virtual certainty the patient's age and sex. His diagnosis can be tested in independent psychiatric examination. His police record can be verified. His state of addiction can be "proven" with medical tests. Witnesses can be called to testify as to the occurrence of the threat.

Likewise, research data and the clinical experience of others can be marshalled to demonstrate to some standard of proof that these characteristics are associated with a certain probability (X) of violent behavior. The lower X is, of course, the easier it is to prove. One might, for example, be able to make a "clear and convincing" case that the probability of violent behavior occurring in our hypothetical patient is at least 1 in 5.

The issue then is whether a .20 probability of violent behavior is sufficient to justify the invocation of the civil commitment law. That question should be resolved not by "proof" but by processes of legislative policy-making and constitutional "interest-balancing." Whether the deprivation of an individual's liberty occasioned by civil commitment is constitutionally acceptable should depend on the individual's dangerousness to society, which in turn presumably depends not only on the *probability* of the predicted harm but also on its *magnitude*. [10] Expectedly, therefore, a potential political assassin or mass murderer could be confined pursuant to a standard of predictive accuracy substantially lower than would be required to confine a person potentially dangerous to property.

Under this analysis, then, one could demonstrate that a mental health professional has *not* proven violence will occur with probability X by showing that (1) the individual does not, in fact, possess the characteristics ascribed to him or her or (2) the characteristics are not, in fact, associated with the probability of violence claimed for them.

Thus, in the example previously given, an attorney defending the patient against commitment could present evidence that the patient was misdiagnosed as a paranoid schizophrenic and a heroin addict, that he never made the threat to kill, or that his arrest record was misconstrued by the mental health examiner. Alternatively, the attorney would grant that the patient fits all the categories ascribed to him, but present testimony derived from research studies or from clinical experience that these characteristics, taken together, predict violence with less than X probability. In either case, the attorney would not be factually contesting the threshold probability necessary for commitment but rather whether his or her client has crossed it. The threshold probability might be challenged, however, by an argument that the constitution should not support coerced confinement to prevent the given harm when that harm is likely to occur with only X probability.

There would, therefore, seem to be no particular "paradox" between the evidentiary standards of proof in civil commitment and the present ability of mental health professionals to predict violent behavior. Nor should mental health professionals always fail even the highest standards of proof in estimating probabilities of future violent behavior. Whether they would or would not fail depends largely on the probability threshold they are asked to exceed. There is no question that mental health professionals (or any one else for that matter) could give estimates of violent behavior in any given case that would exceed the national base rates. All one would need to know is a person's age and sex. Studies have reported as high as a 35%[11] or 40%[12] accuracy rate for prediction among some offender populations. While no research exists which specifically tests the accuracy of prediction in short-term civil commitment,[13] it is conceivable that circumstances exist in which one may demonstrate "beyond a reasonable doubt" that another is "more likely than not" to be violent in the immediate future.

At the moment, most commitment laws do not specify probability thresholds but instead improperly leave it to mental health professionals to make what is essentially a political trade-off between the rights of "false positives" to be free of unnecessary state intervention and the rights of the victims of "false negatives" to be protected from harm. Some have argued that a major analytical advance in mental health law would come about if commitment statutes specified not only what *behaviors* would count as "dangerous" ones but also what threshold *probability* of their occurrence is necessary to trigger commitment.[14]

Some activity in that direction is already apparent. Hawaii,[15] for example, requires for commitment that a court find "beyond a reasonable doubt" that the individual is "likely" (.51?) to do substantial injury to another. Most explicit—and perhaps most significant insofar as it is likely to serve nationally as a legislative guide—is the Mental Health Law Project's Suggested Statute on Civil Commitment.[16] The suggested statute authorizes commitment when it is established "beyond a reasonable doubt" that "it is more likely than not" (clearly translatable to a threshold probability of .51) that in the near future the person will inflict serious, unjustified bodily harm on another person.

If the Mental Health Law Project's suggested statute gains a foothold in American jurisdictions, mental health professionals may be asked to testify—and may be *able* to testify—that a patient should be committed because his potential for dangerous behavior is a "definite maybe."

The renaissance of a mental health forensic heyday may, however, be rather short-lived. As standards of commitment are increasingly converted into probability statements, their thresholds will be increasingly subjected to challenge under a constitutional interest-balancing test. Further, the intricate and complex relationship between *standards of proof* and *standards of commitment* will be open to intense scrutiny and debate. If a probabilistic statement in a standard of commitment is stringent, does that warrant a lesser standard of proof? Or, if a probabilistic statement in a standard of commitment is particularly low, may the commitment standard's constitutionality be salvaged by an exceptionally rigorous standard of proof? Constitutionally, must the deprivation of commitment be measured and balanced in accordance with a formula that would take into account *both* standards of proof *and* standards of commitment? If commitment is justified by proving with .90 certainty that one is .51 likely soon to engage in a given harm, would commitment also be justified by proving with .51 certainty that one is .90 likely soon to engage in that harm?[17]

If there is a clear relationship between standards of proof and standards of commitment, the standard of proof question ought not be litigated in isolation from the operative standard of commitment and from the probability statements, if any, explicitly or implicitly endorsed by the commitment criterion in question. A vivid illustration of the link between the two types of standards is portrayed in the New Hampshire case of *Proctor v. Butler*.[18] There, the state argued against a "reasonable doubt" standard of proof on the ground that, given the uncertainty of psychiatric prediction, such a test would prove "unworkable." The "unworkability" argument, however, did not carry the day. Even assuming the argument's relevance, the New Hampshire court found a "reasonable doubt" test perfectly workable given the state's statutory *standard of commitment*, which was a probabilistic one:

> We note that it is not dangerous in any absolute sense of which the trier of fact must be convinced, but rather "a potentially serious likelihood" of dangerousness. It is not difficult to conceive of circumstances in which evidence of past conduct and mental disability will convince "beyond a reasonable doubt" of a potentially serious likelihood of dangerousness.[19]

In light of the link between standards of proof and commitment standards, the *Addington* case, posing a civil commitment standard of proof question in the abstract, and divorced from any concrete discussion of a commitment standard, was poorly postured before the Court. And by ruling with a broad brush that the "clear and convincing" procedural standard is constitutionally sufficient in commitment cases generally, the Court seems largely to have closed the door to theoretical, but important, arguments that the required standard of proof should perhaps shift according to the substantive standard of commitment at issue.

The *Addington* Court was presumably aware of the fact that the case was poorly postured.[20] If the Court was of that opinion, perhaps it should have simply refused to hear the case.[21] Alternatively, if it wished to give content to the theoretical notion that the deprivation of commitment should be measured and balanced in accordance with a formula that would take into account *both* procedural standards of proof *and* substantive standards of commitment, the Court in *Addington* could have held the *reasonable doubt* test to be constitutionally required. Had it done so, the Court would have shifted the controversy away from the standard of proof question and redirected it to the question of the likelihood of harm required by the substantive criteria of commitment.[22] The litigable question would then read something like this: Is it constitutionally sufficient, for commitment purposes, to prove beyond a reasonable doubt that one "may" be dangerous in the future, or must the state instead prove beyond a reasonable doubt a greater expectation of future dangerousness—such as "likely," "more likely than not," "substantially likely," and so forth?

It is interesting to speculate, then, on why the *Addington* Court took the route it did. Why, for example, did it not require a reasonable doubt standard and then leave for another day the question of the amount of leeway state legislatures would be given in fashioning substantive criteria for commitment? One possibility relates to the general body of law regarding the retroactive application of new Court rulings dealing with standards of proof.[23] Given that body of law, the Court's resolution of the standard of proof question would presumably apply not only to future commitment cases, but would apply even to commitment cases adjudicated prior to the *Addington* decision.

Pre-*Addington*, a number of states followed a reasonable doubt test,[24] but approximately half of the states followed a "clear and convincing" test of committability.[25] Thus, if *Addington* announced a reasonable doubt test, and if that test were to apply retroactively, the new test might wreak havoc, requiring countless releases and recommitment hearings in those many jurisdictions previously following the clear and convincing test. On the other hand, Texas stood virtually alone in adhering to the "preponderance" test,[26] and thus a Supreme Court ruling mandating a clear and convincing standard, even if retrospective in scope, would hardly impact adversely on the administration of justice.

Technically, of course, the Court has said that where the principal purpose of a new rule is to substantially enhance the adjudicatory fact-finding function, the new rule should be given complete retroactive effect without regard to such factors as a potentially severe or disruptive impact on the administration of justice.[27] Nonetheless, although in application the Court has remained rather true to that pronouncement,[28] it seems evident (as perhaps in *Addington* itself) that those "adverse impact" factors may sometimes be smuggled in, and may be quite influential, in determining *whether and to what extent* there will be a "new" rule in the first place. Since a reasonable doubt rule should require retroactive effect but would, in its retroactive effect, be highly disruptive, the potential disruptiveness of such a rule may have led the Court to settle for a clear and convincing standard.[29]

If, because of retroactivity reasons, a reasonable doubt test was impracticable, why did the Court nonetheless apply an across-the-board clear and convincing test and back away from a theoretical position that would have the required standard of proof vary with the operative commitment criterion? Perhaps because, as an intermediate test, the clear and convincing standard is a practical compromise which should, by its very nature, not offend anyone.[30] Moreover, given the shoddy manner in which commitment cases are in practice typically conducted, a shoddiness about which the Supreme Court is acutely aware,[31] the Court probably shied away in *Addington* from endorsing a resolution to the standard of proof inquiry which would be theoretically sound but perhaps sufficiently complex to be ignored in the day-to-day administration of therapeutic justice.

In this chapter, then, we have seen how, for a host of practical reasons, the theory of therapeutic justice must sometimes be sacrificed to accommodate the actual administration of that justice. Interestingly and importantly, however, the sacrifice is not always unidirectional. Often, knowledge about shocking abuses in the daily operation of mental health law, a glimpse of which was provided in Chapter 1, motivates scholars, advocates, and policy makers to rethink—and improve—the theoretical underpinnings of the system. In the next chapter, then, we will shift our emphasis from the theory of civil commitment to a study of the relationship between the theory of therapeutic justice and its actual administration. The vehicle will be a case study: an empirical investigation of the administration of psychiatric justice in a particular (but representative) jurisdiction.

NOTES

[1]99 S.Ct. 1804 (1979).
[2]Brief for Appellant, at 10 n.6.
[3]Texas Rev. Civ. Stats. Ann., Art. 5547-52.

4A. Stone, Mental Health and Law: A System in Transition 33 (1975).

5Cocozza & Steadman, *The Failure of Psychiatric Predictions of Dangerousness: Clear and Convincing Evidence*, 29 Rutgers L. Rev. 1048, 1101 (1976).

6*Id.* at 1099 (emphasis added).

7Kahle & Sales, *Due Process of Law and the Attitudes of Professionals Toward Involuntary Civil Commitment*, in P. Lipsitt & Sales (eds.), New Directions in Psycholegal Research 265, 278 (1980).

8Morse, *Crazy Behavior, Morals, and Science: An Analysis of Mental Health Law*, 51 So. Calif. L. Rev. 527 (1978).

9*See, e.g.*, the discussion *infra* regarding the laws of Hawaii and New Hampshire and the Mental Health Law Project's Suggested Statute on Civil Commitment (1977).

10Cross v. Harris, 418 F.2d 1095 (D.C. Cir. 1969).

11Kozol, Boucher, & Garofalo, *The Diagnosis and Treatment of Dangerousness*, 18 Crime and Delinquency 371 (1972).

12State of Michigan, Department of Corrections, Summary of Parolee Risk Study (unpublished report, 1978).

13Dix, *"Civil" Commitment of the Mentally Ill and the Need for Data on the Prediction of Dangerousness*, 19 Am. Behavioral Scientist 318 (1976); Monahan, *Strategies for an Empirical Analysis of the Prediction of Violence in Emergency Civil Commitment*, 1 Law and Human Behavior 363 (1977).

14Shah, *Dangerousness: A Paradigm for Exploring Some Issues in Law and Psychology*, 33 Am. Psychologist 224 (1978).

15Haw. Rev. Stats.§§334-60(b) (4) (I) & 334-1.

16Mental Health Law Project, *Suggested Statute on Civil Commitment*, 2 Ment. Disability L. Rep. 127 (1977).

17Note that the versions may open the door to markedly different types of testimony—and perhaps in practice to differential rates of false positives. The first version (proving with .90 certainty that one is .51 likely to be violent) would probably best be satisfied by testimony anchored tightly to an *actuarial* base. Rarely would testimony based on "clinical experience, judgment, or intuition" be accorded a .90 level of certainty. On the other hand, the second version (proving with .51 certainty that one is .90 likely to be violent) would favor *clinical* rather than actuarial testimony. Clinicians may not be able to meet a .90 certainty level, but they may well in practice be found to satisfy a .51 or preponderance standard. In practice, therefore, the second version's "probably definite" standard may yield results quite different from the first version's "definite maybe" standard.

18380 A.2d 673 (N.H. 1977).

19*Id.* at 677.

20In fact, the Court cited with apparent approval that portion of an article, from which the present chapter is drawn, making just that point. Addington v. Texas, 99 S.Ct. 1804, 1812 (1979), citing Monahan & Wexler, *A Definite Maybe: Proof and Probability in Civil Commitment*, 2 Law & Human Behavior 37 (1978).

21When it first agreed to hear the case, the Court believed incorrectly that the case was within its "mandatory" appellate jurisdiction. At oral argument, however, it became clear that the case was instead within its mere "discretionary" jurisdiction. The case therefore could have been dismissed without reaching the merits of Addington's argument. *See generally* Addington v. Texas, 99 S.Ct. 1804, 1807 (1979).

22Surely, had *Addington* adopted a reasonable doubt test, mental health professionals and others would have expectedly lobbied their legislators to alter (and loosen) the substantive standards of commitment. If substantive standards required a "substantial likelihood" of future dangerousness, for example, pressure would probably be exerted to reduce the standard to mere "likelihood" or perhaps mere "possibility" of future dangerousness. Legislative acquiescence in that regard would set the stage for vigorous litigation over the constitutionally acceptable probability threshold required in commitment criteria.

[23]*E.g.*, Ivan V. v. City of N.Y., 407 U.S. 203 (1972) (holding retroactive the Supreme Court ruling requiring proof beyond a reasonable doubt in juvenile delinquency adjudications). *See also* Hankerson v. North Carolina, 97 S.Ct. 2339 (1977).

[24]Addington v. Texas, 99 S.Ct. 1804, 1812 (1979).

[25]*Id.*

[26]Brief for the National Association for Mental Health, *et al.*, as Amicus Curiae, at 6–7.

[27]Ivan V. v. City of N.Y., 407 U.S. 203, 204 (1972).

[28]*E.g.*, Hankerson v. North Carolina, 97 S.Ct. 2339 (1977).

[29]Presumably, a clear and convincing standard will also require retroactivity. But since the difference between preponderance and clear and convincing is not enormous, and may in fact be principally symbolic, Addington v. Texas, 99 S.Ct. 1804, 1808–09 (1979), it is arguable that the "major" purpose of a new clear and convincing test is not to "substantially" improve the fact finding process. *See* Ivan V. v. City of N.Y., 407 U.S. 203, 204 (1972) (emphasizing that complete retroactive effect, without regard to "adverse impact" factors, is available where the "major" purpose of the new rule is to "substantially" improve the fact-finding mission). And in those situations in which "the degree to which the [new] rule enhances the fact finding process is small," the Court, in deciding retroactivity issues, *has* "looked to questions of reliance by the State on the old rule and the impact of the new rule on the administration of justice." Hankerson v. North Carolina, 97 S.Ct. 2329, 2345 (1977). Even so, *Addington's* clear and convincing standard should be retroactive. Given the overwhelming rejection of the preponderance standard even pre-*Addington,* and the small number of patients likely, post-*Addington,* to remain confined based on a pre-*Addington* commitment order that was adjudicated under a preponderance standard, retroactivity seems clearly in order. *In re* Scelfo, 406 A-2d 973 (1979).

[30]*See* Addington v. Texas, 99 S.Ct. 1804, 1809 (1979): "We probably can assume no more than that the difference between a preponderance of the evidence and proof beyond a reasonable doubt probably is better understood than either of them in relation to the intermediate standard of clear and convincing evidence."

[31]In its 1979 decision of Parham v. J.R., 99 S.Ct. 2493, 2508 (1979), the Supreme Court, citing studies relating to the practical inadequacies of adversary commitment hearings in practice, relied in part on the practical inadequacies of such hearings to hold that adversary hearings should not be constitutionally required for the commitment of juveniles:

> Common human experience and scholarly opinions suggest that the supposed protections of an adversary proceeding to determine the appropriateness of medical decisions for the commitment and treatment of mental and emotional illness may well be more illusory than real.

Part One
THE COMMITMENT SYSTEM

A. Civil Commitment
II. In Practice

4

The Administration of Psychiatric Justice

A CASE STUDY

INTRODUCTION

As noted in Chapter 1, my students and I, during the 1970–71 academic year, conducted a case study of the administration of therapeutic justice in Arizona. Since at the time of the study that justice system was very much under the control of physicians and psychiatrists, the study was in essence one of "psychiatric justice," and will be refered to as such. The year-long effort required extensive field work, which involved observing many commitment hearings in Phoenix (the state capitol, the state's largest city, and the county seat of Maricopa County) and Tucson (the state's second largest city and county seat of Pima County), examining court files, visiting the Arizona State Hospital and various county hospitals, and conducting interviews with physicians, lawyers, and judges in every Arizona county.

Ultimately, the study led to widespread legislative reform.[1] The present chapter, based on a comparison of the commitment law on the books and in operation during the term of the study, details the application of the civil commitment process from apprehension through the commitment hearing, and pays particular attention to the role played in the process by attorneys and physicians. The documented practice is representative of how nearly all states functioned at that time and of how many states (or areas within many states) still function. Finally, the chapter is important because it demonstrates vividly a problem tra-

ditionally endemic to mental health law: an enormous divergence between the theory and the practice. To convey the full impact of our
findings, I have taken the literary license to write the bulk of this chapter
from the chronological viewpoint of 1970-71—the time when the study
was actually conducted.

PREHEARING PROCEDURE

Petition and Detention Order

Prepetition Screening

In order to set the commitment machinery in motion, a petition
must be filed with the superior court asking that an examination be
made into the mental health of the proposed patient. If the court at that
stage approves the petition, a detention order will usually be issued, the
proposed patient will be detained and examined by physicians or psychiatrists, and a judicial hearing exploring the propriety of commitment
may be held.

In some counties, especially outside of Maricopa and Pima Counties,
the filing of a petition is a markedly uncomplicated procedure: the prospective petitioner, with or without the assistance of the county attorney,[2] simply completes and files the pertinent form. Unless the county
attorney participates in the process and serves as a buffer, no real screening of petitions takes place.[3]

Indeed, even in relatively populous Pima County, a process for
screening has only recently been initiated. Until September, 1970, it was
possible for a petitioner to obtain the requisite petition form at several
locations (including the county courthouse) and to file the petition without further ado. But since that time, when Pima County undertook,
through an ambitious program of community mental health, to reduce
commitments to the state hospital, a screening process has been in operation. Under the new procedure, petition forms are available only at the
Southern Arizona Mental Health Center (SAMHC) and at the county
hospital emergency room. A screening and evaluation unit operates 5
days a week from 8 A.M. to 4 P.M. at SAMHC, and a staff member of that
unit moves to the county hospital emergency room until 11:30 P.M. In
addition, staff members are on call during weekends and early morning
hours. Under such an arrangement, the staff seeks to dissuade the filing
of unnecessary petitions and attempts to explore the propriety of non-
commitment treatment alternatives.

In Maricopa County, although such a complete community mental health model is not yet in operation, a screening system of sorts is administered by the Bureau of Mental Health Services of the County Department of Health (BMHS). Since BMHS is the sole facility in Maricopa County for receiving petitions, every prospective petitioner in Maricopa County is referred there for advice. Often BMHS will recommend that the petition be filed. It is troubling, however, that such a recommendation is almost always made solely on the basis of facts presented by the petitioner—the person who will, at any subsequent commitment hearing, be the principal witness against the proposed patient. Yet, after speaking with BMHS, 60% of potential petitioners decide against instituting commitment proceedings. Many do not file because they are convinced by BMHS that commitment is simply not in order. Often, they are referred instead to various social agencies, to community health clinics, and to other voluntary treatment programs. But, despite its existence, many petitions are filed which BMHS concedes are without merit. Apparently, BMHS personnel do not believe they have the power to refuse to accept and file a petition in superior court if the petitioner insists on it, though BMHS sometimes submits its recommendations to the court in a memorandum accompanying the petition.[4]

Several of the screening problems existing in Arizona (and especially in Maricopa County) have been tackled head-on in California. There, prepetition screening is built into the statutory framework. Each county is required to designate a person or agency to be responsible for preparing and filing mental health petitions, and an individual believing another person to be mentally ill—to the extent that a professional evaluation is in order[5]—is to apply to the designated agency for a petition. But before filing the petition, the designated agency is required to have another approved agency, the prepetition screening agency, "determine whether there is probable cause to believe the allegations" and "whether the person will agree voluntarily to receive crisis intervention services or an evaluation in his own home or in a [designated] facility."[6] When screening by the prepetition screening agency has been completed, the first designated agency "shall file the petition if satisfied that there is probable cause to believe that the person is, as a result of mental disorder, a danger to others, or to himself, or gravely disabled, and that the person will not voluntarily receive evaluation or crisis intervention."[7]

Thus, prepetition screening in California contemplates some sort of factual investigation to test the accuracy and veracity of the petitioner's allegations, contemplates the use of voluntary evaluation in lieu of the petition process whenever possible, and apparently gives the designated agency charged with filing petitions an absolute veto over filing nonmeritorious petitions. Clearly, the California screening approach is worthy of serious consideration in Arizona.

The Petition

Though Arizona law technically authorizes actual commitment only on a showing of dangerousness,[8] a petition requesting that a proposed patient be detained for the purpose of examination need only allege that the proposed patient "is mentally ill and in need of supervision, care or treatment."[9] By contrast, the California provision discussed above requires that a petition for evaluation allege that the proposed patient, as a result of mental disorder, is "a danger to others, or to himself, or is gravely disabled."[10] Yet, notwithstanding the loose Arizona statutory standard, a great number of petitions are defectively drafted. Defective drafting is no surprise, of course, in those cases where the petitions are prepared by laymen. Inadequate lay pleading provides yet another reason why the law ought to insist that the commitment machinery be invoked by a county attorney or, better yet, by a professional mental health screening service.

The primary problem with defective petitions is the pleading of mere conclusions rather than underlying facts. It is quite a different thing to allege "he is violent" than it is to allege "he became angry and beat his brother with a stick on three occasions." Many of the petitions recite the magic words, "he is a danger to himself or others." That, of course, does not make it so.

Many petitions are a series of conclusory statements with one relevant or irrelevant fact alleged. The following is the entire text of a petition on which a detention order was issued:

1. He has shown violent behavior several times.
2. He has memory lapses.
3. He might be harmful to himself and others.
4. Uses credit cards without usual restraint.

If courts issue detention orders on the basis of conclusory petitions, as they frequently do, they are actually improperly delegating to the petitioners the judicial task of determining the sufficiency of the petitions. The law authorizes a court to order a proposed patient detained for examination only "when it appears on a petition . . . *to the satisfaction of a judge . . .* that a person . . . is mentally ill and in need of supervision, treatment or care. . . ."[11] But if the petition speaks only in conclusions, it is, of course, impossible for the judge to decide independently that a proposed patient meets the statutory standard for detention. Judicial reliance on conclusory allegations has long been legally taboo where Fourth Amendment rights are involved,[12] and seems already to have been condemned in the civil commitment area as well, as evidenced in one jurisdiction by a flurry of successful habeas corpus petitions.[13]

In reviewing court commitment files across the state, we discovered many problematic petitions which did not, from the facts presented, adequately convince us that the proposed patient met even the broad Arizona standard of being mentally ill and in need of supervision, care or treatment, let alone a stricter standard such as being dangerous or gravely disabled. Nevertheless, in most of these cases, detention orders were issued, and commitment to the state hospital (perhaps for legally insufficient reasons) was not infrequent.

Some of the insufficient petitions can be categorized according to dominant themes in their allegations. Without in any way attempting to be exhaustive, we devised the following classification of troubling petitions.

The first group may be called *general eccentric*. In these, activities are described which are deviations from the community norm, and perhaps even from the person's particular segment of the community. Viewed objectively, the activity could not be called evidence of need for care and treatment. But if one were drawing inferences a little carelessly, a detention order might well issue, as it did in the case portrayed below (recitals of previous mental illness are often a part of these petitions):

> She is again hyperactive and doing bizarre things. She wants to go take driving lessons thinking that she can get her license one day. She then wants to buy a new car. She talks very fast all the time. She dresses in a bizarre way also. She is not herself and I am sure she is ill again. She has had three previous hospitalizations.

A further step in the direction of judging individuals by their deviation from normative behavior in the community is found in those petitions based merely on the *life style* of the respondent. Consider the following case, where the respondent was detained for several days pending a hearing, at which time the examining psychiatrists testified that he exhibited no signs of mental illness, whereupon he was promptly released. The respondent is a young man whose pattern of living may be described as a blend of Christian simplicity and oriental philosophy. Many people would call him a "hippie." His father, who had not seen him in 4 years, arrived in town, met his son, and shortly thereafter filed a petition alleging the young man to be

> incapable of self-management. He is extremely dirty about himself and his living quarters. He has no utilities or sanitary requirements for daily personal use. He neglects his health, does not eat properly or nourishing food al-

though he receives an ample disability pension from the VA each month. This pension, which should be used for [the respondent's] benefit, appears to be used by his associates, who even try to get his check from the post office. His behavior is inappropriate as he appears to be hallucinating, is extremely religious and identifies with Christ. He recently went on a "vinegar diet," is very thin and unkempt. While he is not dangerous to others, his present way of living and neglect to himself (he's deformed) creates a danger to himself. [14]

Another group of problematic petitions may be termed *aged*, whereby the petitioner seeks to commit a person of advancing years who may be developing senility or who may simply need physical care. Often, this group consists simply of old people in need of nursing care. The following petition, which led to a detention order and to an eventual commitment, was filed for the commitment of an elderly gentleman:

He is incapable of taking care of himself or of living alone at this time. He is confused. He has wandered away from home on several occasions and it has been necessary that he be admitted to a hospital for his own protection as he is a possible danger to himself in his confused state.

The first sentence is conclusory. No facts indicating a true danger are shown, nor is it probable, merely because he wanders away, that he is in need of psychiatric treatment or care. The petition should have described the length of the departures and in what way the departures put the respondent in danger or indicated a need for care.

A final type of petition that presents problems to the court and to the entire commitment process is not as easy to detect as those discussed above. The following petition was filed in Maricopa County Superior Court:

My husband left the family on July 12th. He has disappeared for days on several occasions. He has exhibited a split personality for over 20 years. His attitude and his mood change frequently. He has been violent and threatening to family members, often explodes over nothing. He has often talked about killing himself. He has now been unemployed for three weeks. It has been said that he can no longer get along with people. He is failing to take care of his family and himself in his mental disturbance. I believe that he may be a danger to himself or his family if he gets under more pressure.

Although it contains some unexplained hearsay ("It has been said"), many conclusory statements, and may appear somewhat jumbled to most readers, it is arguable that the petition, if true, creates a probability that the respondent is mentally ill and in need of care or treatment. But if a screening agency is doing its job, the judge need not rely on the petition alone. The Maricopa County Bureau of Mental Health Services submitted the following memorandum with this petition:

> The [respondent and petitioner] have been married almost 24 years. There have been many separations and much trouble. Mr. [Respondent] is currently living with . . . an alleged girl friend. Mrs. [Petitioner] has filed for divorce three times in the past three years. There is one minor child. Neither [the petitioner nor the respondent] have an attorney.

It now becomes apparent that the real charge here is not that the respondent is mentally ill, but that he is disregarding his marital duties. This is a *marital spite* petition, many of which are filed each year throughout the state. Despite the BMHS report, a detention order was issued, and the respondent in the above case was confined for examination and hearing. At the examination, the psychiatrist found him to be "[o]riented, affect appropriate to thought content—judgment and insight intact—no evidence of psychosis." Unfortunately, as a result of the action of his spiteful wife, the man was incarcerated in a psychiatric ward for 5 days. At the hearing, the petition was dismissed. [15]

Judges should learn to recognize the hallmarks of the types of petitions outlined above. Even if the screening agencies are not permitted to veto petitions, they can perform an invaluable service by providing background information which will aid the judge in deciding whether to issue a detention order. When the screening agency believes the facts are legally sufficient to warrant a professional evaluation of a patient, it should assist in drafting a petition that will satisfy the statutory standards.

Sufficient petitions, of course, should not contain conclusory statements. Instead, they should allege facts that show, or from which an inference may be clearly drawn, that the respondent is (1) mentally ill and (2) is in need of care and treatment. Examples of perfect petitions rarely exist. Some, however, do sufficiently allege facts showing a need for care and treatment, if not dangerousness:

> Mrs.———has been a friend of ours for 38 years. Recently she has become very sick. She seemed accidentally to have set her house afire, although she says someone threw a smoke bomb into her house. She was wandering in the neighborhood nude, and drove her car through the wall of her carport so we brought her to our home for her protection. She has no control of bladder or bowel, wanders and puts lighted cigarettes on inflammable surfaces, so we placed her in St. Luke's Hospital to see if they could help. [After discharge from the hospital and a 2-day stay at a nursing home, they returned the respondent to their home.] Since she has been back in our home, she has been very agitated and disturbed. She can't sleep, she wants pain pills, she screams . . . and messes on the floor. She is often incoherent. Now she is stuck in the bath tub and we have been unable to get her out.
>
> I believe Mrs. ———is so sick she is dangerous to herself and needs to be hospitalized immediately.

Perhaps the most common type of sufficient petition involves the recent attempt of suicide:

My son has been emotionally disturbed since his return from
Vietnam....

Today he cut his wrists. He has a violent temper, which is much worse
when he has been drinking. Sometimes he says he is going to kill people and
is very upset about his war experiences. At times he cries, says he needs
help, but today refused to enter a hospital voluntarily.

The Detention Order

Once a petition has been filed and has been found sufficient by the
court, the standard practice throughout most of Arizona is for the court
to issue a detention order, whereupon the proposed patient is apprehended by a deputy sheriff and taken to the appropriate detention
facility[16] for the purpose of undergoing an examination by psychiatrists
or physicians. Sometimes, particularly when the examining physicians
do not have their offices at the detention facility, a day or two can pass
before the examination is conducted. If the patient is examined and
found not to warrant hospitalization, he can, in some parts of Arizona,
be released immediately, although in many other areas of the state he
will be detained until his hearing and will presumably be released at that
time. Patients detained for commitment are held until the hearing and
are then ordered committed, usually to the Arizona State Hospital.
Hearings are held at least weekly, but on occasion a patient's hearing
will be unduly deferred, and Arizona law sets no statutory limit on the
length of time a patient may be involuntarily detained pending a commitment hearing.

To evaluate the Arizona practice, it seems profitable once again to
compare it with California's legislation. In California, as we have seen,
even a person alleged to be mentally ill and dangerous or gravely disabled does not have a petition filed against him, let alone a detention
order issued, unless the person refuses voluntarily to undergo mental
evaluation.[17] Moreover, if the person refuses voluntary evaluation and a
petition is filed, the court, instead of issuing an immediate detention
order, issues a *conditional* order of detention, authorizing the apprehension and detention of the proposed patient only if the patient fails to
appear for evaluation at a certain scheduled time and place.[18] If possible,
the "summons" is to be served by an official wearing plain clothes and
driving an official vehicle other than a police car.[19] If the patient fails to
appear for his scheduled appointment, he is to be apprehended in the
same manner. Finally, if apprehension and detention are necessary,
evaluation is to be had "as promptly as possible" and, except when
Saturdays, Sundays, and holidays intervene, detention shall in no event
exceed 72 hours,[20] at the end of which the patient must either be re-

leased, referred for voluntary treatment, or, as a last resort, certified for a 14-day period of intensive treatment.[21] If a patient is certified for intensive treatment, he is entitled to a judicial hearing within 2 judicial days of filing a petition for a hearing.[22] California's scheme, then, more so than the prevalent Arizona practice, deemphasizes the analogy between the civil commitment process and the criminal process, particularly in the area of uniformed law enforcement officers making "arrests." Significantly, too, California seeks to encourage outpatient mental evaluations rather than resorting to apprehension and detention for that purpose.

Interestingly, although the prevailing practice in Arizona is for the superior court to issue a detention order so that the proposed patient will be confined pending examination and hearing, our field work revealed that in some outlying Arizona counties, respondents, unless violent or likely to flee, are seldom detained prior to hearing. One reason given for such a practice was the lack of adequate detention facilities, though generally it was thought that the best interests of the proposed patient would be served by his being in his home surroundings.

Arizona law with respect to outpatient evaluation is actually far from clear, and perhaps a statutory revision patterned after California procedures is in order. Nevertheless, there is probably room under existing Arizona law for a superior court, in appropriate cases, to fashion its detention order in conditional terms, so that the proposed patient would actually be taken into custody only if he refused or failed to appear for a scheduled outpatient evaluation. Thus, the Arizona statute permits a judge, after a petition has been filed, to "make *orders* which are necessary to provide for examination into the mental health of the person and for his apprehension and safekeeping in the county hospital or other place... which will afford access to designated examiners."[23] This language can easily be read as providing not only for a traditional detention order, but also for other preliminary orders to submit to an evaluation which would result in apprehension and detention only in the event that the patient did not appear at the scheduled evaluation.[24]

There are, of course, certain potential dangers in the legal availability of outpatient evaluations, and the dangers flow in two different directions. First, the outpatient evaluation device might be mistakenly used in situations where persons are in need of immediate detention.[25] Second, the outpatient evaluation device might be used to accomplish the forced evaluation of persons who would be left alone if the more drastic device of detention were the only one available.[26] Nevertheless, sensible administration of an outpatient evaluation provision could quite probably be achieved and the above dangers minimized, particularly if the screening agencies are given an active role by recommending in each case whether an outpatient examination should be conducted.

THE DETENTION FACILITIES

On the issuance of a detention order by the court, the proposed patient is apprehended by an officer and transported to a place designated in the detention order.[27] At the detention facility, the patient is usually evaluated by those who will testify at his commitment hearing. The extent and techniques of treatment available during detention vary in the different counties, but generally the involuntary patient receives little psychiatric treatment other than medication and physical removal from his normal environment.[28]

This section will examine the types of detention facilities used in the 14 Arizona counties and the normal practices of those facilities, which involve limitations on the proposed patient's personal freedom.

Maricopa County

In Maricopa County, patients are detained at the psychiatric ward of the recently constructed Maricopa County General Hospital. The present head of that ward is not satisfied with his new facility. In his words, it "was conceived and designed in the Dark Ages."[29] He indicated that not only is the present facility already overcrowded, but its very design precludes the administration of modern community-oriented psychiatric services. Instead of an accessible center conducive to developing crisis intervention and day care programs, the county has provided the therapists with "a jail for the mentally and emotionally disturbed."

A brief tour of the Maricopa County psychiatric ward supports the doctor's assertions. The ward itself is situated on the third floor of the new hospital and the entrance is kept locked. To gain entry, one must identify himself over an intercom while he is viewed by an invisible doorkeeper by closed circuit television. The halls are long, clean, and barren except that, here and there, a patient may be found sitting on the tile floor alone or with other patients. While the unit's rooms are larger than those of the old facility, they were intended to be occupied by only two patients. Because of overcrowding, three patients are already often assigned to each room.[30]

In keeping with the mythical notion that the mentally ill must be isolated from the civilized world, the ward windows are "pitted" and barely translucent, providing a greenish-grey lumination merely suggestive of the bright Arizona sun that shines outside.[31]

During detention, the patient at Maricopa County General Hospital apparently has ample opportunity for interaction with staff and other patients. There are two day rooms, although the size of one has been diminished by partitioning to create additional office space. Patients may receive visitors from 2 to 4 P.M. and from 6 to 8 P.M. In order to prevent the smuggling of illicit drugs into the ward, however, patients with a history of drug abuse are not allowed to receive guests.

While the new ward has the advantages of air conditioning and additional space, it is unfortunate that its design reflects an architectural assumption that the mentally ill must be removed from society and jailed for their own protection. Furthermore, the fact of its recent construction would seem to preclude politically the creation in the short run of additional facilities less restrictive and more community-oriented in nature.

Pima County

The neuropsychiatric ward of Pima County General Hospital could best be described as an unsuccessful experiment in communal living. A total lack of privacy pervades the unit, which is internally separated by glass partitions into male and female sections. There is, however, interaction of males and females in the common areas. Indeed, there is interaction everywhere as nurses, orderlies, and social workers work and patients live in cramped quarters, locked off from rest of the hospital and the outside world.

Pima County General Hospital provides no exercise areas for its psychiatric patients, although one staff member noted that the hospital would perhaps provide a small outdoor area in the future. Involuntary patients are not allowed passes, while voluntary patients are allowed to leave the ward only for a "constructive or useful purpose," such as job hunting or family visitation. If the patient is merely tired of cramped quarters and desires to leave the ward for a short period, a request for a pass will presumably be denied.

The day room, which doubles as the courtroom for commitment hearings, is too small to permit any type of occupational or manual therapy, and is not so used. There is a television set as well as some reading matter for patient use. Each patient is allowed to keep his own toiletries and other personal items, except razors or potentially dangerous instruments. Violent patients are apparently quieted by the use of medication, mechanical restraints, or are placed in one of the ward's seclusion rooms.

It appears that the Pima county detention facility is very much inferior to that of the Maricopa hospital, which at least provides semiprivate rooms and more space. Both facilities, however, are woefully inadequate both in providing pleasant surroundings and therapeutic activities for those who have been detained against their will.

The Twelve Rural Counties

In the 12 less populous counties, patients are detained in either the available hospital facilities or the county jail. Use of the jail as the primary detention facility occurs in a few of the rural counties, although all counties use their jail facilities in certain circumstances. In the common situation, the limited number of psychiatric beds are filled to capacity, so that detention of an additional patient must be at the county jail. Often, violent patients will be incarcerated in the jail, although at least one county's sheriff prefers to transfer violent patients to the local hospital where they can receive tranquilizing medication.

It is worthy of note that in one of the most populous of the 12 "rural" counties, proposed patients are generally detained at the county jail, even though some hospital facilities are available. We were told that the county jail is used because county officials were concerned about the additional expense represented by the hospitalization of proposed patients. In certain other counties, officials reported that local hospitals were simply not physically equipped to deal with mental patients and had insufficient staff trained in caring for the mentally ill.

Our research team members either visited the detention facilities in each county, interviewed officials about conditions in those institutions, or did both. The reports revealed the following information about detention under commitment petition in Arizona's 12 less populous counties.

Detention in Hospital Facilities. Where the local hospital facilities provide beds for psychiatric detention, the rooms are generally comparable to normal hospital rooms. The windows may be barred, however, and the rooms underfurnished. It is the normal practice in several counties to keep the door locked while a room is occupied by a proposed patient, although a private facility that is used for detention in one county is equipped with "half-door" rooms. That appellation refers to the fact that the top part of the door of these rooms may be left open while the bottom is latched from the outside. The proposed patient is thus provided with the impression of contact with the world beyond the locked door.

Although security facilities are available in one hospital, staff members informed project interviewers that, if at all possible, the proposed patients are kept on the general wards and, with certain limitations, are treated as ordinary hospital patients. In another county, however, patients awaiting commitment hearings are kept in the same detention unit as are inmates of the county jail who have been hospitalized for physical illness.

Most of the interviewers reported that there is little opportunity for detained patients to exercise. Apparently, however, in at least one hospital, a proposed patient is allowed to walk about the hospital if the doctor believes the patient would not abuse the privilege. Hospitalized patients are generally afforded the same rights and privileges as are other patients regarding visitation, mail, and telephone use. In this regard, hospitalized patients fare far better than those who are detained in county jails.

Detention in the County Jail.   While many counties regularly detain proposed patients in their county jails, there is little uniformity in the type of cell used for this purpose. The patient may be held in a normal single cell, an elaborate padded section of the jail, or merely thrown in with the inebriates who occupy the "drunk tank." There is no therapy for those detained in jail facilities, and individual rights are considerably more restricted than they would have been had the patient been taken to a hospital.

As was previously mentioned, one fairly populous county uses its jail for the primary detention facility. In that county, patients are isolated in one of two padded cells. Both cells are adjacent to a central station, enabling deputy sheriffs to observe closely, through a slide-back, metal screen door, the patients' activities. If a patient manifests extreme dangerousness to himself, a straitjacket may be employed in addition to crisis level dosages of medication. Complete censorship of mail and phone use is the rule, together with prohibition of radio and television use. Visitors are generally not allowed, although a patient may receive members of the immediate family on the doctor's recommendation. While the sheriff of this county has been described as "compassionate" and "overly cautious" toward those sequestered, it was the widespread view of interviewed officials that the local hospital should be used for detention purposes. Apparently, however, the county has been unwilling to accept the financial burden this would entail.[32]

The problems of additional expense and inconvenience to hospital staff notwithstanding, it is clearly unreasonable to maintain that jail detention for nonexplosive patients is ever justified if hospitalization is an available alternative. Furthermore, even with patients who present some degree of dangerous behavior, it is difficult to accept the argument that the staff of a hospital in one county is incapable of dealing with such a problem, when the mentally ill are cared for, apparently without incident, in other county hospitals. However considerate and humane a sheriff's deputy may be when dealing with proposed patients, the fact remains that, under the guise of help and treatment, individuals are regularly being apprehended by law enforcement officers and detained in county jails. Obviously, jail incarceration may have a deleterious effect on an already disturbed person and is thus at odds with the philosophical basis for commitment. It should be equally clear that this practice, which is probably a function of habituation, could be easily discontinued. At the very least, the judge issuing the detention order should, before authorizing jail detention, have to be convinced that hospitalization would be a grossly unsuitable detention alternative and that jail detention is an absolute necessity in the particular case.

THE HEARING

AN OVERVIEW

After detention and psychiatric examination, the next step in the commitment process is the judicial hearing. The hearings in all Arizona counties comply at least superficially with the broad statutory requirements: a hearing is always held, the requisite number of witnesses always attend to testify, and the doctors or psychiatrists are always present to make their recommendations. But, as will be seen, superficial compliance hardly insures adequate protection to the proposed patient. Interestingly, the atmosphere of the hearing seems to differ in the various counties.

Maricopa County

Hearings in Maricopa county are conducted before the probate judge[33] twice a week, on Mondays and Thursdays. A large number of cases are commonly heard on each day. On one occasion, for instance, the project observed the processing of 18 cases during a single afternoon sitting.[34]

The hearings, which are not transcribed,[35] progress in rapid fire fashion, averaging 4.7 minutes each, with some not longer than 3 minutes. They begin with the judge announcing the name and case number of the first patient and then the calling and swearing of the witnesses.[36]

Next, the patient is ushered into the hearing room—a small room on the psychiatric ward of the county hospital.[37] On some occasions the patient may not be present.

After the patient is seated, a court-appointed attorney asks the witnesses if they have read the petition, whether they feel it is "substantially" true, and whether they wish to amend or change anything in it. The witnesses almost invariably answer that the petition is substantially true and that they have nothing to add.

After the testimony of the witnesses is given, the appointed attorney asks one of the psychiatrists for his opinion of the patient. The standard answer of the first psychiatrist is approximately the following: "Patient is suffering from a major psychiatric disorder," followed by other conclusory statements such as "he is psychotic, depressed, and demonstrates inappropriate affect. I recommend that he be committed to Arizona State Hospital as an incompetent."[38] Very seldom is any evidence given concerning the factual basis of the conclusions. In the hearings observed, a history was given only if the patient had been previously hospitalized.

The attorney then asks the second psychiatrist, "Do you agree and concur with Dr. ———?" The usual answer of the other psychiatrist is, "Yes, I concur completely with Dr. ———," followed by the second psychiatrist generally repeating some of the same conclusions about the patient's mental disability.

Ordinarily, the judge then says to the patient, "That's all,"[39] and the patient is removed from the hearing room without being asked to give a statement. In some cases, however, the patient asks to be heard, in which case permission is always given.

After the patient has left the room, the judge enters an order, ordinarily to "commit to Arizona State Hospital as an incompetent." And the next case is called.

In order to better demonstrate the summary procedures that exist in Maricopa County, the following chronologies[40] of observed hearings are offered. They are representative of the typical hearing.

Case 1

ATTORNEY: Are you the petitioner?
SOCIAL WORKER: Yes.
ATTORNEY: Is the petition true?
SOCIAL WORKER: Yes, to the best of my knowledge.
ATTORNEY (*to patient's wife*): Have you read the petition?
WIFE: Yes.

ATTORNEY: Is it true?

WIFE: Yes.

ATTORNEY: Doctor, have you had a chance to examine the patient?

PSYCHIATRIST I: Yes, this patient is hallucinatory, judgment markedly impaired. He would be dangerous to others and should be committed as an incompetent.

PSYCHIATRIST II: I concur. He has poor impulse control. He suffers from a major psychiatric illness and would be dangerous to others.

COURT: It is ordered that the patient be committed to Arizona State Hospital or the Veterans Hospital as an incompetent. No costs; maintenance as VA may provide.

Case 2

ATTORNEY (*to patient's father*): Did you sign the petition?

FATHER: Yes.

ATTORNEY: Is the petition true?

FATHER: True and correct.

ATTORNEY (*to patient's mother*): Is the petition true?

MOTHER: Yes.

ATTORNEY (*to doctor*): Dr. ———, would you give us your findings?

PSYCHIATRIST I: Patient shows all the symptoms of a major psychiatric disturbance. He may be dangerous to himself and others.

PSYCHIATRIST II: He is suffering from a major psychitric illness and may be dangerous to himself and others.

[*Patient is removed from hearing room*] COURT: Is he a veteran?

PSYCHIATRIST II: Yes.

COURT: The patient is ordered committed to Arizona State Hospital or VA as an incompetent; no costs; maintenance as VA may provide.

Case 3

ATTORNEY (*to patient's mother*): Is the petition true?

MOTHER: Yes, it is true.

ATTORNEY (*to patient's stepfather*): Is the petition true?

STEPFATHER: Yes, it is true.

PSYCHIATRIST I: The patient demonstrates poor impulse control; is suspicious, evasive, hostile, and has poor judgment. The patient is a danger to himself and to others. I recommend commitment to Arizona State Hospital as an incompetent.

PSYCHIATRIST II: [*Gave similar statement.*]

[*Patient is removed from hearing room.*]
COURT: It is ordered that the patient be committed to Arizona State
Hospital as an incompetent.[41]

Pima County

Not long ago, hearings in Pima County, which have long been held
only once a week, closely approximated the Maricopa model. But since
September, 1970, when Pima County initiated a community mental
health model and drastically reduced commitments to the Arizona State
Hospital, the nature of the hearings have changed considerably. Now,
with 2 to 3 hearings per week, instead of the previous 15 to 20, speed is
not nearly as essential as before. Consequently, the hearings observed
by the project in Pima County averaged 27 minutes each, compared to
the 4.7-minute average duration of those observed in Maricopa County.
And the Office of the Public Defender, which now represents patients in
Pima County, participates in the hearing to a considerably greater extent
than do the court-appointed attorneys in Maricopa County. Nonetheless, the preparation and participation provided by the public defenders
does not begin to approximate acceptable standards of advocacy.

The Pima County hearing procedure as observed by the project is
described below. It should be noted, however, that since Pima County
superior court judges rotate in taking responsibility for commitment
hearings, the nature of the hearing may well differ from judge to judge.

Hearings in Pima County are held in a small recreation room at the
county hospital once a week on Thursdays. The hearing begins with the
patient present. If the patient is without counsel, which is usually the
case, a public defender is appointed.[42]

After appointment of counsel, the court asks the lay witnesses their
names and asks them to be sworn. The court ordinarily then proceeds to
describe the prospective hearing:

> The purpose of this hearing is to determine whether John Doe suffers
> from a mental illness that makes him dangerous to self, others, or property.
> The doctors will testify and then the patient's attorney will examine the
> doctors.

After the lay witnesses are sworn, the psychiatrists are asked to
testify. Their testimony is presented in greater depth than in Maricopa
County. A history of the patient is usually given, and factual support for
the diagnosis and recommendation is much more common.

After the testimony of the psychiatrists, the court usually asks the
public defender if he has any questions. In the hearings observed, the

public defender ordinarily did have a few questions going to the basis of the diagnosis and the recommendations. The fact that some questions were addressed to the psychiatrists represents a significant departure from the Maricopa model, where in none of the observed hearings did the attorneys ask the psychiatrists for anything more than their recommendations.

Following the cross-examination of the psychiatrists, the lay witnesses give their testimony.[43] Their statements are not simply that the petition is true or correct as is the case in Maricopa County, but are usually narrative of the behavior they have seen in the day-to-day activity of the proposed patient.

The public defender is not the only participant in the hearings to question the lay witnesses; the judge often asks questions also. In fact, in Pima County, the judge often proved to be a rather active participant in the hearings.

After the attorney finishes the cross-examination of the witnesses, the judge will ask the patient if he or she has anything to say. If no statement is offered, or after a statement is given, the judge gives his or her determination and order.

In the case of Maricopa County, it was relatively easy to give examples of typical hearings. The summary nature of the proceedings made selection a simple process. In Pima County, however, each hearing is rather unique. Therefore, the following chronologies are not typical in the sense of being recurrent, but they are satisfactorily representative of Pima County hearings.

Case 4

COURT: Do you have an attorney?
PATIENT: No.
COURT: The law requires that you have an attorney. His purpose is to see to it that your rights and interests are protected. Do you understand this?
PATIENT: Yes.
[*Court appoints public defender.*]
COURT: Who will testify?
MOTHER OF PATIENT: I am her mother, we will testify.
[*Father and mother sworn.*]
COURT: The hearing is to determine if ———— suffers from a mental illness that makes her dangerous to herself, others or property.
PSYCHIATRIST I: Patient is 19 years old. She was previously committed in

September with an acute psychotic illness. At the time of commitment ——— was pregnant. On October 10th she left Arizona State Hospital unauthorized and went to New Mexico with her father for an abortion. Patient was discharged while she was in New Mexico. The characteristics of her disease: she was under pressure; she had uncontrolled behavior, bizarre behavior, belligerent, auditory hallucinations, no suicide attempt. She was confused, thought process disorganized. She has been fighting, setting fires. When at home, she manifested uncontrolled behavior. Diagnosed as schizophrenic.

PSYCHIATRIST II: I have examined her and concur.

PUBLIC DEFENDER: Dr. ———, was there any improvement [since her previous commitment]?

PSYCHIATRIST I: Under large doses of medication there was improvement. But treatment was interrupted by the abortion.

PUBLIC DEFENDER: What kinds of acts constituted uncontrollable behavior?

PSYCHIATRIST I: Frequent arguments, fighting, running out of the house. She was found by the police in a confused state.

COURT: [Asked the patient's mother to testify.]

MOTHER: She has been spending nights with me and days with her father. We are giving her Thorazine. The abortion upset her. The Thorazine tended to confuse her. Whatever medicine they are giving her now seems to help.

COURT: Without medication how did she act?

MOTHER: She had flashbacks, she was nervous. Her problems are related to drugs that she took at college. She was very nervous or sensitive but she didn't throw temper tantrums.

COURT: Has she thrown temper tantrums?

MOTHER: No.

COURT: Would she get violent?

MOTHER: No, she resented being taken to the gynecologist; she tried to run away.

COURT: What do you mean upset?

MOTHER: She wanted to get away. She refused to let the doctor examine her. That day I did not give her any medication. She seemed good. I told her to take a bath and set her hair. She said, "I will take a bath, but I won't set my hair." I said, "If you don't set your hair, I'll set it for you."

COURT: Did you bring her to the hospital?

MOTHER: No, the police found her in a vacant house and brought her here.

COURT: (*to public defender*): Do you have any questions?

PUBLIC DEFENDER: Mrs. ————, was there any marked improvement on medication? Could you control her on medication?

MOTHER: Yes.

PUBLIC DEFENDER: Do you think it is natural to be upset by an abortion?

MOTHER: Yes, I would be.

COURT (*to father*): Mr. ————, I understand [the patient] spent days with you?

FATHER: Yes, I helped her go to New Mexico. She seemed confused, but only after the abortion did she seem confused. She seemed confused from the transition from days at my house and nights at her mother's. She has been a problem ever since.

COURT: How did she act?

FATHER: Once she stepped off a high place and fell down. She was erratic with her speech.

COURT: Could she carry on normal conversation?

FATHER: Yes, but sometimes erratic. She couldn't be trusted. She jumped in a truck and drove down the street and ran a stop sign.

COURT: Do you feel that if she were not hospitalized she would need someone to take care of her at all times?

FATHER: Absolutely. Someone would have to watch her constantly. She was very unpredictable.

COURT: Behavior unpredictable?

FATHER: Yes.

MOTHER: She was unpredictable before the abortion.

PUBLIC DEFENDER: Are you two separated?

MOTHER & FATHER: Yes.

PUBLIC DEFENDER: Have you ever seen your daughter set fires, as Dr. ———— stated?

MOTHER & FATHER: No.

PUBLIC DEFENDER: Would the patient be OK if she were at home?

MOTHER: Yes, if she were on medication.

PUBLIC DEFENDER: Do you feel you could care for her?

MOTHER: Yes, I am a home nurse. I am experienced. I could take care of her. I think it would be better for [the patient].

COURT: Do you feel you can do a better job than the Arizona State Hospital?

MOTHER: Yes.

COURT: Who will take care of her medicine? Who will prescribe it? A doctor should be on call.

MOTHER: I can administer the medicine, I can't prescribe it.

COURT (*to social worker*): You signed the petition, didn't you?

SOCIAL WORKER: Yes. I filed on the advice of a physician. I have seen her. She remains withdrawn. She seems a *little* confused, a *little* hostile, unpredictable. I am aware of the fire she set.

COURT: Doctor ———, you heard Mrs. ——— [mother] say she could take adequate care of [the patient]?

PSYCHIATRIST I: I don't think at this time she has completed her treatment. She gets most upset when she interacts with her mother or her mother comes to see her. There is a definite conflict between the mother and the girl.

PSYCHIATRIST II: [The patient] told me she would rather live with her friend than her mother.

MOTHER: That couldn't be because she doesn't have any friends.

PUBLIC DEFENDER (*to patient*): Do you think commitment to Arizona State Hospital a couple of months ago was beneficial?

PATIENT: Yes, it did help me. But there are certain things that go on at the state hospital that push my ideals too far. They allow an open ward for therapeutic reasons. A lot of times the therapeutic ward does not function therapeutically. At times like that I become disgusted and explode.

PUBLIC DEFENDER: Do you think their facilities would be more beneficial than if you went home to your mother?

PATIENT: No, my mother is an experienced nurse. I feel with the help of a doctor on call and with the help of the health care program at the mental health center—I think that would be more beneficial than Arizona State Hospital, with the possibility of going to the mental health center at times of friction with my mother. Hospital is no better than home.

MOTHER: She has been an outpatient at the mental health center and has done very well.

COURT: Apparently not well enough.

PSYCHIATRIST I: This is actually her third hospitalization. The past few days she has looked better. But she still looks withdrawn and preoccupied. It is my own personal feeling that treatment out of the hospital would not be good. I would strongly recommend Arizona State Hospital.

MOTHER: How do you propose to keep my daughter at the hospital? She can walk out any time she wants.

PSYCHIATRIST II: The same thing can be said when she lives at your house.

COURT: In many respects Arizona State Hospital leaves a lot to be desired. But they are trying to do the best they can with the personnel and funds available. This is the only institution we have in this case.

There is no doubt in my mind that your daughter needs care and treatment. At least until she functions on her own. Experience is all we have to go on.

Let the record show that the patient suffers from a mental illness and if left at liberty is likely to be dangerous to herself and/or others or property. It is ordered that the patient be committed to Arizona State Hospital.

Case 5

COURT: Do you have an attorney?

PATIENT: Yes, Mrs. ———— [a staff member] called him but he never called back.

COURT: Do you know who she called?

PATIENT: He didn't call back. She left a message. I thought he would be here, that he would call her in the evening. But he is not here.

COURT: Apparently he doesn't want to represent you.

PATIENT: No, he has other . . .

COURT: Cases?

PATIENT: Yes, cases.

COURT: The court will appoint the public defender to represent you and protect your interests.

PATIENT: Fine.

[*The lay witnesses are identified and sworn.*]

PSYCHIATRIST I: Where is the patient's husband? He is the petitioner.

SOCIAL WORKER: He is not coming. He was not subpoenaed.

COURT (*to patient*): Where is your husband?

PATIENT: Where is he? He didn't come? He told me he would come later on, that there would be other hearings before mine and that they take a long time, but that he would be here for mine.

COURT: He was mistaken.

PSYCHIATRIST I: I can clarify this with my testimony.

COURT: Well, let's have it.

PSYCHIATRIST I: Patient is 24, married, and well known to this service, as well as to Arizona State Hospital. She has five children, including two sets of twins. She has had 13 hospitalizations since 1964. In January, 1970, she was released. All five children are in foster homes. Her husband brought her to the walk-in clinic. He said she demonstrated bizarre behavior. He was unable to leave her alone. He said they were not living together. Their relationship is stormy, but he doesn't want her to go to Arizona State Hospital. Welfare said it has no plans to return her children to her. She was cooperative but agitated and tangential. Affect constricted and inappropriately argumentative. She struck a lab technician who was going to take a blood sample. . . .

PATIENT: [*Interrupting.*] I've apologized to her, Doctor. I've seen her before. She is a cousin of my husband or the cousin of a friend. I've seen her.

PSYCHIATRIST I: She could be quite volatile. There is no evidence of organic brain disease. She is suffering from a chronic psychosis but she needs to be committed to Arizona State Hospital.

PATIENT: The welfare people said I would get my children back. They gave me a paper to get them back. They didn't think I was crazy.

PSYCHIATRIST I: The attorney she speaks of represented her when she broke her foot at Arizona State Hospital and sued them.

PATIENT: ——— represented me when I broke my foot.

COURT: We will get back to you.

PATIENT: Excuse me. My brother says that you shouldn't send me to Arizona State Hospital because they gave me money for my foot.

COURT: We will get back to that.

PSYCHIATRIST II: She is quite anxious. She told me to get in touch with her husband, but I couldn't reach him at the number she gave me. She indicates that she could get her children, which is quite contrary to fact. She can't take care of herself at this time.

COURT: Left to her own devices, would she cause trouble for herself?

PSYCHIATRIST II: She would be a nuisance to others.

COURT: Her behavior is unpredictable?

PSYCHIATRIST II: Yes.

PATIENT: I did say to my husband and the nurse that I'd give up my children, rather than go to Arizona State Hospital. That is why they took my children away. Give me a chance. I've never harmed anyone. I've never cut my wrists. Look at my wrists. I had my boy for a year. I washed clothes by hand. I used to take in laundry and iron white shirts. I used to make corn bread. I didn't fight him. I just left him at my mother-in-law's.

COURT: Let me interrupt. This has nothing to do . . .

PATIENT: [*Begins to speak unintelligibly.*]

COURT: I've heard all I want to hear. Be quiet.

PATIENT: I'm sorry.

COURT: When I tell you to be quiet, be quiet.

COURT (*to mother*): Mrs. ———, prior to the time she was hospitalized, was she in your house?

MOTHER: Yes.

COURT: How did she happen to be sent to the hospital?

MOTHER: She was nervous, she wanted to argue.

PATIENT: I . . .

COURT: She doesn't want to shut up?

MOTHER: Yes, she doesn't want to do much of anything.

COURT: If left alone, could she take care of herself?

MOTHER: I think so. She stayed by herself all while I worked.

COURT: Why is she here?

MOTHER: I don't know.

PSYCHIATRIST I: She was brought to the walk-in clinic by her husband

COURT (*to witness*): Mrs. ———, when was the first time you saw the patient?

WITNESS: About 3 weeks ago.

COURT: How was she acting?

WITNESS: I don't know anything about her. You shouldn't ask me. She seemed normal to me. I don't know.

COURT (*to public defender*): Any questions?

PUBLIC DEFENDER: I don't think so.

COURT (*to nurse*): You have observed her on the ward?

NURSE: Yes.

COURT: Will you be sworn?

[*Nurse is sworn.*]

COURT: You are familiar with [the patient's] prior visits?

NURSE: Yes, and I helped admit her this time.

COURT: How was she different?

NURSE: Well, she thinks she is changing into a man and was highly agitated.

PUBLIC DEFENDER (*to nurse*): Was she agitated when she talked about turning into a man?

NURSE: No, . . . well she is agitated all the time.

PUBLIC DEFENDER: Is she agitated now?

NURSE: Well, she is talking; yes, she is agitated.

PUBLIC DEFENDER: Have you known anyone else on the ward to strike anyone?

NURSE: Yes, they've struck me, but that doesn't have anything to do with this.

PUBLIC DEFENDER: Is there any pain associated with taking blood?

NURSE: Yes, sometimes.

COURT (*to psychiatrist*): Do you think she needs Arizona State Hospital?

PSYCHIATRIST I: In view of her lack of support at home, I would be concerned with her taking medication and taking care of herself. We need to resolve her situational problems. If there was proper supervision and control . . .

PATIENT: What do you mean proper supervision and control?

PSYCHIATRIST I: She is on Thorazine four times per day.
PUBLIC DEFENDER: What does that do?
PSYCHIATRIST I: It decreases agitation and organizes behavior.
PATIENT: I won't hurt anyone.
COURT: With the amount of medication you are taking now, you are still upset. I find that without supervision or control you would be a danger to yourself.
PATIENT: No.
COURT: The patient is ordered committed to Arizona State Hospital.
PATIENT: There is a mental health center here. I could get help there.
COURT: You must not have been following their treatment.
PATIENT: Yes, I have.
(*Patient is helped from the room.*)[44]

THE ROLE OF COUNSEL

In Arizona, there is a statutory right to counsel that provides: "At the time of apprehension or during detention, but before the hearing, the proposed patient apprehended shall be permitted to consult an attorney to represent him at the hearing. If he is not represented by an attorney, the court shall, before the hearing, appoint an attorney to represent him".[45] A literal interpretation of the statute has led most Arizona judges to the conclusion that mere appointment of an attorney "before the hearing" meets all of the necessary statutory requirements. In Maricopa and Pima Counties, one attorney is usually appointed to represent all of the indigent cases on the docket for the same day. In Maricopa County, hearings are scheduled in the afternoon and lawyers usually try to interview patients the previous evening or the morning before the hearing. In Pima County, during hearings which we observed, a public defender was appointed *at* the hearing and had no opportunity to preinterview the patients.

While it might appear that the practice of first appointing counsel at the hearing itself is the lowest standard by which any "right to counsel" could be enforced, an interview uncovered in one of the counties where Indians sometimes come before the civil commitment court an even graver deprivation of the right to counsel:

JUDGE: I have absolutely no jurisdiction over an Indian to commit him to the State Hospital. But I do it anyway—I do it all the time. It's illegal *ab initio*. So why appoint an attorney?
PROJECT: So commitment is for his benefit?
JUDGE: Yes, it's for his benefit, but if I have no jurisdiction, I see no point in appointing an attorney, because it's all illegal anyway.

Not surprisingly, the statute is silent concerning the role of the attorney before or during the hearing. The legislature has served its function by providing for legal representation, leaving the development of the functions to be performed to the expertise of the bar, guided by its own code of ethics and professional responsibility. But, unlike its performance in the criminal arena, the bar has not comfortably defined its role in the area of mental commitments.

While both criminal trials and commitment hearings have accusatory elements and may result in the deprivation of liberty, the attorney in the criminal setting seems to step more easily into the role of an advocate for the client (guilty or innocent) and to zealously prepare a defense to support the client's cause. In the area of civil commitment proceedings, although the petitioner may be present, observations have shown that the state is seldom represented at the hearing;[46] thus the traditional adversary (the prosecution) is absent. In addition, the lawyer may have limited experience in the civil commitment area and little or no professional training in the medical and psychological areas involved. While the testimony of two physicians or psychiatrists was presented in every observed commitment case, in the more than 50 hearings observed the patient's counsel seldom presented any such testimony or actively cross-examined the testifying doctors. It is difficult to imagine a competent attorney representing a client in a personal injury action or in any other case involving medical or technical questions without at least consulting his own professional experts and cross-examining the adverse experts. Indeed, it is disheartening to realize that when we deal not with the liberty-threatening situation of commitment, but instead with lucrative cases such as will contests and traumatic neurosis personal injury matters, lawyers hardly seem unduly deferential to—or bewildered by—the damning pronouncements of adverse psychiatrists.

It is understandable that such conditions prompted one writer who examined the function of counsel at commitment hearings to describe the average attorney as "a stranger in a strange land without benefit of guidebook, map or dictionary."[47] Contending that "any decision concerning a deprivation of liberty, perhaps for life, must be made openly with full exploration of all the issues,"[48] the same author concludes:

> The perfunctory performance of the "roleless" attorney is a major factor in the sterility of the commitment hearings, and it is the competent attorney who must be responsible for the development of meaningful prehearing and hearing procedures.[49]

Observation of commitment hearings in Maricopa and Pima Counties, combined with extensive interviews in all counties with judges, county attorneys, patients' attorneys, and doctors involved in prehearing examination and courtroom testimony, has disclosed some disquieting data concerning the commitment process in Arizona. Probably the most significant conclusions which can be drawn from the data concern the role of counsel and the general lack of any adversity to the proceedings. Most debasing to the adversary role is the procedure followed in Maricopa County, where the appointed counsel assists the court by virtually presenting the case *against* the patient.[50] Indeed, in those outlying counties where the county attorney participates in the proceedings on behalf of the *petitioner*, his performance is indistinguishable from the performance of the *patient's* attorney in Maricopa County.

Interviews with attorneys who represent patients at commitment hearings throughout Arizona disclosed that most saw their role as one of guarding the procedural rights of the patient. One attorney expressed the common view that his role was to see that "only those patients needing commitment were committed." Interestingly, a committee appointed by the Pima County Board of Supervisors to study local commitments rightly noted that a lawyer's role surely should extend beyond simply insuring fairness, for such a limited function would be a superfluous duplication of the role of the judge.

Another attorney similarly felt that a lawyer should become an advocate only when the patient was not actually in need of treatment. When questioned concerning how such determinations were made, he, like his colleagues, disclosed that he relies on the examining doctors' recommendations. When the doctors recommended commitment, attorneys felt they should do nothing to interfere with the patient's opportunity to receive "needed treatment." In one hearing observed in Maricopa County, the attorney actually requested that he be sworn, whereupon he proceeded to testify against his client.[51]

The limited concept of the role of counsel in the commitment process helps to explain, but cannot justify, other data collected. Attorneys are often appointed the morning of the trial and have, at best, only a few minutes before the hearing to meet with the patient. In many instances, the attorney never meets with the patient until the case is called. In one observed instance, counsel was appointed the morning of the trial, and the doctors testified that the patient was too ill to attend, whereupon the attorney promptly waived his unseen and unknown client's right to be present at the hearing. In another observed instance, where a statutorily required witness failed to attend, the patient's counsel attempted to waive the witness requirement, but was admonished by the court that the requirement was jurisdictional and thus could not be waived.

The length of hearings in the more populous counties is an indicator of the "sterility" of most commitment hearings. In the hearings observed in Maricopa County, the average length was less than 5 minutes, during which an average of slightly over four questions were asked by the patient's counsel. The questions most frequently asked of the petitioner: (1) "Are the facts which you have stated in this petition correct to the best of your knowledge?" (2) "Do you have anything to add?" Of the witness: (1) "Do you know the facts in the petition to be true?" (2) "Do you have anything to add?" In Pima County, the average hearing took considerably longer (27 minutes) and the average number of questions asked by patient's counsel was 6.3 per hearing.

It appears from the data that not even the most elementary legal questions are explored, such as (1) whether the decision to commit is to be based on dangerousness to self or to the person or property of others; (2) whether there is any real factual basis for such a conclusion; (3) whether possible alternatives to involuntary commitment exist or have even been explored; (4) whether medical examinations were thorough (a matter of particular significance in rural counties where examining physicians are usually not psychiatrists); and (5) whether the doctor's recommendation is based on factual or conclusory data.

The effectiveness of counsel at a commitment hearing will depend heavily on his or her efforts prior to the proceeding. But compensation for appointed counsel in Arizona is so grossly inadequate that attorneys are unquestionably discouraged from investigating facts, preparing a defense, exploring possible alternatives to commitment, and seeking outside psychiatric opinions. For example, Maricopa County allows $10 per case. Pima County, which previously allowed $5 per case, now uses the services of the public defender.[52] Significantly, some states have begun to recognize that patients at commitment hearings deserve to receive effective representation, and that quality services are far more readily obtained when attorneys are compensated adequately.

Actually, the sort of payment scheme most likely to provide patients with meaningful legal representation would compensate counsel by the hour, rather than by the case. When counsel is compensated a certain amount per client, he may not have as much incentive to labor over the case as he would if his compensation were tied to time expended in preparation.[53] Since Arizona's counsel compensation statute specifies that appointed attorneys may receive "such amount as the court in its discretion deems reasonable, considering the services performed,"[54] an hourly fee schedule could easily be achieved in this state simply by judicial implementation of the existing legislation.

The minimal compensation now available for appointed attorneys in commitment cases is indicative of a lack of understanding of the true role of counsel, and represents a most perfunctory compliance with the statutory requirement to provide counsel. Effective representation requires at least the following activities on the part of counsel. The attorney should make a thorough study of the facts of the case, which should include court records, hospital records, and information available from social agencies. Communication with the patient is, in the ordinary case, a must. The family and friends of the patient should also be contacted to ascertain the true facts behind the petition. It is essential that the attorney have a full understanding of the events preceding the filing of the petition. An investigation of the financial condition of the patient and his family—including their hospitalization insurance—is necessary to determine if certain alternatives to hospitalization should be explored. Finally, the attorney should explore the treatment and custodial resources of the community, should understand the various services offered by social agencies, and should know the avenues by which these resources can be applied to meet the needs of the client as alternatives to involuntary commitment.

The attorney has a responsibility to consult with the examining physicians concerning the medical history of the patient, the diagnosis, the proposed treatment, and the prognosis. The lawyer can insist that the doctor use lay language in explaining the patient's condition and in giving reasons for the recommendations concerning the criteria for commitment. In many of the rural counties in Arizona, interviews of examining physicians disclosed that many of them have only the vaguest comprehension of the standard of dangerousness required by the statute.

As will be demonstrated in the following section, crucial decisions in the commitment process are made by the physician, and his or her recommendations carry more than considerable weight with both judges and patients' counsel. The decisions made in the medical area are largely responsible for the mechanical processing aspects of the commitment hearing. If the attorney becomes an active advocate, the doctor will be faced with the necessity of justifying a recommendation to commit. That could result in a reduction of the tendency of doctors to recommend commitment whenever they are in doubt.[55]

Indeed, there is much that concerned, competent counsel can do even short of seeking the release of a client. Even if the propriety of hospitalization seems beyond question, counsel can press for the most favorable type of commitment and can play an important role in the determination of civil legal competency that, in some counties, usually accompanies a determination of committability.

With respect to counsel's possible role regarding the type of commitment, consider the following observed example.

"Jim," the 15-year-old son of relatively wealthy parents, was suffering from organic brain damage. Because he was exceptionally hard to handle at home, Jim had been placed in a foster home, where he resided until a member of the foster family became ill, necessitating Jim's departure. To the parents, the prospect of Jim's returning home seemed out of the question. His father testified that "the family couldn't function as a unit with him around," that he upset the normal routine, and that his presence at home was particularly taxing on the mother.

According to the doctor, Jim wanted *voluntarily* to go to the state hospital, but no one was available to transport Jim there and, in the absence of a court commitment, the sheriff's department felt it lacked the statutory authority to transport the patient.[56] Jim's lawyer then asked him whether he thought it would help him to go to the hospital, and when Jim responded affirmatively, the court promptly ordered him involuntarily committed and the hearing terminated—to everyone's apparent satisfaction.

Jim's lawyer must obviously have been relieved to hear Jim say he desired hospitalization, for that must have plainly altered the lawyer's conception of his role. Yet, with only a mild assertiveness, the lawyer could have markedly helped his client.

He could have inquired, for example, into the suitability of another foster placement, thereby possibly short-circuiting hospitalization altogether. But even if hospitalization seemed inevitable, there was much for the lawyer to do. He could, for instance, have challenged the sheriff's interpretation of the transportation statute and might have persuaded the court to issue an order directing the sheriff's department to transport Jim as a voluntary patient. Or he might have asked Jim's parents whether they would either provide or arrange for the necessary transportation. Moreover, since the doctors felt hospitalization was warranted and Jim and his parents concurred, Jim seemed clearly eligible for commitment under Arizona's "non-protesting" admission statute,[57] which is in many principal respects similar to voluntary admission, but which is included in the county-provided transportation statute.

Had the attorney truly represented his client, therefore, he could seemingly have arranged for an admission to the hospital pursuant to statutory provisions far less threatening to liberty than the ordinary involuntary civil commitment provision. Further, voluntary admission may in many cases be desirable simply because available evidence indicates that nurses and attendants find voluntary patients "more attractive" than committed patients, and such attitudes may be perceived by the voluntary patients and may affect their self-concepts and eventual recovery.[58]

As suggested earlier, counsel can, in some counties, perform an important function (even for clearly committable clients) when civil legal competency is put in issue at the commitment hearing. Arizona's statute properly recognizes that the standards for commitment should differ from those of competency, and that a determination of committability should not in itself result in a finding of incompetency.[59] In some counties, such as Pima, the statute is closely adhered to. In fact, patients committed from Pima County are virtually never declared incompetent and deprived of their civil rights.[60] But in Maricopa County and some of the outlying counties, the situation is otherwise: nearly all committed patients are declared incompetent. In those counties, counsel should strive to persuade the courts to separate these two determinations.

Thus, even if commitment seems inevitable, the lawyer should investigate and argue the question of competence. In so doing, the following factors are relevant: How much and what type of property does the patient possess? A patient may well be capable of handling a small and simple estate even though he would be incapable of handling a large and complex one. How much control and guidance are provided by other members of the patient's family? Despite a physician's opinion of incapacity, how has the patient *actually* performed in handling his own affairs? Would it be psychologically detrimental to deprive him of that right? What assumptions has the doctor made in finding that spending patterns have not been in the patient's best interests? Is it more in the interest of elderly persons to increase their spending in order to enjoy their last years or to keep their estates intact for their heirs?[61] These issues could and should be explored in Arizona proceedings, but they are not being aired.

Although the situation described here is not markedly different from the situation in many other jurisdictions, some jurisdictions have begun to provide true legal services for the mentally ill. In New York, for example, the American Civil Liberties Union has undertaken a law reform project on behalf of the mentally ill, and the Mental Health Information Service has undertaken an effective servicing role.[62] Arizona must strive to provide comparable legal services.

THE ROLE OF THE PHYSICIAN

The judge who signs the commitment order is the most significant figure in the commitment process by only a small margin. The physician's recommendation is probably the most important single factor in the commitment decision. In Arizona's rural counties, judges have indicated that they almost always follow the doctor's recommendation. Of

396 cases studied in Maricopa County, the physician's recommendation was followed in 97.9% of the cases. A similar study of 367 cases in Pima County indicated that action taken by the court conformed with the physician's recommendation in 96.1% of the cases.[63] This extraordinary correlation, coupled with data gleaned from interviews with judges throughout the state, can lead to only one conclusion: nearly total reliance is placed on the recommendation of the physician.[64]

The power of the medical profession becomes especially significant in view of the vagueness of the Arizona statutes. Provision for examination prior to a commitment hearing is found in the following statutory language:

> The judge shall also appoint and require two or more designated examiners [physicians] to be present at the examination [hearing]. On the basis of the testimony and a personal examination of the proposed patient, the designated examiners shall make a written statement under oath stating their opinion as to the mental health of the proposed patient, whether he has a mental illness likely to be dangerous to himself or to the person or property of others if he is permitted to be at large, and whether the mental illness is likely to be temporary or permanent.[65]

"Designated examiner" is defined as "a licensed physician selected by the superior court. Whenever possible, the designated examiner shall be a licensed physician experienced in the diagnosis, treatment and care of mental illness."[66]

One apparent flaw in the implementation of the statute is attributable to the shortage of trained psychiatrists in Arizona.[67] Psychiatrists are actually used only in Arizona's four most populous counties. Most counties use ordinary physicians who are for the most part lacking in the psychiatric training necessary for an accurate diagnosis and recommendation.

In two rural counties using physicians, no actual examination of the proposed patient is made. In direct contravention of the statutory "personal examination" requirement, the doctors, acting much like jurors, merely attend the hearing and form their recommendations based on observations made at that time.[68] They apparently feel, too, that they should not ask any questions at the hearing, which is in sharp contrast with the practice in another county, where the examining doctors sit with the county attorney during the hearing and actively participate in questioning witnesses. In many other rural counties, well-meaning physicians indicated during interviews that their decision was most often based on whether the patient needed treatment rather than the criterion of "dangerousness" required by the statute. In one instance, a general surgeon, used frequently by the court to examine proposed patients, indicated that his actual decision was based on whether the patient needed psychiatric evaluation. It was his feeling that by recommending commitment, he was merely sending the patient to the Arizona State Hospital for psychiatric evaluation by qualified psychiatrists who could release the patient if treatment was not needed.

Even in the more populous counties, where psychiatrists are used, a study of 342 medical reports submitted in commitment cases indicated that 154 (45%) were based on conclusory information taken from the petition relative to allegedly "dangerous conduct" of the patient.

Since the psychiatrist who is called on to testify as a witness at commitment hearings is, in some of the more populous counties, also involved in many of the community-based outpatient treatment programs, problems may arise which are similar to Dr. Szasz's vision of the "dual role" of institutional psychiatrists—therapist for the patient and agent for the state.[69] A committed patient may be released from the hospital and, immediately or after a while, desire or need outpatient or supportive psychiatric services in his home community. When he looks into the availability of those services, however, he may find that his proposed therapist is the very person who, as agent of the state and protector of society, testified in the past as to his mental illness, dangerousness, and need for total confinement. Under such circumstances, the patient may forego the community-based treatment, as much as he may require it, for fear that his therapist will betray him.[70]

Another significant problem concerning the role of the psychiatrist relates to the prediction of antisocial behavior. Since failure to commit a patient who later becomes violent and dangerous usually makes the headlines, psychiatrists are, in commitment recommendations, particularly prone to overprediction of the need for hospitalization.[71] Nevertheless, there are many instances where examining physicians will conclude that a proposed patient is not mentally ill or in need of hospitalization. Such a diagnosis seems to lead to differing prehearing responses in Arizona's two most populous counties.

In Pima County, a system has been informally devised to permit the immediate release of patients who have been medically determined not to be in need of hospitalization. On reaching such a diagnosis, the examining doctor asks a county psychiatric social worker to contact the court, to inform the court of the medical finding, and to request that the petition be immediately dismissed. The petition is then dismissed, the patient is released, and a form letter is transmitted from the doctor to the court for insertion in the patient's legal file.[72] Although the doctors in

Pima County seek to have the petitioner acquiesce in the dismissal of the petition, the petitioner's consent is by no means considered a necessary prerequisite to the operation of their prehearing discharge procedure.

In Maricopa County, there also exists a procedure for releasing patients prior to hearing who, in the opinion of the doctors, are not in need of hospitalization. But the procedure is more limited than in Pima County because, as learned in interviews with the judge and a testifying psychiatrist, a Maricopa County petition will not be dismissed without the petitioner's consent unless it is completely frivolous. Accordingly, a recalcitrant petitioner can block the prehearing dismissal of a Maricopa County commitment petition—thereby necessitating the continued custody of the patient on the county hospital psychiatric ward until the date of the hearing—even though both examining psychiatrists feel hospitalization is not in order. That impediment to release seems particularly curious in view of the fact that, at the commitment hearing, the doctors will no doubt testify against involuntary hospitalization, and the petition will invariably be dismissed at that time.

Unfortunately, some psychiatrists apparently do not practice any sort of prehearing release procedure, as evidenced by a commitment hearing observed in one of the state's Veterans Administration Hospitals.[73] In that case, the patient had been in custody against his will for several days awaiting his hearing. At the hearing, however, the psychiatrists asked if they could testify first and both concluded that the patient showed no signs of mental illness, whereupon he was promptly released by the court.

It is apparent that there is a need for the development of effective prehearing discharge procedures in many parts of Arizona. Such procedures would not only result in speedier justice for persons not needing hospitalization, but would also enable the examining physicians to play a role more in keeping with medical theory: they would be permitted to release, rather than be required to hold and treat, "patients" not needing hospital treatment.

But, with respect to the many patients who would not be released even under a fully developed prehearing discharge procedure, the physician will be called to testify at the commitment hearing. It is important, therefore, to discuss his appropriate role at that stage of the proceedings as well.

If commitment is truly viewed as a legal rather than as a medical determination, it would seem logical to limit the psychiatrist's role in the commitment hearing to merely presenting evidence.[74] The psychiatrist might be required only to delineate the various factors which are determinative of the commitment question and not be asked specifically whether or not the patient meets the legal criteria for commitment. Rather, the court, after consideration of the various factors presented by the psychiatrist and other relevant evidence, would, as it should in any case, determine whether the patient meets the legal standards for commitment. To insure independent and reasonable judicial decision making, it would be helpful to require the court to make findings of fact and conclusions of law for each case.

The greatest danger of permitting a psychiatrist to testify in conclusory fashion about legal criteria is that the doctor may have his or her own notion of the substantive legal standards required for commitment. And that notion may differ markedly from that of the court, but the difference may easily go unnoticed and unexplored at the hearing, particularly if neither the court nor the patient's lawyer vigorously questions the doctor. Consider the following hypothetical situation: A patient, the subject of a commitment hearing, is suffering from depression and has, because of his depression, stayed home from work rather frequently. If the doctor is permitted to testify in legal conclusory terms, and if the doctor believes that endangering one's employment is equivalent to "injuring oneself," the doctor could easily testify that "this patient is very depressed, is a danger to himself, and should be committed." Such perfunctory testimony—by no means atypical in Arizona commitment proceedings—could readily lead to the involuntary hospitalization of the patient even by a judge who believes that the statutory requirement of danger to self contemplates some risk of suicide. The court, in light of the psychiatrist's testimony, might simply assume that he and the doctor are using the legal standard similarly, and might, without probing and without giving the matter a great deal of thought, routinely order commitment.

The confusion is compounded even further when the testifying physicians are completely bewildered, as they often are, by the various legal concepts of committability, competency, and the insanity defense. For example, one psychiatrist, who regularly examines proposed patients and testifies as to their committability at weekly Maricopa County hearings, demonstrated complete confusion as to the various concepts. In an interview with us, he repeatedly used the terms "competency" and "committability" interchangeably. When pressed as to the requirements of committability, he responded, "As you know, Arizona follows the *M'Naghten* test of incompetency. That is, he [the proposed patient] must be so mentally ill as to be a danger to the person or property of others." Perhaps confusing civil incompetency standards with the name of the ancient test of criminal responsibility is pardonable. But the belief that competency is a function of the commitment test surely is not, particularly when this very psychiatrist often testifies in conclusory terms that "the patient should be committed as incompetent."[75]

The role of the psychiatrist at the hearing should consist simply of providing information on which the court would base its decision. Such a procedure could be defended based on the tendency of psychiatrists to overpredict dangerousness and the need for hospitalization, and on the possibility that a doctor could otherwise usurp judicial functions. The procedure would also be consistent with the underlying assumption that indeterminate commitment should be, in the final analysis, a legal and not a medical determination.

Probably the greatest weakness in the statutory role prescribed for the physician is the lack of psychiatric training required on the part of the examining physician.[76] This is especially apparent when one considers the strides which have been made in recent years in mental health theory and practice. Available psychiatric knowledge raises serious doubts concerning the qualifications of the average physician to make any kind of accurate diagnosis and prognosis of mental illness in all but the most typical cases, and that knowledge casts equally serious doubt on the exclusion of psychologists as qualified designated examiners.

In that regard, it is noteworthy that physicians in some of the outlying counties mentioned that although they testified as experts in civil commitment hearings, they declined to do so in criminal cases where competency to stand trial or the insanity defense is at issue, necessitating the appearance in those cases of out-of-town psychiatrists. Apparently, those physicians believe that "criminal commitment" cases are, in comparison to "civil commitment" cases, sufficiently complex or consequential to warrant real expertise.

CONCLUSION

It is true, as the next chapter notes, that criminally committed patients typically suffer, more so than civilly committed patients, stigmatization and special security status. Those factors, however, should not be sufficient for us to depreciate the need for forensic understanding in the civil commitment process.

Indeed, an understanding, through empirical study, of the Arizona situation as it existed a decade ago (the situation documented above) led, during the mid-seventies, to major law reform in Arizona.[77] Now, far from its bleak origins, Arizona boasts a mental health law considered by some to be one of the best. Even so, given the tendency in this area for practice to fall well below theory, periodic study is necessary to learn how the system might be misfiring and how it might be modified to improve its functioning or to bring it back on course.[78]

Now that the reader is hopefully fairly informed about the civil commitment system, however, the time has come to shift our attention to the system of criminal commitment. Indeed, as the next chapter notes in its opening passages, a patient's presence in one system rather than in the other one is often a matter of fortuity—or of finances.

NOTES

[1]Many of the recommendations have now been enacted into law. See generally Shuman, Hegland, & Wexler, Arizona's Mental Health Services Act: An Overview and an Analysis of Proposed Amendments, 19 ARIZ. L. REV. 313 (1977). Similar studies have led to reform in other jurisdictions. See the discussion in Contemporary Studies Project, Involuntary Hospitalization of the Mentally Ill in Iowa: The Failure of the 1975 Legislation, 64 IOWA L. REV. 1284 (1979).

[2]According to ARIZ. REV. STAT. ANN. § 36–509(B) (Supp. 1970–71), "[t]he county attorney shall prepare the petition. . . ." It appears that in the metropolitan communities the assistance of the county attorney is never sought, but in some of the rural counties, the county attorney does participate in the pleading stage—and sometimes in the hearing itself.

[3]But it has been shown in a study of midwestern commitment proceedings that rural procedures provide more screening, and stress rationality in decision making, far more than do urban procedures. Some of the rural rationality is attributed to the fact that the proposed patient is often known to the decision-making officials. Scheff, Social Conditions for Rationality: How Urban and Rural Courts Deal with the Mentally Ill, 7 AMER. BEHAVIORAL SCIENTIST 21 (Mar., 1964). In some of Arizona's outlying counties, the county attorney will interview the petitioner and determine whether a physician has been contacted who concurs in the petition, and in one county the prior acquiescence of a physician seems to be insisted on.

[4]See infra p. 77 for a copy of one such memorandum. Cf. CAL. WELF. & INST'NS CODE §5202: "If the petition is filed, it should be accompanied by a report containing the findings of the person or agency designated by the county to provide prepetition screening."

[5]Actually, the California standard requires the petition to allege the respondent to be mentally ill and gravely disabled or dangerous to himself or others. CAL. WELF. & INST'NS CODE §5201.

[6]Id. §5202.

[7]Id.

[8]ARIZ. REV. STAT. ANN. §36–514 (C) (Supp. 1970–71).

[9]Id. §36–509 (A) (Supp. 1970–71).

[10]CAL. WELF. & INST'NS. CODE §5201.

[11]ARIZ. REV. STAT. ANN. §36–510(A) (Supp. 1970–71) (emphasis added).

[12]Aguilar v. Texas, 378 U.S. 108 (1964). See also Spinelli v. United States, 393 U.S. 410 (1969).

[13]Prefender, Probate Court Attitudes toward Involuntary Hospitalization: A Field Study, 5-J. FAM. L. 139, 150 (1965):

> [O]f the 221 petitions for a writ from Kalamazoo Hospital . . . only 23 were denied. This means that 198 of the 221 patients were released because of imperfections in the way

they were orginally [sic.] admitted. Sixty-one of these cases showed defects in the petition, chiefly due to insufficient facts cited by the petitioner. Nineteen cases involved improper petitioners, and in 127 cases the physicians' certificates were defective, the majority because of conclusions and hearsay evidence.

[14]*See In re* Sealy, 218 So. 2d 765 (Fla. App. 1969) for a similar case. *Sealy* also indicates that psychiatrists as well as laymen sometimes confuse matters of lifestyle with matters of mental health, especially with respect to young people. It seems that certain time-honored tools of psychiatric diagnosis (such as concern for appearance) clash head on with the youth culture.

[15]Another example of a petition seemingly filed for improper motives was uncovered in an interview with an examining physician. In this particular case, the petitioner was a social worker rather than a spouse, and the respondent was eventually committed. In a taped interview, the physician related the following:

> One time I can remember a lady who was alcoholic but not crazy. The fault was the social worker who was the child welfare worker. He was kind of a "go-getter." He wanted to take the kids out of the house. Instead of presenting her as an unfit mother which would have been the course to take, ... he had her brought into court for alcoholism to be commited to the state hospital. ...
>   Well, she was an alcoholic, but she was not endangering the kids in the sense that she even meant them harm or that she was insane by the legal definition of it. She was perfectly capable [and] put on a defense of herself in the courtroom. ... [S]he was capable of giving a pretty strong defense of herself and she did. One of the complaints was that she believed in the supernatural and this and that. I think I made the statement in court that if they put up everyone that believes in the supernatural they are going to put up half the people in the room. That's no grounds for commitment. They found her drunk a couple of times. Fine, but that wasn't grounds for finding her insane. They should have brought her up under a different rule, unfit mother or something.

[16]This is usually a county hospital or a county jail.

[17]CAL. WELF. & INST'NS CODE §5202.

[18]*Id.* §5206. In California, the court implements the evaluation procedure by issuing a single "Order for Evaluation or Detention." The appropriate form may be found in *id.* §5207. In practice, a copy of the California order for evaluation is given to the designated examination facility, and if the proposed patient fails to appear at the scheduled time and place, the facility notifies the authorities, who then pick the patient up and bring him to the facility.

[19]*Id.* §5212.

[20]*Id.* §5206.

[21]*Id.* §5206 & 5250.

[22]*Id.* §5276.

[23]ARIZ. REV. STAT. ANN. §36-510 (Supp. 1970-71) (emphasis added).

[24]*Id.* Note that while section 36-510 speaks of the court making various "orders," section 36-511 provides for an officer apprehending a proposed patient pursuant to an "order for detention." Reading the two sections together leads to the inference that section 36-510 provides for certain orders in addition to strict unconditional detention orders.

[25]An obvious example might be the case of a recent serious suicide attempt.

[26]Surprisingly, our research disclosed a possible third danger of outpatient evaluations. Apparently, in some communities, the fact that a member of the community has been detained pending a commitment hearing may operate in his favor to avoid a wrongful commitment. In one rural county, an attorney informed us that when neighbors or friends of a proposed patient think the person is being wronged, they will call the attorney or even the judge and inform him of the circumstances. Perhaps if outpatient evaluations become the rule, neighbors and friends of docile or distressed patients may

never learn of the pending commitment until the patient departs with the sheriff for the Arizona State Hospital in Phoenix.

[27]ARIZ. REV. STAT. ANN. § 36-511 (Supp. 1970–71).

[28]Sometimes, detention serves the additional purpose of extralegal social control. A student who investigated mental health processes in one outlying county filed this report:

> Mention was made of a long-haired bearded 'hippie-type' person who was confined for bizarre behavior thought to be drug induced. While he was detained he was given a haircut and a shave, but no mention was made as to the method of persuasion that was used to obtain such results. There was no hearing because the proposed patient escaped from the hospital early in his confinement. The interviewer's impression was that the patient was not given a choice about receiving a haircut. This interviewer also had a beard and long hair and made his escape a few minutes later.

[29]The new facility, designed in 1959, opened on February 27, 1971.

[30]Full occupancy of the ward was to be 36 patients. During our examination of the facility, only 2 months after it opened, there were 47 patients on the ward.

[31]Normal window glass is used throughout the rest of the hospital, with the exception of the jail security ward on the fourth floor where "pitted" glass is also utilized.

[32]Individuals who are able to afford the hospital costs, however, may be placed there with a doctor's approval.

[33]In Maricopa County, a single judge hears all civil commitment cases. The practice is different in Pima County, where the judge who happens to be the assignment judge for a particular month, pursuant to a rotation schedule, hears all commitment cases during that month.

[34]While holding all commitment cases on certain days has obvious advantages, such as the efficient use of the testifying psychiatrists' time, the clear-cut pressure to process all current cases by the end of the court day must inevitably work against the contemplative exploration of pertinent legal, factual, and medical issues. Where deprivation of liberty is at stake, it seems in order to follow the model of the criminal process and depart from a rigorous time schedule.

[35]The right to a transcript of the hearing has been raised by some advocates of patients' rights. In the District of Columbia, Mental Health Commission hearings are now transcribed and a copy of the transcript is made available to the patient and his or her counsel. In Arizona, however, the proceedings are not transcribed and only minute entries are made in the file record of the court.

It might be thought that since the hearing determines committability at the time of the proceeding rather than guilt or innocence of a past act, a transcript is probably not as crucial in mental health proceedings as it would be in criminal proceedings: If the patient is committed and later petitions for a periodic reexamination and release hearing pursuant to ARIZ. REV. STAT. ANN. § 36-516 (Supp. 1970–71), it will be his mental condition at the time release is sought that will be crucial, not his past mental state. Indeed, facts relating to the patient's mental state at the time of his original commitment hearing, even if recorded in a verbatim transcript, might seem remote and irrelevant if the courts take advantage of the provision in Section 36-516 that reexamination by petition "shall not be required to be conducted if the petition is filed sooner than one year after the issuance of the order of commitment."

It must, however, be recognized that a transcript of the commitment proceeding might prove extremely useful to a patient preparing for a Section 36-516 judicial reexamination by enabling him to compare his current mental condition (and his possible improvement) with the very points that were in issue at the time of his earlier commitment. Such a comparison, if favorable, should no doubt carry considerable weight with the reexamining court. Moreover, an involuntarily confined patient might seek release not through a Section 36-516 reexamination proceeding but via habeas corpus, contending, for example, that the committing court failed to ventilate the issue of possible treatment alternatives less drastic than full-time compulsory state hospitalization. To litigate such a contention, the commitment proceeding transcript would seem highly advantageous if not essential.

Because a confined patient's opportunities for release can rest heavily on the availability of a transcript, Arizona commitment proceedings should be recorded. Precedent for recording state-initiated actions possibly leading to the loss of liberty can be found in Arizona's Juvenile Code, which calls for a court reporter in most juvenile hearings (ARIZ. REV. STAT. ANN. § 8-234 (Supp. 1970-71)).

Under the doctrine of Gardner v. California, 393 U.S. 367 (1969), transcripts of the proceedings should be made available free of charge to indigent patients who are committed. In *Gardner*, which dealt with an equal protection claim to transcripts in a postconviction context, the court rejected a state argument that the petitioner, having been present at his superior court hearing, could draw on his memory in preparing an application for further judicial review. Considering that patients at commitment hearings are usually under sedation and are mentally troubled, *Gardner* would seem to govern *a fortiori* in a commitment context.

[36]In one observed hearing, a witness failed to appear. Another "interested" party was present and volunteered to testify. The volunteer was asked if he was familiar with the case, and when an affirmative answer was given, he was sworn.

In some Pima County cases observed by the author prior to the project's actual inception, ward attendants were sometimes called as witnesses to satisfy the statutory two-witness rule, ARIZ. REV. STAT. ANN. §36-514(B) (Supp. 1970-71), when one of the two required lay witnesses failed to appear. Similar cases in Maricopa County are frequent.

[37]Hearings are also held at the county hospital in Pima County, though in many of the outlying counties they are held in courtrooms, in chambers, or in courthouse libraries.

[38]By this statement the psychiatrist is actually recommending that the judge take two actions: (1) that he commit the patient and (2) declare him to be civilly incompetent. It appears, however, that in some cases the psychiatrist confuses the separate legal requirements for the two judicial actions.

[39]Or more often, the bailiff merely taps the respondent on the shoulder and ushers him from the room.

[40]The chronologies were taken by having two project members observe each hearing. The observers rapidly took notes, which they compared for accuracy after the hearings. The chronologies are believed to be virtually verbatim replicas of the observed hearings.

[41]This entire hearing, including the time taken to remove the patient from the hearing room, consumed three minutes.

[42]Sometimes, but by no means always, the public defender will have conferred with his client prior to his formal appointment at the hearing.

[43]Note that this chronological sequence is violative of the statute, which requires the testifying physicians to base their opinions not only on the psychiatric examination, but also on the testimony presented at the hearing, ARIZ. REV. STAT. ANN. § 36-514(B) (Supp. 1970-71). Accordingly, the physicians should testify last.

[44]We were unable to observe hearings in the rural counties, but the principal participants in the commitment process in those counties were interviewed. By and large, commitment hearings in the outlying counties were not markedly different from the metropolitan hearings, though they are generally more formal and legalistic. Hearings are fre-

quently conducted in the courthouse, and the county attorney often presents the case against the proposed patient. Average hearing lengths seem to vary widely from county to county, ranging from a low of 3 to 4 minutes to a high in some counties of 30 to 40 minutes or over an hour.

[45]ARIZ. REV. STAT. ANN. §36-514(A) (Supp. 1970-71).

[46]A survey of Arizona counties indicated that the county attorney's office is only represented at commitment hearings in six rural counties where commitment hearings average fewer than 25 per year. The judge of one outlying county, apparently unaware of the practice of six of his bretheren, indicated that he wishes that the county attorney could be allowed to participate in commitment hearings.

[47]Cohen, *The Function of the Attorney and the Commitment of the Mentally Ill*, 44 TEX. L. REV. 424 (1966).

[48]*Id.* at 425.

[49]*Id.*

[50]The questions most frequently asked by the patients' appointed counsel consisted of asking the petitioners if the facts stated in the petition were true and whether the petitioner had anything to add. These same questions were also asked of the lay witnesses.

[51]The attorney testified that during his interview with the proposed patient, the latter had attempted to hit the attorney. In the attorney's opinion, the patient was dangerous.

[52]By statute, the public defender is required to represent patients at commitment hearings, at least where appointed by the court to do so, ARIZ. REV. STAT. ANN. §11-584(2) (Supp. 1970-71). But this statute has not been implemented in Maricopa County where private attorneys tend to be appointed to represent proposed patients.

[53]*Cf.* Tumey v. Ohio, 273 U.S. 510, 532 (1927) (judicial payment scheme unconstitutional when it runs counter to defendant's interest in a fair trial). *See also* Ison v. Western Veg. Distrib., 48 Ariz. 104, 59 P.2d 649 (1936).

[54]ARIZ. REV. STAT. ANN. § 13-1673 (1956).

[55]Dershowitz, *The Psychiatrist's Power in Civil Commitment: A Knife that Cuts Both Ways*, PSYCHOLOGY TODAY 43 (Feb., 1969). A powerful theoretical justification for commitment counsel to act in an adversary capacity appears in Note, *The Role of Counsel in the Civil Commitment Process: A Theoretical Framework*, 84 YALE L. J. 1540 (1975). Technical adversary training itself, however, may be insufficient to achieve adversary behavior by attorneys in such cases. Poythress, *Psychiatric Expertise in Civil Commitment: Training Attorneys to Cope with Expert Testimony*, 2 L. & HUMAN BEH. 1 (1978). Perhaps technical adversary training coupled with a heavy dose of training in the theory and ethics of advocacy might make a difference.

[56]*See* ARIZ. REV. STAT. ANN. § 36-518 (Supp. 1970-71) (providing for transportation for persons committed under sections 36-505, -507, & -514, but not under the voluntary admission procedure of section 36-502). If county-provided transportation for voluntary patients cannot be arranged informally or administratively, statutory revision seems clearly in order.

[57]*Id.* § 36-505 (Supp. 1970-71).

[58]Denzen & Spitzer, *Patient Entry Patterns in Varied Psychiatric Settings*, 50 MENTAL HYGEINE 257 (1966). Unfortunately, the judge of one Arizona county discourages voluntary admissions because he feels they "hamper the proper care of the patient." Accordingly, he tells prospective petitioners that if they want to explore the voluntary admissions route, they will have to "go through the routine themselves" and would have to make their own arrangements to transport the proposed patient to the state hospital.

[59]Ariz. Rev. Stat. Ann. §36- 514(D) (Supp. 1970-71).

[60]The few incompetency determinations in Pima County were usually cases where a single elderly person required a guardian to care for substantial real and personal property.

[61]See Allen, Ferster, & Weihofen, Mental Impairment and Legal Incompetency 118-19, 133-35 (1968).

[62]Note, The New York Mental Health Information Service: A New Approach to Hospitalization of the Mentally Ill, 67 Colum. L. Rev. 672 (1967). For an extensive bibliography on the right to counsel at commitment hearings, see A. Brooks, Law, Psychiatry, and the Mental Health System 113-116 (Supp. 1980).

[63]Also, the two examining physicians virtually always agree with each other with regard to recommendations. In many cases, this may be attributable to the fact that only one physician actually examines the patient and that physician then "briefs" his colleague before the hearing. It should be noted that in many of those cases where the doctor's recommendation was not followed, the judge was precluded from doing so because the doctor had recommended a type of disposition not provided for by the statute.

[64]At one observed hearing, a patient questioned the correctness of a diagnosis, which prompted the following revealing retort by the judge: "I don't guess you want to put your judgment over these doctors. I don't like to do it myself."

[65]Ariz. Rev. Stat. Ann. §36-514(B) (Supp. 1970-71).

[66]Id. §36-501.

[67]Arizona has only 75-80 psychiatrists, with all except three or four located in either Phoenix or Tucson. It is ironic that psychologists are excluded as qualified examiners since they too are obviously qualified professionals in the field of mental health. The shortage of psychologists, however, is equally acute in Arizona's rural counties.

[68]One of those doctors made the following comment in a taped interview:

> I am supposed to form an opinion on what I hear in the courtroom only. Sometimes I feel that I am the jury and the judge both. I don't examine the patient. I only listen to testimony in the courtroom unless it happens to be a patient of mine. There have been several times when I have said I don't have enough information [to have an opinion] but the judge sent them up anyway.

[69]Szasz, Hospital Refusal to Release Mental Patients, 9 Clev.-Mar. L. Rev. 220 (1960).

[70]Cf. id. See also Ross, Commitment of the Mentally Ill: Problems of Law and Policy, 57 Mich. L. Rev. 945, 964, (1959).

[71]T. Scheff, Being Mentally Ill (1966).

[72]The letter reads as follows:

> Dear Judge _____:
> The above-named person was admitted to the psychiatric service of the Pima County General Hospital on _____, 197___(date) by petition of _____.
> We have examined the patient and do not feel that he (she) meets the statutory requirements for commitment at this time. The patient is not considered psychotic nor dangerous to himself (herself) or to others. We feel the patient has received maximum benefits from hospitalization, and recommend that the patient be released from the hospital and the petition dismissed at this time. Thank you for your cooperation.
> Sincerely yours,
> _____, M.D.
> _____, M.D.

[73]Eligible persons may be committed by state courts to the Veterans Administration. See Ariz. Rev. Stat. Ann. §36-514(C) (Supp. 1970-71).

[74]Cf. Washington v. United States, 390 F.2d 444 (D.C. Cir. 1967) (doctors prohibited from testifying whether an offense was a "product" of a mental illness under the Durham rule, for otherwise the jury's function would be usurped).

[75]It would be unfortunate enough if the doctor had confused two concepts—civil commit-

ment and civil incompetency—but he clearly confused four: the two civil standards, the criminal standards for competency to stand trial, and not guilty by reason of insanity. No doubt his confusion, coupled with his unscrutinized conclusory testimony, bears heavily on why an enormous number of patients committed in Maricopa County are also declared legally incompetent.

[76]It would be interesting to determine empirically whether their lack of behavioral knowledge leads nonpsychiatrist physicians to "overpredict" mental illness to an even greater extent than do psychiatrists. From the interview data gathered in Arizona's rural counties, greater overprediction on the part of physicians would be anticipated.

[77]*See* note 1 *supra.*

[78]Repeated studies have, for example, been needed in Arizona and in Iowa. *See* note 1 *supra.*

Part One
THE COMMITMENT SYSTEM

B. Criminal Commitment

5

The Criminal Commitment System

ITS STRUCTURE AND COMPONENTS

INTRODUCTION

While conducting the empirical inquiry into the administration of psychiatric justice in Arizona (which formed the basis of the preceding chapter) we learned, from an interview with a superior court judge, of the following interesting incident: A criminal defendant in a rural county had been committed to the Arizona State Hospital as incompetent to stand trial (IST). After the defendant had been confined as IST for a few months, the superior court judge was visited by the County Board of Supervisors, who successfully urged the judge to dismiss the criminal charges and to recommit the patient pursuant to the *civil* commitment process.

The decision to dismiss the charge and to recommit the patient civilly rather than to continue the IST commitment had certain enormous consequences. In addition to avoiding the prospect of eventual criminal trial, confinement pursuant to a "civil" rather than a "criminal" commitment label would have much to do with the patient's security status while in the hospital, influencing, for example, whether he would be housed on an open ward or instead on the far less attractive maximum security unit.

Was the board of supervisors' recommitment request grounded in such humanitarian and clinical considerations? Hardly. Instead, the supreme motivating force, according to the judge who agreed to the recommitment, was the fact that the cost of hospitalizing an incompetent criminal defendant falls by statute on the county in question while the comparable cost of maintaining a civilly committed patient is, in Arizona, shouldered by the state. In that interview, we had stumbled on a clear-cut example of what today's proponents of mental health unified services systems describe as "decisions affecting care... based on jurisdictional jockeying generated by fiscal considerations that are irrelevant to the patient's needs."[1]

As it turns out, various incentives (fiscal or otherwise) that are purposely or often unintentionally built into the criminal commitment system, and the consequences that flow from those incentive patterns, are generally of far more interest and importance than are the tests for determining whether one is incompetent to stand trial, not guilty by reason of insanity, and so forth. Accordingly, the present chapter will examine the criminal commitment system and its components ("special" offenders, defendants found incompetent to stand trial, defendents found not guilty by reason of insanity, and prison-to-hospital transferees) with a particular focus to mesh theory and practice (and law and behavioral science) by looking closely at incentives operative in the area of criminal commitment, especially insofar as those incentives or contingencies focus on nonclinical criteria or tend to produce countertherapeutic effects.

"SPECIAL" OFFENDERS SUBJECTED TO INDETERMINATE CONFINEMENT

Though they follow widely divergent patterns, laws in several states call for the commitment, outside of the traditional correctional setting, of designated offenders, typically ones who have been involved in prohibited sexual activity and who are accordingly labelled "sexual psychopaths" or "mentally disordered sex offenders." Laws providing for the commitment of "special" offenders (such as "sexual psychopaths" and "defective delinquents") typically provide that the commitment should be for an indeterminate period and should terminate only when the offender may be safely released. These laws have been subjected to heavy criticism by commentators, often on the ground (among many others) that they promote "shamming" rather than genuine rehabilitation.

When viewed from the perspective of a contingency analysis, matters are even worse, for efforts at shamming—and a fortiori at genuine rehabilitation—are often frustrated by the absence of clear-cut criteria for improvement and discharge. Hugo Adam Bedau, a philosopher, has described four possible correctional models which vary from one another in terms of the type of sentence and release standards: (1) a fixed sentence where release is contingent simply on reaching the expiration date; (2) an indeterminate sentence where release is gauged by objective conditions (e.g., obtaining a high school equivalency diploma); (3) an indeterminate sentence where release is gauged by subjective criteria (e.g., expressing "socially constructive attitudes"); and (4) an indeterminate sentence where the inmate population is never informed of the release criteria.[2] While most administrators of special and security institutions operating under an indeterminate sentence probably purport to follow Model 2 (objective release criteria), the indeterminate sentence in practice probably conforms most closely to Model 3 (vague and subjective release criteria) and not infrequently to Model 4 (unspecified release criteria).

If indeterminate confinement is to be continued in any form, it ought at least to conform to Model 2. Models 3 and 4 are examples of bad psychology as well as bad law. In a report to the National Prison Project, for example, Bernard Rubin, M.D., criticized on psychological grounds the "Control Unit Treatment Program" at the United States Penitentiary at Marion, a program which is in some ways analogous to an indeterminate sentence program.[3] The Marion control unit program operated to place hostile prisoners in indefinite special confinement (with progressive tiers of increasing privileges) in order to alter their behavior and attitudes so that they might eventually reenter the general prison population. To begin with, Rubin noted that progression and release had to operate capriciously, for the stated release criterion was simply one which "reflects the committee's confidence that the offender has matured beyond the point of being a probable danger to other persons."[4] The absence of objective criteria for entering or exiting the program and for range progression within the program led Rubin to conclude that the Marion control unit system could not even be rightfully termed a "program." Moreover, in Rubin's view the "program" worked actual *harm*: It corrupted the inmates by encouraging dishonest game-playing and shamming, and the lack of specified objective criteria was demeaning to the inmates and led to feelings of helplessness, frustration, and outright rage.

Many observers agree with Rubin's assessment of programs which do not clearly specify behavior necessary to trigger the valued contingency of release. Ralph Wetzel, for example, has noted that the success and efficiency of contingency management programs can be greatly facilitated by the utilization of cues, prompts, and models relating to expected behavior patterns.[5] And Albert Bandura, in a provocative piece,[6] notes that contingencies function to motivate and to impart information. Contingencies operate best, then, "after individuals discern the instrumental relation between action and outcome,"[7] and "behavior is not much affected by its consequences without awareness of what is being reinforced."[8] In sum, Bandura concludes:

> Not surprisingly, people change more rapidly if told what behaviors are rewardable and punishable than if they have to discover it from observing the consequences of their actions. Competencies that are not already within their repertoires can be developed with greater ease through the aid of instruction and modeling than by relying solely on the successes and failures of unguided performance.[9]

These principles are, as Bandura admits, hardly surprising. That they make considerable intuitive sense is reflected in the anecdote about a father who, disturbed by his young son's propensity for foul language, went to a psychologist for advice on how to handle the problem. "Use principles of behavior modification," the psychologist suggested. "Punish your son contingent on his use of nasty language." Armed with that advice, the father the next morning asked his son what he would like for breakfast. The son replied, "I think I'll have some of those f——' cornflakes." The father promptly spanked the boy and sent him to his room for an hour of "time-out." At the expiration of that hour, the father brought the boy back to the table and said, "Now, let me ask you again, what do you want for breakfast?" "Well, " the boy responded, "I sure as sh—— don't want any of those f——' cornflakes!"

If we are to expect patients and inmates to learn something other than to forego cornflakes in order to seek release from indeterminate confinement, it is evident that we must move toward a model of objective and clearly specified criteria for progression and release. Even if indeterminate confinement laws were abolished and a lid were clamped on the permissible length of confinement, clear and objective release criteria would be necessary if we had any hope of developing a fair system of parole or other type of system allowing for release prior to the expiration of the maximum permissible confinement period.

DEFENDANTS FOUND INCOMPETENT TO STAND TRIAL (IST)

A defendant charged with a crime who, at the time of the trial, is mentally incapable of understanding the nature of the proceedings or of assisting counsel with the defense is incompetent to stand trial. Until very recently, the typical situation involving IST defendants could have been portrayed as follows:

Defendants alleged to be IST would be automatically confined, often in a maximum security institution, for a rather lengthy period of evaluation. Ultimately, a court hearing would be held, and those persons judicially found to be IST would automatically be committed to a security hospital for an indefinite period (until competent to stand trial), perhaps to last a lifetime.[10]

Because of a highly significant Supreme Court decision and certain other developments, the IST legal confinement portrait is now undergoing a radical alteration. Invoking equal protection and due process considerations, the Court, in the 1972 case of *Jackson* v. *Indiana*,[11] ruled unconstitutional the *indefinite* confinement of ISTs pursuant to procedures and substantive standards which fall below the standards employed for the civil commitment of the mentally ill. Accordingly, the mere filing of criminal charges and a determination that a defendant is incompetent to stand trial cannot, without a further showing (such as a civil commitment type hearing or a showing of dangerousness, for example), authorize long-term hospitalization of ISTs. The *Jackson* Court did, however, approve a limited commitment of persons holding IST status.

A related development is a growing awareness that IST *evaluations* need not consume a lengthy period of time and need not generally occur in secure facilities. While IST evaluations have usually been conducted in secure institutions over a 30- to 90-day period, recent studies have concluded that fully 70% of those evaluations can adequately be conducted on an outpatient basis.[12] Finally, because of growing acceptance of the "least restrictive alternative" concept, it is becoming increasingly evident that a defendant found to be IST can often avoid hospitalization and can be treated instead as an outpatient. The "least restrictive alternative" doctrine is, of course, a general doctrine of constitutional law. Very generally, it holds that the government should not broadly infringe on liberties when the government's end could be achieved by means which infringe on liberties in a less restrictive manner. In the context of commitment, the doctrine calls for exploring and exhausting alternatives to hospitalization (outpatient therapy, etc.) before ordering hospitalization.

But now contrast the contingencies of the revised model with the traditional picture of indefinite secure confinement: If there is a prohibition against bringing to criminal trial a person who is IST and if a person who is IST can be treated on an outpatient basis in his home community, psychologists, psychiatrists, and sociologists might be concerned with certain potential antitherapeutic implications of that psycholegal incentive system. Concern could be expressed over what psychologists might call a "contingency structure" which could induce continued IST status, and psychiatrists might refer to the "secondary gain" advantages that could flow from a patient continuing to play what sociologists refer to as the "psychiatric sick role." In other words, by *remaining* clinically IST while at large in the community, a patient may indefinitely postpone "pending" criminal proceedings without sacrificing liberty.

Although it is not specifically aimed at overcoming the secondary gain advantages of outpatient IST status, the interesting Burt and Morris proposal[13] to abolish the incompetency plea—and to criminally try defendants despite their incompetence—would surely deal a crippling blow to any antitherapeutic aspects of the above-described incentive structure.

DEFENDANTS FOUND NOT GUILTY BY REASON OF INSANITY (NGRI)

The insanity defense relates not to a defendant's mental condition at the time of trial, but to his or her mental condition at the time of the alleged offense. Jurisdictions differ with regard to specific tests of the insanity defense (what type of mental condition need be shown to render the defendant nonresponsible for the crime). Once again, however, the consequences of a successful insanity defense are of far greater interest—and practical importance—than are the differences in the contents of the various insanity defense tests.

Traditionally, persons who have been found not guilty by reason of insanity (NGRI) have been subsequently committed, often to secure institutions. Typically, however, NGRI patients have been rather few in number, a fact explained by the relative rarity of cases in which the insanity defense has even been raised, let alone raised with success. And the relative rarity of raising the insanity defense can in turn be explained by the previously prevailing legal disincentives to its assertion: Until rather recently, the "successful" invocation of the insanity defense would often lead to *automatic* and *indefinite* confinement in a secure mental institution. Under those legal contingencies, the practice of criminal defense lawyers was, as might be expected, to recommend raising the defense only to clients charged with the most serious offenses (such as those carrying a possible penalty of capital punishment or lifelong confinement).

But recent years have witnessed a diminishing of the legal disincentives to the defense's assertion. With the realization that an NGRI verdict establishes simply a *reasonable doubt* about sanity at the time of the crime or at best a proof of insanity at that *prior time*, courts have, on due process and equal protection grounds, begun to find unconstitutional those statutes which authorize *automatic commitment* of persons found NGRI.[14] Since commitment should be premised on a finding of *present* mental illness and dangerousness, due process requires, those courts assert, a post-NGRI verdict hearing relating to present mental status, and equal protection requires that that hearing conform roughly to procedural and substantive standards set by law for civilly committed patients.[15] Further, with the emergence of statutory and constitutional limits on the length of commitment, defendants who successfully raise the insanity defense are becoming less concerned with the fear of *indefinite* hospital confinement.[16] Accordingly, with the emergence of more favorable legal contingencies surrounding the successful assertion of the insanity defense, we should expect to see the defense raised more often, which will increase the number of NGRI verdicts and accordingly force us to pay more attention to procedures relating to the commitment and release of NGRI acquittees.

Typically, state procedures relating to NGRIs have been different from civil commitment procedures. Usually, NGRI acquittees have had an easier route into and a more difficult route out of institutions than have their civilly committed counterparts. As we have seen, NGRI acquittees have often been automatically committed, without a separate civil-commitment-type hearing relating to present mental condition and dangerousness. And NGRI release procedures have often been extremely cumbersome. In Arizona, for example, where civilly committed patients have always been able to be released by the unilateral action of the hospital superintendent, a now-defunct 1968 law provided that NGRI committees could be released not simply in the discretion of the hospital director, but only after two psychiatrists certified the patient to be no longer dangerous, and after a jury, presumably drawn from the county where the crime occurred, found, with the patient bearing the burden of persuasion, that release was warranted.[17] Compared to civilly committed patients, NGRIs had to bear a tremendously heavy release burden, and "the potential for meting out community vengeance by an unforgiving jury"[18] was apparent. For example, in one Arizona case reported in a field study,

> the patient, charged with assault with a deadly weapon, had originally been found NGRI on October 9, 1969, and was committed to the Arizona State Hospital. On July 30, 1970, two psychiatrists filed certificates to the effect that

the patient was no longer a danger to herself or others. The release trial occurred on December 7–9, 1970, but the patient failed to meet her burden of proof, and the jury hung six–six. Thus, despite being hospitalized for fourteen months, being certified as recovered by two staff psychiatrists, and obtaining the favorable votes of half the jurors, she was retained at the hospital.[19]

Those serious disparities in procedural treatment between NGRIs and civilly committed patients have recently led courts to hold, principally as a matter of equal protection, that NGRIs are entitled to admission and release procedures that are *closely comparable* (though not necessarily identical) to admission and release procedures for the civilly committed.[20] State legislatures have responded by according to NGRIs procedures that are comparable or identical to civil commitment procedures. Thus, spurred on by cases such as *Bolton* v. *Harris*,[21] many jurisdictions are doing away with automatic commitment of NGRIs and are instead funneling those persons through the ordinary civil commitment process. Similarly, many jurisdictions (now including Arizona) currently release NGRIs according to the same release procedures that apply to ordinary civilly committed patients (typically the unilateral discretionary action of the hospital director).

There may be, however, an adverse latent consequence of releasing NGRIs according to procedures *identical* to civil commitment release procedures. According to hospital officials and staff interviewed by this writer in Arizona, where previously existing disparate release procedures for NGRIs and for the civilly committed have now been changed to provide for completely equivalent release procedures for the two groups, the hospital is fearful of the adverse publicity and public reaction that might ensue if an NGRI patient were to be released "too soon" or, worse yet, if a released NGRI patient were to soon commit another violent act. The hospital is thus reluctant to release, *completely on its own say-so,* NGRIs who seem to the hospital clinically capable of uneventful community adjustment following discharge. Although the matter is of course one for empirical investigation, it may be that, because of the reluctance stemming from sole responsibility for release decisions, the average length of time that NGRIs are now held prior to their release may actually *exceed* the average period of time that, under prior law, comparable NGRIs were held before being "certified" by the hospital as ready for referral to a jury charged with making the ultimate release decision. The new procedure, therefore, may not have removed from consideration the visible nonclinical, extralegal, and probably unconstitutional[22] factors that were potentially operative in the jury-release structure, but may have instead simply concealed them from view by transferring them (or others like them) to the new decision-making structure of unilateral hospital discharge.

Despite the awareness of the operation of nonclinical release-inhibiting factors, it is often difficult to structure a legal system that will remove or lessen the impact of those factors. The establishment of durational limits on commitment will of course help, for those limits will at least ensure that unwarranted delays in release will not continue indefinitely; but a durational limit will only lessen the problem, not solve it, for it will not address the question of unwarranted confinement of a patient who deserves release *before* the expiration of the period of commitment. To the extent that hospitals or therapists might delay or prevent release of particular patients because of the fear of financial liability that might be incurred should such released patients commit violent acts in the community, statutes could—and should—be enacted immunizing institutions and therapeutic staff from liability for release decisions made in the good faith exercise of professional discretion.[23] But the problems (and fears) run deeper than the question of legal liability. Seemingly, the main concern is with taking full responsibility (in a nonlegal sense) for making difficult decisions about future dangerousness in an area where accurate predictive tools are absent and where, when an "incorrect" decision is made, adverse public and press reaction can be very severe. Psychological studies suggest that if a legal decision-making structure could be designed in which NGRI release responsibility is shared or diffused, the decision to release might be made with fewer inhibitions.[24]

Ordinarily, strong policy objections exist with respect to taking advantage of the psychological consequences of diffusing responsibility, for diffusion can easily lead to the uninhibited making of *culpable* decisions.[25] But diffusion can more readily be justified where the decisions to be made are necessary and difficult, and where diffusion is necessary to weaken or eliminate the contaminating (or even paralyzing) impact of nonclinical, extralegal, and unconstitutional factors—such as the wrath or vindictiveness of the community.

If a case for diffusion can be legitimately made with respect to hospital release decisions, the next matter of concern would be to determine the type of body that should be designated to share release decision-making authority and responsibility with the hospital. A release jury, such as was once operative in Arizona,[26] would obviously not be satisfactory, for it would relieve the hospital of unwarranted inhibitions but would, far more patently than the hospital, be itself subject to similar influences. A court, rather than a jury, might, however, be an acceptable authority-sharing institution. Ideally, courts would be less subject than juries to influences of sheer community vindictiveness. If hospitals were required to secure judicial approval prior to releasing NGRI patients, the hospitals would presumably refer to the courts without inhibition those patients deemed by the hospital to be ready for release.[27] In most instances, the courts could be expected to read and rely on the hospital psychiatric reports and to approve the hospital release decision without holding a full-blown hearing. In selected instances of troublesome cases, the courts might hold hearings and either accept or disapprove the hospital's release recommendation.[28] In any event, the sharing of release responsibility might well work to lessen improper inhibitions: The hospital will know that a court will scrutinize the hospital release recommendation and will know that the court will serve as an additional safety valve in the release process; the court, on the other hand, will know that the hospital's release recommendation is based on the evaluative judgment of therapeutic professionals who have had a considerable amount of time to observe the patients proposed for release.

If court approval, rather than purely unilateral hospital action, is regarded as appropriate with respect to NGRI patients, the question remains whether equal protection would authorize, for NGRIs, a release procedure that differs from the procedure employed with regard to ordinary civilly committed patients. If equal protection were offended by the distinction, it might be necessary, to accomplish court approval of NGRI releases, to require court approval of the release of *all* hospital patients, thus avoiding the problem of unequal treatment of the NGRI group, though perhaps creating a more cumbersome release mechanism than is really desirable.

It is unlikely, however, that equal protection would be read to require the *identical* procedural handling of NGRI and other patients. Equal protection may require close comparability of procedural treatment, but it ought not to be read to require complete equivalency. Thus, even *Bolton* v. *Harris*,[29] the liberal District of Columbia decision which has spoken most forcefully about according NGRI patients procedural rights that compare closely to civilly committed patients, requires only "reasonable" rather than "rigid" application of the equal protection clause.[30] *Bolton* recognized that some differences in procedural treatment between NGRI and civil patients could be warranted. And the propriety of court-approved release can, according to *Bolton*, be one of those warranted distinctions:

> We uphold the release provisions of §24-301 (3) even though they differ from civil commitment procedures by authorizing court review of the hospital's decision to release a patient. We do not think equal protection is offended by allowing the Government or the Court the opportunity to insure that the standards for the release of civilly committed patients are faithfully applied to Subsection (d) [NGRI] patients.[31]

A system of court-approved release of NGRIs may, therefore, be advantageous both to NGRI patients (by reducing the hospital's inhibitions regarding release) and to society (by ensuring that release standards have been "faithfully applied" to patients who escaped criminal conviction only by the successful operation of the insanity defense). If the system is advantageous both to society and to patients with a history of dangerous behavior, however, it seems curious that it should be employed only with NGRIs and with no other patient categories. It would seem that the crucial distinction, for release structure purposes, ought not to be between NGRI patients and all others, but ought instead to be between *dangerous* and *nondangerous* patient categories or, in more technical legal language, between *police power* patients and *parens patriae* patients (see Chapter 2). Serious legislative consideration should be given, in other words, to permitting unilateral hospital release of *parens patriae* patients, but to requiring (for the sake of society and for the affected patients) court approval of the hospital release recommendation before discharging patients committed pursuant to the state's police power.

PRISON-TO-HOSPITAL TRANSFEREES

Although most of the legal controversy surrounding prison-to-hospital transfers centers around the procedural trappings that must accompany involuntary transfers, an emerging area of importance concerns *voluntary* transfer procedures for prisoners desirous of obtaining treatment unavailable in the prison context. Voluntary transfers to mental hospitals or prison psychiatric units do not, of course, require the procedural trappings mandated for involuntary commitments or transfer. Nonetheless, the voluntary transfer area is often riddled with problems and is in considerable need of reform. In many (though not all) jurisdictions, for example, voluntary hospital admission, even with the approval of both the prison and the hospital, is simply not a legally available option insofar as prison inmates are concerned: Involuntary commitment is the only permissible route.[32] That in itself constitutes a legal disincentive to seeking transfer, for if transfer can be effectuated only through commitment, a prisoner who seeks commitment will, at least in the number of jurisdictions which do not yet have durational limits on the length of civil confinement, be exchanging his definite sentence expiration date for an indefinite therapeutic release date. Add to that the confusing situation regarding good time allotments in mental hospitals, parole board policies disfavoring conditional release of prisoner-patients, and policies in some states mandating maximum security confinement of transferred prisoners (even of those who have served in prison as responsible outside trustees), and virtually all incentive for an emotionally disturbed offender to seek treatment is undercut by the contingencies of the legal system.[33]

All of those adverse legal contingencies deserve reconsideration. Surely, there should be no problem regarding the authorization of voluntary admission for prison inmates, so long as the proposed admission is screened by prison and hospital officials to ensure that the applicant is not simply seeking to avoid a term of penal incarceration. Good time credits—both "ordinary" credits and, under some circumstances, "extra" credits—should be made available to prisoner-patients whether those prisoner-patients have been voluntarily or involuntarily transferred.

Since "ordinary" credits are typically earned by a prisoner not only while he is physically in a given state prison, but are earned also while he is standing trial on an out-of-state detainer[34] and while he is serving a given state sentence out-of-state concurrently with the sentence of another jurisdiction,[35] there seems little reason to deny such credits to a prisoner serving his sentence in a state mental hospital.[36] The availability of "extra" credits is slightly more difficult, for most states reserve those credits for inmates who perform certain assignments or who hold positions of confidence and trust. Nonetheless, some such positions are already available in a mental hospital setting and others could easily be made available. Transferred prisoners holding such positions should accordingly be entitled to earn those credits. Moreover, if a prisoner was holding such a position, and earning "extra" credits, prior to the worsening of his mental condition that triggered his transfer to a hospital, he should presumably be permitted to continue earning those extra credits at the hospital even if, because of his mental condition, he is now unable to perform the required activities. In that connection, it is significant that the policy of many prisons is such that prisoners who undergo treatment for *physical* problems are not deprived of "extra" credits for the period of time they spend at the county general hospital. In fact, one federal court found an equal protection violation in the denial of certain credits to a prisoner medically unable to perform prison labor.[37]

The parole problem is easily as troubling to prisoner-patients as is the problem of good time allowances. Parole boards often have a flat policy against authorizing the conditional release of prisoners who are confined in mental hospitals.[38] Such a firm policy, however, seems unwarranted. Especially in the context of *committed* prisoner-patients, it is important to recognize that

> granting the prisoner-patient parole would not in this setting be equivalent to setting him free: Rather, the parole from his penal sentence would signify simply that, *when* he is discharged by the hospital, he will be released rather than returned to the prison—a fact that should surely provide a powerful incentive for the patient to take full advantage of the psychiatric care available and thus to regain his liberty.[39]

Indeed, even with respect to *voluntary* patients, where the hospital traditionally has no control over the patient's decision to leave, the parole preclusion policy is unpersuasive, for the board, if it deems a further period of hospitalization to be necessary prior to the patient's discharge to the community, could parole the patient *to the hospital*, leaving in the hospital's hand the ultimate decision whether to release the patient prior to the expiration of his "parole" status.[40]

That point was underscored by a lower New York court which, on equal protection grounds, declared unconstitutional that state's outright policy against conditionally releasing prisoner-patients, and which ordered the parole to a civil hospital of a Dannemora State Hospital inmate who had been denied parole solely because of his mental patient status.[41] The record in that case contained the testimony of the director of the secure mental hospital, who claimed that a substantial number of prisoner-patients at the facility could be paroled safely to a civil mental hospital or, in some cases, to outpatient treatment in their home communities. He thought, too, that such action would greatly enhance the patients' chances for complete psychiatric recovery. The court, noting that no flat parole prohibition exists with respect to persons suffering from *physical* disabilities, and noting further that physically disabled prisoners are often paroled to general hospitals for treatment, ruled squarely that, whether dealing with the physically or mentally disabled, "self-sufficiency is not a requirement of parole."[42]

Recent state statutes have addressed, to varying degrees, the legal problems associated with prison-to-hospital transferees. A rather recent Arizona statute (which unfortunately was later adversely amended) addressed specifically the issues of voluntary hospital admission, good time credits (both "ordinary" and "extra"—double time—credits), and parole. The pertinent provisions are set out below:

> E. A prisoner may apply for voluntary admission to the state hospital under the provisions of Section 36-531. His application, when submitted to the prison physician, shall be forwarded to the superintendent of the state hospital by the prison physician together with the report of the prison physician

and such material, if any, provided by the prisoner in support or in explanation of his application. A prisoner hospitalized in the state hospital as a voluntary patient shall be in the legal custody of the superintendent of the prison.

F. All prisoners transferred to the Arizona State Hospital pursuant to this section (relating to commitments and to voluntary admissions) shall remain eligible to accrue [ordinary] good-time credits pursuant to section 31-251. Double-time deductions pursuant to section 31-252 shall be allowed any prisoner who was earning the deductions immediately prior to transfer to the state hospital, and to any prisoner performing any assignment of confidence or trust at the state hospital.

G. No prisoner otherwise eligible shall be denied parole solely because he is confined at the state hospital pursuant to this section.[43]

CONCLUSION

It seems that lawyers, behavioral psychologists, and others have reached the stage where they may begin cooperating to formulate a "behavioral jurisprudence." Such a jurisprudence could involve "contingency consciousness raising" with regard to the legal system, applying behavioral principles in analyzing and revising that system, clarifying vague legal concepts by attempting to redefine them in behavioral terms, and explaining from a behavioral perspective the existence of rights and rules.[44] The following chapter looks, in the context of a concrete case, at various elements of the commitment process (criminal and civil), and at how a defense lawyer's knowledge of the process—and of the operative contingencies—may be essential to effective representation.

NOTES

[1]Testimony entitled, "The Need for Unified Services Amendments," presented on behalf of June Jackson Christmas, M.D., Commissioner, New York City Department of Mental Health and Mental Retardation Services, to the Select Committee on Mental and Physical Handicap, Albany, New York, December 3, 1974, p. 1. Because of tightened civil commitment laws, we are now seeing some instances opposite to that mentioned in the text: because civil commitment is now unavailable in many jurisdictions to nondangerous persons, such persons who were in days past civilly committed are now arrested on minor charges and found incompetent to stand trial. Dickey, *Incompetency and the Nondangerous Mentally Ill Client*, 16 CRIM. L. BULL. 22 (1980).

[2]Bedau, *Physical Interventions to Alter Behavior in a Punitive Environment*, 18 AMER. BEHAVIORAL SCIENTIST 662 (1975). *Cf.* Haymes v. Regan, 525 F.2d 540 (2d Cir. 1975), holding that, so long as a prisoner is given reasons for the denial of parole, the parole board is not constitutionally obligated to disclose the release criteria observed in its

parole decisions. *See also* Greenholtz v. Inmates of Nebraska Penal & Correctional Complex, 99 S.Ct. 2100 (1979).
[3]The program was also condemned on constitutional grounds by federal court action in Adams v. Carlson, 368 F.Supp. 1050 (1973).
[4]Rubin, *Report of Visit to Control Unit Treatment Program* (Unpublished Report, Nov. 25, 1973).

   In the context of indeterminate sexual psychopath legislation, the capriciousness may be particularly pronounced. As contrasted with *committed* sexual psychopaths, persons who are simply criminally *convicted* as sex offenders typically serve *determinate* terms roughly reflecting the moral blameworthiness of their crimes, In re Lynch, 105 Cal. Rptr. 217, 503 P.2d 921 (1972). If one accepts the research findings that convicted sex offenders are behaviorally and clinically comparable to committed sexual psychopaths (Morrow & Peterson, *Follow-Up of Discharged Psychiatric Offenders—"Not Guilty by Reason of Insanity" and "Criminal Sexual Psychopaths,"* 57 J. CRIM. L., CRIM., & P.S. 31 (1966)), it is difficult to justify on due process and equal protection grounds—and surely on grounds of sound social policy—the propriety of wholly indeterminate confinement for the category of sexual psychopaths. From a constitutional and public policy standpoint, it is therefore important to recognize that, if two sexually deviate groups are in fact virtually indistinguishable, the decision whether a sexual deviate will serve a determinate term as a convicted criminal or an indeterminate term as a committed patient must in actuality rest on prosecutive, psychiatric, or judicial whim. The constitutional and policy objection can be reduced, of course, if the ceiling on convicted sex offender confinement is carried over to the category of committed sexual psychopaths—and perhaps if potential committees are given the option of criminal confinement as a sex offender or of therapeutic confinement as a sexual psychopath.
[5]Wetzel, *Behavior Modification in the Social Learning Environment,* unpublished manuscript, undated. *See also* at pp. 3–4: "Cues in learning need to be clear and should specify behavior. When we say to a child 'I want you to be good and behave yourself' we are not giving a very specific behavioral cue. What are the behaviors of 'being good' and 'behaving one's self'? The ability to give clear, specific noncritical and nonprovocative cues for behavior is a quality of a good trainer."
[6]Bandura, *Behavior Theory and the Models of Man,* 29 AMERICAN PSYCHOLOGIST 859 (1974).
[7]*Id.* at 860.
[8]*Id.*
[9]*Id.* at 862.
[10]A 1965 study of patients at the Matteawan State Hospital in New York revealed that 645 of the 1,062 IST committees had been hospitalized for longer than 5 years, and one-fifth of the total had been "awaiting trial" for over 20 years. A. MATTHEWS, MENTAL DISABILITY AND THE CRIMINAL LAW: A FIELD STUDY 214–15 (1970). A question remains regarding whether a defendant is truly competent if the competence is maintained through psychotropic medication. A negative answer would, of course, greatly increase the hospital stay for many defendants. For an affirmaive answer, see Winick, *Psychotropic Medication and Competence to Stand Trial,* 1977 AM. B. F. RES. J. 769.
[11]406 U.S. 715 (1972).
[12]de Grazia, *Diversion from the Criminal Process: The 'Mental Health' Experiment,* 6 CONN. L. REV. 432, 436 (1974).
[13]*See generally* Burt & Morris, *A Proposal for the Abolition of the Incompetency Plea,* 40 U. CHI. L. REV. 66 (1972).
[14]*E.g.,* Bolton v. Harris, 395 F.2d 642 (D.C. Cir. 1968).
[15]*Id.*

[16]Persons who are found NGRI might, in appropriate cases, be subsequently civilly committed pursuant to a *parens patriae* or a police power rationale, depending on the particular clinical situation. But even if different durational limits are set for the two classifications (as seems appropriate), and even if an NGRI defendant is committed pursuant to the police power (with an authorized duration that would presumably be lengthier than would be the case with *parens patriae* commitments), the NGRI committee should not be held for a period exceeding the maximum criminal penalty for the charged offense. *See* Burt & Morris, note 13 *supra* at 66, 74 n.30 (1972).

[17]A discussion of the 1968 law and its defects appears in Wexler & Scoville, *The Administration of Psychiatric Justice: Theory and Practice in Arizona*, 13 ARIZ. L. REV. 1, 154–58 (1971).

[18]*Id.* at 157.

[19]*Id.* at 158.

[20]*E.g.*, Bolton v. Harris, 395 F.2d 642 (D.C. Cir. 1968).

[21]*Id.*

[22]*Cf.* Olson v. Pope, No. 8361, Superior Court of Solano County, California (March 28, 1973) at 9, where the court, in an unpublished opinion, said that "despite all indications in favor of parole the record suggested that the Adult Authority (parole board) had denied parole because of the vindictive attitude of some residents of the community where the offenses were committed and that if this were established as a fact, it was tantamount to the authority's acting on whim, caprice and rumor."

[23]*Cf.* ARIZ. REV. STAT. §36-543(D): "The medical director of the agency shall not be held civilly liable for any acts committed by the released patient." *See also* Ennis, *Civil Liberties and Mental Illness*, 7 CRIM. L. BULL. 101 (1971).

[24]*Cf.* Bandura, *supra* note 6; Fischhoff, *The Silly Certainty of Hindsight*, 8 PSYCHOLOGY TODAY 71 (April, 1975). For constitutionality, *see* Martinez v. California, 100 S. Ct. 553 (1980).

[25]Thus, Bandura, *supra* note 6, discusses diffusion with disapproval:

> A common dissociative practice is to obscure or distort the relationship between one's actions and the effects they cause. People will perform behavior they normally repudiate if a legitimate authority sanctions it and acknowledges responsibility for its consequences. By displacing responsibility elsewhere, participants do not hold themselves accountable for what they do and are thus spared self-prohibiting reactions. Exemption from self-censure can be facilitated additionally by diffusing responsibility for culpable behavior. Through division of labor, division of decision making, and collective action, people can contribute to detrimental practices without feeling personal responsibility or self-disapproval.

[26]It is interesting to note that the scheme of jury release of NGRIs was actually proposed by Arizona hospital officials who were reluctant to release unilaterally patients who had been committed as NGRI.

[27]This writer is aware of instances at the Arizona State Hospital where patients with a past history of violence have been deemed by the hospital staff to be ready for release but where the staff was reluctant to exercise its unilateral release authority. In such instances, the staff often advised the patient or the patient's counsel to seek release by petitioning the court for a hearing. At the hearing, the hospital staff would happily testify in favor of the patient's release. *See also* the recently enacted Arizona statute which, while mechanically involving the courts in some release decisions, actually retains release authority in the hand of the hospital. ARIZ. REV. STAT. §36-543.

[28]That judicial disapproval will sometimes occur is clear. *See* United States v. Ecker, 543 F.2d 178 (D.C. Cir. 1976). *See generally* Note, *Constitutional Standards for Release of the Civilly Committed and Not Guilty by Reason of Insanity: A Strict Scrutiny Analysis,* 20 ARIZ. L. REV. 233 (1978). Cases like *Ecker* do not necessarily mean that the requirement of judicial approval is generally an extra hurdle in the road to release. *Ecker* may simply be the

visible evidence of rare cases where judicial approval did not occur. In the great bulk of cases, judicial approval may be routine, and were there no judicial approval requirement, many patients might linger for longer periods in hospital wards awaiting a favorable hospital discharge decision.

29395 F.2d 642 (D.C. Cir. 1968).

30*Id.* at 651.

31*Id.* at 652.

32*See generally* Wexler & Scoville, *supra* note 17, at 174–88.

33*See generally id.*

34Walsh v. State *ex rel.* Eyman, 104 Ariz. 202, 450 P.2d 392 (1969).

35Wexler & Scoville, *supra* note 17, at 185.

36*See* People *ex rel.* Brown v. Herold, 29 N.Y.2d 939, 280 N.E. 2d 362, 329 N.Y.S.2d 574 (1972). *Brown* involved a suit against the Director of Dannemora State Hospital, challenging the Department of Corrections' policy denying good-time allowances to all mentally ill prisoners. *Brown* held the departmental policy to be violative of the statutory scheme and of the equal protection clause, at least as applied to prisoners who have not been declared legally incompetent, and who thus may be competent to weigh the risks and benefits of electing the New York good-time allowance plan.

37Sawyer v. Sigler, 320 F.Supp. 690 (D. Neb. 1970).

38*E.g.,* United States *ex rel.* Schuster v. Herold, 410 F.2d 1071 (2d Cir. 1969); People *ex rel.* Slofsky v. Agnew, 68 Misc. 2d 128, 326 N.Y.S. 2d 477 (Sup. Ct., Clinton Co., 1971).

39Wexler & Scoville, *supra* note 17, at 186 (emphasis added).

40*See id.*:

> The mechanism of parole-to-hospital is not simply a legal euphemism for parole denied. It can significantly affect the "parolee's" living conditions. In Arizona, for example, transferred prisoners are placed automatically in the Maximum Security Unit of the state hospital and—for security reasons—are usually retained in that unit during their entire stay at the hospital. If a prisoner-patient were granted parole, however, he would seemingly no longer constitute a "special" security or escape risk, and might well be transferred to the general hospital population, where living conditions are less restrictive and more pleasant and where chances for psychiatric recovery seem substantially greater. The possibility of leaving the Maximum Security Ward and entering the general hospital population is raised not only by the granting of parole, but also by the expiration of a transferred inmate's penal sentence—which is another reason why prisoners contemplating transfer to the hospital ought to be concerned with the computation of their "good time" credits.

41People *ex rel.* Slofsky v. Agnew, *supra* note 38.

42*Id.*

43Ariz. Rev. Stat. §31-224.

44Vargas, *Rights: A Behavioristic Analysis,* 3 Behaviorism 178 (Fall, 1975); Goldiamond, *Toward a Constructional Approach to Social Problems,* 2 Behaviorism 60 (Spring, 1974).

Part One
THE COMMITMENT SYSTEM

C. The Relationship between the Systems of Civil and Criminal Commitment

6

The *Crouch* Case

EXPLORING PROBLEMS OF CIVIL AND CRIMINAL COMMITMENT THROUGH AN ACTUAL EXAMPLE

INTRODUCTION

Much of the material previously discussed regarding civil and criminal commitment can perhaps best be grasped if it is reviewed in the context of a concrete case. The present chapter will attempt that review and will seek also to introduce certain other important issues in the commitment process. Finally, as the culminating chapter in the commitment portion of the book, this chapter will explore, through the case example, some salient aspects of the relationship between the systems of civil and criminal commitment.

THE *CROUCH* CASE—A VEHICLE FOR DISCUSSION

On February 5, 1976, an emotionally troubled University of Arizona student who had been jailed a few days earlier on disorderly conduct charges was found strangled to death in his cell. His cellmate, William Crouch, was charged with murder. Crouch was acquitted of the homicide by reason of insanity but was committed to the Arizona State Hospital. A newspaper account[1] of the proceedings provides a factual foundation sufficient to serve as a springboard for the discussion that follows:

> William T. Crouch was found innocent yesterday because of insanity in the beating death early last year of his cellmate at the County Jail and was ordered committed to Arizona State Hospital.

Two psychiatrists testifying at the short Superior Court trial said that although Crouch does not appear psychotic now, he could suffer a recurrence of a psychosis that led him to beat and strangle to death Paul Simon on February 5, 1976.

Dr. Harrison Baker, a psychiatrist at the state hospital, agreed with the prosecutor's classification of Crouch as a "time bomb."

Crouch still suffers from amnesia, which Baker described as "protection."

"Any effort to tinker with it could be harmful outside of a safe environment," he said.

Judge Robert Roylston acquitted Crouch at the end of the three-day trial, during which only three psychiatrists and a psychologist testified. The trial also served as a civil commitment hearing, and the four witnesses were asked if they thought Crouch should be committed.

Two psychiatrists, Baker and Dr. John LaWall, and the psychologist, Dr. Martin Levy, said Crouch had recovered from the paranoid schizophrenia they said he suffered from the time of the murder and the January 28, 1976 robbery of a grocery.

But Dr. Jacob Hoogerbeets said "common sense" would indicate that Crouch could again become dangerous. He said that although Crouch does not exhibit as many psychotic symptoms as he formerly did, "I think he could get psychotic again. I feel strongly that really nothing has changed."

Thomas Welch, one of Crouch's two attorneys, said he believes Hoogerbeets' testimony had convinced the judge to order Crouch committed.

Baker, LaWall and Levy said Crouch apparently had sexual fantasies about Simon and had a "homosexual panic reaction," thinking Simon was going to make sexual advances toward him.

Crouch came to Tucson from El Paso, his home town, about a week before his arrest on the armed robbery charge. Several of the doctors said he apparently had been psychotic since leaving El Paso, based on reports that he had behaved strangely.

About a week before the murder, jail detention officers tried to have Crouch placed in the psychiatric ward at the County Hospital because of his frequent combativeness, police records show. However, a doctor and social worker at the hospital both said they thought Crouch was not psychotic but just had social problems.

Crouch's attorneys said yesterday that his father wants to have Crouch transferred to a psychiatric hospital at Big Spring, Tex. Roylston approved the move, subject to the proceedings necessary to transfer a patient from one state to another.

Under Arizona law, a hearing on Crouch's commitment to the state hospital must be held every six months. If he is transferred to Texas, Welch said, he would be subject to that state's commitment law. Welch said he does not know the details of that law.[2]

PREDICTIONS OF DANGEROUSNESS AND STANDARDS OF PROOF

As a result of the critique of the older Arizona standard discussed in Chapter 4, commitment in Arizona now generally requires, among other things, a finding that the proposed patient is dangerous.[3] If the journalistic account mentioned above is reasonably accurate, Dr. Hoogerbeets's "common sense" predictive judgment regarding Crouch's dangerousness was a necessary basis of Crouch's commitment. It is not necessary, however, to recount here the fallibility of psychiatric and psychological predictions of dangerousness; many others have already undertaken the task of marshalling the empirical evidence.[4]

Closely related to the question of predicting dangerousness is the question of the standard of proof in a commitment proceeding. As detailed in Chapter 2, the Supreme Court in *Addington* v. *Texas*[5] has held the "clear and convincing" evidence standard to be constitutionally required in commitment cases.

There is, however, a potential chasm between the mere recognition of a constitutionally grounded right to a stringent standard of proof and the realization of such a right in actual practice. The Arizona *Crouch* case is again illustrative. Arizona statutes authorize commitment only "if the court finds by clear and convincing evidence that the proposed patient is, as a result of mental disorder, a danger."[6] Both "danger"[7] and "mental disorder"[8] are further defined, the latter roughly requiring a condition of psychosis. The difficulty of establishing future dangerousness, especially when a stringent standard of proof is employed, has already been discussed. In *Crouch*, however, according to the newspaper account of the testimony, the finding of "mental disorder" appears even more questionable than does the finding of dangerousness.

Although they thought that he could suffer a recurrence of the psychosis that led to the death of his cellmate, two psychiatrists and a psychologist testified that Crouch no longer suffered from the paranoid schizophrenia that had afflicted him at the time of the crime. The court's finding of "mental disorder" apparently rests, then, as Crouch's attorney concluded, on the testimony of the remaining psychiatrist, who testified simply that "I think he [Crouch] could get psychotic again. I feel strongly that really nothing has changed."[9]

If the portrait painted above is reasonably accurate, one could confidently state that a rational trier of fact could not have found by "clear and convincing evidence" that Crouch was "mentally disordered" within the meaning of the legislative mandate. Despite the standard of proof required by state statute or by Supreme Court doctrine, however, commitment courts will expectedly feel enormous pressure to "do something" with a person who has brutally taken the life of another or who has otherwise demonstrated dangerous behavior.[10] (Contrast this position with that taken in Chapter 5 relating to the court's role in releasing already confined patients.)

Indeed, the pressure is probably stronger still in states, unlike

Arizona, where judicial office is attained (and retained) primarily through the electoral process. While state appellate courts might be able to apply legal rules with greater detachment than can their counterparts on the trial level firing line, even those appellate tribunals may be unable or unwilling to apply particular rules in particular instances, especially if those rules emanate from a federal forum.[11]

If a committed patient such as Crouch expeditiously[12] but unsuccessfully sought relief in the state appellate system, he might, having exhausted his state remedies, next seek to vindicate his constitutional claims via a habeas corpus petition in a federal district court.[13] Ironically, however, even given the *Addington* insistence that commitment courts adhere to a standard of proof that meets at least a "clear and convincing" standard,[14] and even assuming that the record will indicate that the state fell far short of meeting that standard, it was, until very recently, by no means clear that the confined patient could secure relief in federal court. While the legal development in this area may be of interest and importance for the legally trained reader, its significance for the nonlaw reader may be considerably less. Accordingly, the technical discussion is set off in brackets for the benefit of those who wish not to immerse themselves in the nuances of the development of legal doctrine.

[Traditionally, when federal courts reviewed state convictions, they took the position that, so long as there was *any* evidence to support the conviction, they would not weigh the sufficiency of evidence produced in state criminal trials.[15] Similarly, in a commitment context, courts following the traditional rule would presumably have held that so long as there was *any* evidence to support the commitment (which there arguably was in *Crouch*) the decision to commit would not be set aside simply because the evidence did not achieve a clear and convincing status.

As we shall soon see, however, the Court in 1979 discarded the traditional rule, which is traceable to the 1960 case of *Thompson* v. *City of Louisville*.[16] There, Justice Black, writing for a unanimous Court, held that petitioner's police court convictions, which were totally void of evidentiary support, violated the due process clause. Justice Black's opinion in *Thompson* stressed that the question "turns not on the sufficiency of the evidence, but on whether this conviction rests upon any evidence at all."[17] It is important to note that, at the time of *Thompson*, standards of proof in criminal cases had not yet been technically constitutionalized. Not until a decade later, in *In re Winship*,[18] did the Court, in the context of criminal convictions and juvenile delinquency adjudications, hold that the standard of proof beyond a reasonable doubt is to be part and parcel of the due process clause. Yet, because he found virtually no independent constitutional potency in the due process clause itself, Justice Black (the author of *Thompson*) dissented in *Winship*.[19]

Obviously, there immediately erupted considerable tension between *Thompson* and *Winship*. If *Thompson* survived, and forbade federal courts from weighing the sufficiency of evidence underlying state court convictions and commitments, *Winship's* role would be restricted to overturning state proceedings only when state statutes specify a constitutionally insufficient standard of proof[20] or when juries are instructed that they may convict (or commit) pursuant to a constitutionally substandard measure of proof.[21] Under that view, *Winship* (and *Addington*) would have minimal impact in the area of commitment where state statutes generally provide for satisfactorily stringent standards of proof, and where juries are rare and are probably not constitutionally required. Under that view of *Winship*, state commitment courts would in practice be able to ignore, with virtual impunity, the Supreme Court's *Addington* pronouncement regarding the constitutional necessity of a clear and convincing standard of proof.

In the 1979 Supreme Court case of *Jackson* v. *Virginia*,[22] however, *Winship* was, by a divided Court, read as sounding the death knell for *Thompson*. According to *Jackson*, the relevant inquiry for a federal habeas corpus court reviewing the evidence underlying a state court conviction is "whether, after viewing the evidence in the light most favorable to the prosecution, *any* rational trier of fact could have found the essential elements of the crime beyond a reasonable doubt."[23] If the new *Jackson* v. *Virginia* test is held applicable to federal habeas corpus proceedings reviewing state civil commitment proceedings,[24] cases like *Crouch* may successfully vindicate *Addington* claims in federal court.[25]]

CONSEQUENCES OF NGRI VERDICTS

The consequences of a verdict of not guilty by reason of insanity (NGRI) vary from one jurisdiction to another. In some states, mandatory commitment is the consequence. Increasingly, however, commitment is authorized only after the trier of fact finds it to be warranted by the proposed patient's *present* mental condition. In many jurisdictions, minor variations of the ordinary civil commitment process are invoked, sometimes augmented by a requirement of mandatory mental evaluation of persons found NGRI.[26]

The particular procedural commitment mechanism employed following an NGRI verdict can be of considerable importance in individual cases. It is nonetheless clear that in every jurisdiction there exists some technique for at least focusing on the question of committability of a defendant acquitted as NGRI. Yet, certain commentators have long been concerned that

> [i]n virtually all jurisdictions, the jurors are told nothing at all about the prospect of commitment or release following upon an acquittal by reason of insanity, just as they are told nothing about the sentences which may follow upon a guilty verdict. Yet the issue unquestionably nags when the insanity defense is under consideration. Unless told otherwise, the jury may be under the impression that it is being asked to release a man who has established both his incapacity and his dangerousness.[27]

Had *Crouch* involved a jury trial rather than a bench trial, the issue might have been very important in that case. Fearful that juries might convict simply to circumvent the spectre of a dangerous defendant walking the streets, some scholars have urged that jurors be given "informative instructions" regarding the consequences of an NGRI verdict. To date, however, the District of Columbia Circuit appears to be in the distinct minority in requiring such an instruction in the absence of defense objection.[28] Moreover, a study conducted by Rita Simon, using experimental jurors to hear and decide simulated, abbreviated cases, reached the startling result that "information as to disposition of the defendant is *not* a crucial consideration in the jury's decision."[29]

Simon's study, although well executed, can be criticized on the ground that it might not predict the actions of decision makers who must determine the *actual* fate of criminal defendants. Further, to the extent that uninstructed jurors may be misinformed regarding the consequences of an NGRI verdict, it is possible that the jurors are misinformed in a direction that benefits the *defendant* rather than the state. In Simon's study, for example, the large majority of both instructed and uninstructed "jurors" believed that a defendant found NGRI would be *automatically* and *indefinitely* committed to a mental hospital.[30] Might uninstructed jurors adhere to that view even though jurisdictions are rapidly departing both from automatic and from indefinite commitment? Would jurors be less inclined to find a defendant NGRI if they knew such a defendant would be confined only if, following examination and a subsequent court hearing, the defendant were found to be currently mentally ill and dangerous?[31] What if they were instructed that a defendant found NGRI could be held for no longer than 90 days unless, during the 90-day period of hospitalization, he again acted in an overtly dangerous manner?[32]

What all of this suggests, it seems, is that the Simon study has merely scratched the surface of needed research. Much remains to be done even in simulated settings,[33] let alone in the natural environment. Ideally, too, such research should be undertaken in a number of jurisdictions.

Whether or not jurors should be informed of the consequences of an NGRI verdict, defense lawyers should be thoroughly versed in that area of law. In deciding whether the insanity defense should be raised, for example, it is particularly pertinent, as we saw in Chapter 5, for defense counsel to be familiar with the legal contingencies that will flow from a successful invocation of the defense. Obviously, if a "successful" insanity plea leads to automatic and indefinite confinement in a secure mental institution, the defense should be raised only in the most serious of offenses. But in jurisdictions where commitment is not automatic but rests instead on a finding of present mental illness and dangerousness, and where sharp durational limits are placed on the length of mental institutionalization, the insanity defense may be considerably more popular.

Lawyers raising the insanity defense are no doubt generally well schooled in the commitment schemes of their particular jurisdictions.[34] Subtle and complex problems can arise, however, when the defendant is a nonresident of the jurisdiction in which he is being tried. Once again, the *Crouch* case can serve as a springboard for discussion.

Following a verdict of NGRI in Arizona, a separate determination of committability is made,[35] and commitment is for a more or less fixed period of up to 180 days.[36] Given that commitment structure, coupled with substantial psychiatric testimony that Crouch lacked criminal capacity at the time of the crime but was presently free from psychosis, the assertion by counsel of the insanity defense seemed imperative. Indeed, considering that, on conviction, Crouch would have received a sentence of death or life imprisonment, the defense of insanity presumably should have been raised even if *automatic* and *indefinite* commitment were to follow. It would even have been excusable for Crouch's attorneys to have raised the defense without inquiring into whether, as a resident of Texas, Crouch could have been returned by Arizona to Texas, and whether, under Texas law, Crouch could have then been committed for a period of time considerably in excess of the limit prescribed by Arizona law.

Had the criminal charge been a substantially less serious one, however, it would have been important for an attorney representing a nonresident to explore the above issues as an indispensable part of the strategic decision whether to recommend raising the defense of insanity.[37] In many states, commitment standards are notoriously slippery, and commitment may be for an indefinite period of time. A cursory examination of Texas law reveals that Texas probably falls within both of those categories.[38]

The fact that a nonresident defendant's home state (*e.g.*, Texas) has a law facilitating long-term commitment may lead a defendant charged elsewhere (*e.g.,* Arizona) with a less serious crime to forego raising the insanity defense *if,* on being committed following an NGRI verdict, the defendant can be involuntarily transferred by the charging state to the defendant's state of residence. Accordingly, the transfer power of the charging state is another factor that should be investigated by counsel in connection with the decision to invoke the defense of insanity.

Constitutionally, because of right-to-travel considerations, a state is unable to transfer an unwilling *resident* patient to the patient's state of *former* residence, regardless of how long—or short—the patient has resided in the committing state.[39] In other words, for mental hospital interstate transfers, statutory durational residency requirements have been held unconstitutional. Although even newcomer residents cannot constitutionally be returned "home" by the committing state, the constitutional proscription does not apply to "patients who are concededly *non-residents* but who happen to require mental hospitalization while temporarily"[40] in the committing state. The power of states to transfer *nonresidents* (such as Crouch) seems then to be purely a matter of statute.

Statutory patterns for the return of nonresident patients run the entire gamut. Some jurisdictions, for instance, *require* nonresidents to be returned home.[41] Others leave the matter to the discretion of the superintendent.[42] Several states belonging to the Interstate Compact on Mental Health[43] have "statutorily vowed to resolve such questions clinically rather than on the basis of cost."[44] Still others (such as Arizona) have no statutory provisions for transfer, necessitating that such transfer occur, if at all, only if both states *and* the patient agree to it.

Thus, in Crouch's case, because of Arizona's absence of an involuntary transfer statute, Crouch would presumably be in a position to block a transfer to Texas if he perceived such a transfer to be against his best interests. Had Arizona belonged to the category of states in which the involuntary transfer of nonresidents is mandatory or in the institution's discretion,[45] the matter would have been quite different. In such a case, invoking the insanity defense might have worked a real disservice to a defendant charged with other than a serious offense.

LEAST RESTRICTIVE ALTERNATIVE

In an interesting recent article, the late Dr. Browning Hoffman, together with his associate Lawrence Foust, explores the statutory and case law that has developed with respect to the principle of the "least restrictive alternative."[46] The article pays close attention to the vagueness and incompleteness of the statutory law, where questions as basic as who carries the burden of proving what go unaddressed. Hoffman and Foust conclude that the existing lackluster legislation leaves the "least restrictive alternative" principle a practical sham, and they seek statutory surgery to make the principle clear and meaningful. Hoffman and Foust are surely correct in their assessment of the general vagueness of "least restrictive alternative" statutes.

Because others have not done so, it may be worthwhile to focus on a narrow but important "least restrictive alternative" problem quite different in emphasis from the aspect of vagueness. There are certain state statutes that defeat the "least restrictive alternative" principle (or at least its supposed spirit) by their very *precision* rather than by their ambiguity. Statutes referred to in the preceding section are illustrative.

For example, statutes that *require* nonresident patients to be returned home can work extreme hardship in certain cases. This is particularly true in cases involving elderly people, without friends or family in their home states, who require hospitalization while visiting their children who are longtime residents of another state. In those transfer statutes, merely changing the word "shall" to "may" could work a major change (a less restrictive disposition of sorts) for a number of patients. Further, states enacting the Interstate Compact on Mental Health permit transfers of nonresidents only when such transfers are demonstrably in the best interests of the patients.

Another illustration of precise statutory departure from the spirit of the "least restrictive alternative"—again with interstate transfer implications—is found in those state statutory provisions patterned on section 18 of the Uniform Veterans' Guardianship Act. That section allows the commitment of veterans to the Veterans Administration and permits that agency to place the patient in any agency hospital facility "within or without [the committing] state."[47] A state enacting that provision of the Uniform Act would typically also enact a related provision giving "force and effect" in the enacting state to the judgments of courts of other states committing eligible persons to the care and custody of the Veterans Administration.[48]

The twin provisions were believed to be desirable by the drafters "[b]ecause of the necessity for transfer from one institution to another, depending upon the type of affliction and availability of treatment therefor, and because of possible lack of sufficient facilities in a given area."[49] In practice, the provisions authorizing the out-of-state transfer—and particularly the *involuntary* out-of-state transfer—of committed veterans seem to have worked therapeutic and legal harm. Because those sections validate practices which are both low in effectiveness and high in restrictiveness, those explicit statutory provisions indisputably fly in the face of a "least restrictive alternative" rationale and accordingly warrant prompt repeal.

Many states (including Arizona) have *general* Veterans Administration (VA) hospitals that provide inpatient psychiatric services as well as more traditional medical services. Psychiatric units of VA general hospitals are, however, typically small, acute-care facilities that provide intense, short-term care. They serve both voluntary patients and committed patients, but are unable to serve patients likely to require inpatient treatment for periods longer than one month.

To care for long-term patients within the VA system, the agency has established a number of large, exclusively *psychiatric* hospitals, often in remote, rural locations. Patients committed to the VA by Arizona courts are often transferred to VA psychiatric hospitals in Ft. Lyon, Colorado, Roseburg, Oregon, American Lake, Washington, and Sheridan, Wyoming.

A relatively recent study of VA psychiatric services, conducted by a legal scholar and commissioned by the Administrative Conference of the United States, urged the demise of the large, remote institutions.[50] The report emphasized that the geographical isolation of the institutions makes community psychiatry and family therapy programs impossible. The author noted that the geographical, professional, and academic isolation of the institutions, coupled with the clinical sterility of a chronic, all-male population, makes very difficult the recruitment of vigorous and skilled therapists.

Not mentioned in the report, but nevertheless of considerable concern, at least to involuntarily transferred committed patients, are the immense legal complications that accompany transfer.

Technically, according to section 18(1) of the Uniform Act, "[j]urisdiction is retained in the committing... court... at any time to inquire into the mental condition of the person so committed, and to determine the necessity for continuance of his restraint."[51] But if a committed patient is transferred to an out-of-state VA hospital, the physical separation of the patient and his attending physicians from the commitment court and the patient's attorney renders unworkable the statutory retention-of-jurisdiction provision. If the state of commitment authorizes *indefinite* confinement, if that state's commitment order is given "force and effect" in the receiving state, and if the receiving state courts refuse to review the propriety of continued confinement on the ground that jurisdiction for such inquiry resides exclusively in the courts of the committing state, a patient can obviously be held for unwarranted periods without opportunity for meaningful review.

Even if the state of commitment sets durational limits on confinement, there is no assurance that a patient transferred out-of-state will be released on the expiration of the commitment period. The patient could, for example, be recommitted under the laws of the receiving state—laws which may be considerably more lax in terms of standards, procedures, and length of confinement than those of the home state. In the *Crouch* case, for example, even if the defendant had been an Arizona resident, had he also been a veteran, his commitment following a verdict of NGRI might have resulted in his involuntary transfer to a VA hospital in another state and in the possibility of recommitment pursuant to the laws of that state.[52] Further, a recommitment for any transferred veteran would presumably be accomplished without the court being informed of the current availability and propriety of less restrictive facilities in the patient's far-away home community.

Worse yet, it is possible that the receiving institution will overlook (or be unaware of) the durational limit specified by the law of the committing state and that the patient will simply languish in that institution beyond the expiration of his commitment order. Indeed, given the fact that a VA psychiatric institution will be receiving patients committed under the laws of a variety of states, it seems unlikely that the institution could accord each patient the particular rights (regarding discharge, review, treatment, refusal of treatment, privacy, mail, and visitation) specified by the law of his particular jurisdiction. In that respect, transferred veterans, unlike nonveterans committed to state hospitals, are surely disadvantaged—perhaps unconstitutionally—by their classification as veterans.

The incidence of patient transfers to distant psychiatric hospitals seems heightened by the Veterans Administration's propensity to think of treatment only in terms of VA-provided services. Although the agency does provide outpatient treatment, other aspects of the panoply of services less restrictive than full-time mental institutionalization (*e.g.*, day hospitals, halfway houses, etc.) seem not to be available through the VA itself. There appears to be a clear tendency to ignore other treatment possibilities, even when they are available in the community through state or local funding, when VA doctors examine a veteran in connection with commitment proceedings. That tendency, coupled with the fallibility of psychiatric science, can lead to unwarranted intrusions on liberty. The practice ought to raise the hair (and the ire) of reformers who argue that the "least restrictive alternative" mandate should be read as requiring even the governmental *construction* of alternative facilities, let alone as requiring the mere *use of already available* facilities.

On point is one "close-call" case with which this writer is familiar. In that case, psychiatrists examined a proposed patient at the VA general hospital in Tucson and recommended commitment and long-term hospitalization in an out-of-state VA psychiatric hospital 1,000 miles from the patient's home. The patient's lawyer obtained a court order authorizing an examination of the patient by a psychiatrist connected with local treatment facilities. The psychiatrist concluded that the patient was a perfect candidate for treatment in a Tucson halfway house. The VA commitment petition was promptly withdrawn, and the patient was successfully and uneventfully treated in his home community.

The possibility of out-of-state transfer to large VA psychiatric institutions should be sharply curtailed if not abolished. At best, such out-of-state institutions should be available only to voluntary patients and to committed patients who are found, at a pretransfer court hearing, to have personally given competent, informed, and voluntary consent to a transfer to such an institution.[53] Under such a scheme, a nonconsenting committed patient could insist on being treated at a state hospital rather than being sent to an out-of-state VA facility. Another possible solution would take the form of legislation which would entirely preclude a committed veteran from being transferred from the state. Under that arrangement, short-term veteran patients would be treated at psychiatric units of local VA general hospitals, and longer-term patients would be treated at state hospitals.[54]

Legislation limiting the power to transfer a committed veteran from the state is the most obvious and effective way of overcoming the interstate transfer problem. Another technique, at least in those 24 or so jurisdictions that have VA psychiatric hospitals, is to repeal or refuse to enact the legislative provision giving "force and effect" to the commitment orders of other states. California apparently enacted the Uniform Act without the "force and effect" section.[55] The effect of that action, perhaps coupled with the stringency of California's own commitment law, is that Arizona VA hospitals transfer to California long-term VA facilities only veteran patients who are not under commitment and who agree to enter California institutions as voluntary patients.

Indeed, the "force and effect" section was proposed at a time when commitment orders in most states provided for *indefinite* periods, for its rationale was to permit interstate transfers and yet "avoid the detrimental effect on the patient of new commitment proceedings in the second State and the expense incident thereto."[56] Now that the trend is toward placing durational limits on commitment, receiving states with large out-of-state patient populations may find themselves bearing the financial burden of numerous recommitment hearings. Perhaps the inconvenience and expense of shouldering such recommitment hearings will encourage receiving states to repeal their "force and effect" statutes and to accept only voluntary out-of-state veterans.

If that course of action is followed, many committed veterans will find themselves in the less restrictive environment of a state hospital in their home state. It is interesting that such a less restrictive course of action may be fueled by the rise in recommitment hearings resulting from the waning of indefinite confinement.

LENGTH OF CONFINEMENT

We are now experiencing an evident trend away from indeterminate confinement not only in criminal law, but also in the area of civil commitment. In the latter area, where limits on confinement cannot properly be based on their "proportionality" to the "moral blameworthiness" of the "offender," restrictions on the length of confinement are emerging instead as part and parcel of the due process notion that "the nature *and duration* of commitment bear some reasonable relation to the purpose for which the individual is committed."[57] In the context of a civil commitment case, the Supreme Court has emphasized in 1975 that "even if [a patient's] involuntary confinement was initially permissible, it could not constitutionally continue after that basis no longer existed."[58]

From the language quoted above, it seems easily arguable that states must, under constitutional mandate, set reasonable limits on the period of civil confinement. In addition, they must, at the end of such a period, review each patient's status and make a decision to release or to recommit.[59] Yet, as is evident from the discussion of the *Crouch* case involving length-of-confinement comparisons under Arizona and Texas law, state statutes differ markedly over the necessity of mandatory periodic recommitment hearings.

Texas, it will be recalled, authorizes indefinite commitment, whereas Arizona has joined a small number of states that allow only determinate commitments. Arizona's commitment law authorizes confinement for a maximum period of 180 days,[60] at the expiration of which a patient may be involuntarily retained only on recommitment. But the legislative uneasiness over the maximum 180 day period, as applied to persons who have been demonstrably dangerous to others, led the legislature in effect to hedge on the determinacy of confinement by easing, for such persons, the standards and proof of recommitment.

As a basis for commitment or recommitment under Arizona law, "danger to others" is narrowly defined to encompass only incidents where substantial bodily harm was inflicted or attempted on another within 12 months preceding the commitment hearing.[61] The requirement that a finding of current dangerousness be made on the basis of behavioral indicators occurring within the preceding 12 months is dispensed with, however, in cases where the bodily injury inflicted or attempted was "grievous or horrendous,"[62] and in cases where the patient "has existed under conditions of being restrained by physical or pharmacological means, or of being confined, or of being supervised, which have deterred or tended to deter him from carrying out acts of inflicting or attempting to inflict bodily harm upon another person."[63]

Dispensing with the 12-month period in *initial* commitments may be warranted in cases where a criminally charged patient, eventually found NGRI, was confined for a lengthy period in jail or in a hospital as temporarily incompetent to stand trial. Rigid adherence to the 12-month requirement in those cases would preclude commitment of NGRI defendants whose trials had been delayed—or strategically stalled—for more than a year following the criminal incident.

Dispensing with the 12-month period in the context of *recommitments*, however, and thereby authorizing recommitment after recommitment on the basis of the patient's *original* act of dangerousness, serves to make a sham of the 180 day durational limit. Indeed, if patients who have demonstrated substantial dangerous tendencies (or at least "grievous or horrendous" tendencies) are generally not thought to be ready for release after only six months, it might be more sensible, and candid, for the legislature to set a durational limit for such "police power" commitments that *exceed* the durational limit set for commitments pursuant to the state's *parens patriae* power. Focusing on specific legal and clinical categories (or even subcategories) in the setting of durational limits is surely a more sensible legislative practice—better law and better behavioral science—than is fudging on the durational limit by in turn fudging on the standards for recommitment.

COMMITMENT STANDARDS

Whether we speak of recommitment or of initial commitment, it is clear that the *criteria* for commitment, the commitment standards, are a matter of current concern to courts and to legislatures. As the earlier discussion of the *Crouch* case reveals, states differ considerably in their standards for commitment. Texas, for example, seems to have rather loose criteria, while Arizona more closely approximates the modern trend toward tightened commitment criteria.

Although many states authorize commitment on a mere showing that a patient is in "need of care and treatment," concern over abuses in the process have led to considerable legislative activity, and "[r]ecent statutory enactments appear to indicate a trend toward restricting involuntary civil commitment to the dangerous mentally ill and toward limiting the type and increasing the severity of harm necessary to support a finding of dangerousness."[64]

That statement, coupled with increased procedural protections, accurately reflects the major developments in the commitment process over the past decade. Since we have now discussed the most important issues in commitment law, it is appropriate to conclude the "commitment" portion of this volume and to proceed to Part Two of the book, a discussion of the "other" major compartment of issues that have confronted mental health law in the past decade—issues relating to law and therapy.

NOTES

[1] Arizona Daily Star, Mar. 8, 1977, § B, at 1, col. 3.

[2] *Id.*

[3] ARIZ. REV. STAT. § 36–540.

[4] *See, e.g.,* Cocozza & Steadman, *The Failure of Psychiatric Predictions of Dangerousness: Clear and Convincing Evidence,* 29 Rutgers L. Rev. 1084 (1976); Ennis & Litwack, *Psychiatry and the Presumption of Expertise: Flipping Coins in the Courtroom,* 62 CALIF. L. REV. 693 (1974).

[5] 99 S.Ct. 1804 (1979).

[6] ARIZ. REV. STAT. § 36–540 (A) & (B).

[7] *Id.* § 36–501 (3) & (4).

[8] *Id.* § 36–501 (18).

[9] *See* text accompanying note 2 *supra.*

[10] Indeed, in *Crouch,* the defendant waived a jury trial and raised the insanity defense in a bench trial. A judge who takes the position that "something" must be done with such a defendant may understandably seek the more humane result of commitment—even if that result requires a stretching of the evidence—rather than the harsher result of rejecting a murder defendant's insanity defense. However, relatively speaking, the rejection of the defense might not have appeared to be as transparent a departure from legal standards as was the determination of committability.

[11] The Supreme Court seems reluctant to confront the factual question of the influence of institutional constraints on the judicial decision-making process. For example, the Court, while purporting to be "fully cognizant of the critical importance of life tenure, particularly when judges are required to vindicate the constitutional rights of persons who have been found guilty of criminal offenses," proclaimed in the next paragraph of its opinion that "elected judges of our state courts are fully competent to decide federal constitu-

tional issues." Swain v. Pressley, 97 S. Ct. 1224, 1230–31 (1977). *See also* Stone v. Powell, 428 U.S. 465, 493 n.35 (1976). *But see id.* at 502 (Brennan & Marshall, JJ., dissenting).

[12]ARIZ. REV. STAT. § 36–546.01 (expedited appeal available in commitment cases).

[13]Federal habeas corpus is a remedy for challenging the constitutionality of one's confinement. It is typically employed by prisoners but is available to challenge any unconstitutional confinement, including unconstitutional civil commitment. *See* United States *ex rel.* Schuster v. Herold, 410 F.2d 1071 (2d Cir. 1969). Note that the Supreme Court's curtailment of federal habeas corpus jurisdiction to hear Fourth Amendment claims, Stone v. Powell, 428 U.S. 465 (1976), should not affect jurisdiction to hear claims, such as standard of proof issues, that go to the integrity of the fact-finding process.

[14]The standard of proof question is somewhat more complicated in the context of the commitment of persons previously acquitted by reason of insanity. *See* German & Singer, *Punishing the Not Guilty: Hospitalization of Persons Acquitted by Reason of Insanity*, 29 RUTGERS L. REV. 1011, 1032–33 (1976).

[15]Thompson v. City of Louisville, 362 U.S. 199 (1960).

[16]*Id.*

[17]*Id.*

[18]397 U.S. 358 (1970).

[19]*Id.* at 377 (Black, J., dissenting) (discussing his view of the due process clause). See also *id.* at 372 n.5 (Harlan, J., concurring) (expressing "bafflement" at Justice Black's position regarding the due process clause).

[20]This is more or less what occurred in *In re Winship.*

[21]Freeman v. Zahradnick, 97 S. Ct. 1150, 1152 (1977) (Stewart, J., dissenting from denial of *certiorari*).

[22]99 S.Ct. 2781 (1979).

[23]*Id.* at 2789 (emphasis in original).

[24]*See id.* at 2799 n.11 (separate opinion of Justices Stevens, Burger, and Rehnquist).

[25]*See also* Moore v. Duckworth, 99 S. Ct. 3088 (1979).

[26]*See* A. GOLDSTEIN, THE INSANITY DEFENSE 143 (1967); D. WEXLER, CRIMINAL COMMITMENTS AND DANGEROUS MENTAL PATIENTS 48–49 (1976).

[27]A. GOLDSTEIN, *supra* note 26, at 143–44.

[28]Lyles v. United States, 254 F.2d 725 (D.C. Cir. 1957).

[29]R. Simon, THE JURY AND THE DEFENSE OF INSANITY 93 (1967).

[30]*Id.* at 94.

[31]*Cf.* Bolten v. Harris, 395 F.2d 642, 651 n.50 (D.C. Cir. 1968) (revising the *Lyles* instruction in light of procedural changes wrought by the *Bolten* decision).

[32]*Cf.* CAL. WELF. & INST. CODE § 5300 (90-day limit).

[33]Thus, the difference in result, if any, from giving a mandatory indefinite commitment instruction, a 90-day instruction, and no instruction at all could be undertaken in a simulated setting. Even if it were established, in a jurisdiction where commitment is difficult and limited, that uninstructed jurors mistakenly place too much faith in the commitment process and therefore "over-acquit," it by no means follows that detailed and explicit informative instructions ought to be given. Such instructions might indeed cause some juries to "over-convict," and if that is the case, we are probably wise to leave matters where we found them (or, perhaps, to give instructions that indicate merely that an acquitted defendant's mental condition will be examined to ascertain the propriety of commitment).

[34]*E.g.,* State v. Karstetter, 110 Ariz. 539, 521 P.2d 626 (1974) (propriety of prosecutor and defense counsel addressing, in closing argument, the consequence of a verdict of NGRI).

[35]17 ARIZ. REV. STAT. ANN., R. Crim. P., rule 25.

[36]ARIZ. REV. STAT. § 36-540 (B).

[37]The matter is analogous to a criminal lawyer's inquiry, in connection with the representation of an alien criminal defendant, of the deportation consequences of a criminal conviction. *See* Wexler & Neet, *The Alien Criminal Defendant: An Examination of Immigration Law Principles for Criminal Law Practice*, 10 CRIM. L BULL. 289 (1974). As the next section of this chapter indicates, a lawyer handling a commitment case or a possible insanity-defense criminal case should also inquire whether his client is a veteran.

[38]M. ROSENTHAL, INTERPRETATION OF THE MENTAL HEALTH CODE 13 & 17 (5th ed. 1976) (handbook dealing with Texas Mental Health Code).

[39]Vaughan v. Bower, 313 F. Supp. 37 (D. Ariz.), *aff'd*, 400 U.S. 884 (1970).

[40]Wexler, Scoville, *et al.*, *The Administration of Psychiatric Justice: Theory and Practice in Arizona*, 13 ARIZ. L. REV. 1, 87 (1971) (emphasis added).

[41]*Hearings on the Constitutional Rights of the Mentally Ill Before the Subcommittee on Constitutional Rights of the Senate Committee on the Judiciary*, 91st Cong., 1st & 2d Sess. 157-58 (1970) (testimony of Patricia Wald, Esq.).

[42]*Id. See also* Vaughan v. Bower, 313 F. Supp. 37, 39 (D. Ariz.) *aff'd*, 400 U.S. 884 (1970) (setting forth Arizona's since-repealed discretionary statute).

[43]*E.g.*, N.Y. MENTAL HYG. LAW § 67.07.

[44]Wexler, Scoville, *et al.*, *supra* note 40, at 87.

[45]In fact, until 1974, when the Arizona legislature revised its commitment law and repealed its transfer statute, Arizona belonged to the category of states permitting involuntary transfer of nonresidents at the discretion of the superintendent of the Arizona State Hospital.

[46]Hoffman & Foust, *Least Restrictive Treatment of the Mentally Ill: A Doctrine in Search of Its Senses*, 14 SAN DIEGO L. REV. 1100 (1977). For a brief introduction to the doctrine of the least restrictive alternative, *see* Chapter 5.

[47]UNIFORM VETERANS' GUARDIANSHIP ACT § 18(1).

[48]*Id.* § 18(2).

[49]*Id.* (Commissioners' Prefatory Note).

[50]Burt, *Admission and Release Processes of Veterans Administration Psychiatric Hospitals* (unpublished manuscript).

[51]UNIFORM VETERANS' GUARDIANSHIP ACT § 18 (1).

[52]*See* ARIZ. REV. STAT. § 36-548 (C) & (D). Cognizant of some of the abuses of interstate transfer, the Arizona legislature precluded out-of-state transfers of nonconsenting veterans without an explicit court order authorizing the same. *Id.* § 36-548 (D). That represents a departure from the more freewheeling transfer provisions of the Uniform Act. Like section 18 (3) of the Uniform Act, however, Arizona has long required court approval of the transfer to *any* VA facility (within or without the state) of a patient who has been *criminally* committed. *Id.* § 36-548 (C). No patient may be committed or transferred to the VA without the VA's consent, and the agency is understandably reluctant to accept "criminally" committed persons. However, it does accept such people on occasion. Thus, if Crouch were a veteran, if the VA agreed to accept him, and if the commitment court approved an out-of-state transfer, he could have been sent involuntarily out of the state. That result would contrast sharply to the result that would be reached if Crouch were not a veteran.

[53]A related question, yet to be analyzed in the specific context of out-of-state transfers of committed veterans, is whether procedural due process requires some sort of hearing prior to the involuntary transfer of a patient to an out-of-state VA facility. *Compare* Wolff v. McDonnell, 418 U.S. 539 (1974) *and* Clonce v. Richardson, 379 F. Supp. 338 (W.D. Mo. 1974) *with* Meachum v. Fano, 427 U.S. 215 (1976) *and* Montanye v. Haynes, 427 U.S. 236

(1976). *See generally* O'Brien, *Tokens and Tiers in Corrections: An Analysis of Legal Issues in Behavior Modification*, 3 NEW ENG. J. PRISON L. 15, 36–40 (1976) (discussing those decisions). *See* Vitek v. Jones, 100 S. Ct. 1254 (1980).

[54]Hopefully, a VA voucher system could reimburse the state for the treatment of such veterans. However, even failing such a financial arrangement, the spirit of the least restrictive alternative teaches that the state should, if necessary, absorb that cost.

[55]*See* UNIFORM VETERANS' GUARDIANSHIP ACT § 18 (indicating California omission).

[56]*Id.* at 644 (Commissioners' Prefatory Note).

[57]Jackson v. Indiana, 406 U.S. 715, 738 (1972) (emphasis added). *See also* McNeil v. Director, Patuxent Inst., 407 U.S. 245 (1972).

[58]O'Connor v. Donaldson, 422 U.S. 563, 575 (1975). *See also id.* at 580 ("confinement must cease when those reasons no longer exist.") (Burger, C.J., concurring).

[59]A recent case so holding is Fasulo v. Arafeh, 173 Conn. 473, 378 A.2d 553 (1977) (decided on state constitutional grounds).

[60]ARIZ. REV. STAT. § 36–540.

[61]*Id.* § 36–501 (3).

[62]*Id.* § 36–501 (3) (b).

[63]*Id.* § 36–501 (3) (a).

[64]*Developments in the Law—Civil Commitment of the Mentally Ill*, 87 HARV. L. REV. 1190, 1205 (1974).

Part Two
LAW AND THERAPY

A. Outpatient Therapy

7

The *Tarasoff* Case and the Controversy over Its Therapeutic Implications

INTRODUCTION

By now, the case name *Tarasoff v. Regents of the University of California*[1] has become a household word in American mental health law circles. *Tarasoff*'s familiarity is no doubt attributable in part to the fact that the case was twice heard by the Supreme Court of California.[2] More important, however, is the rule of law established in the opinion.

In *Tarasoff*, a mental health outpatient at a University of California hospital successfully carried out his intention, previously confided to his therapist, to kill a particular victim. In the ensuing lawsuit, brought by the victim's parents against the University of California and certain of its therapists, the California court startled mental health professionals when it announced that a psychotherapist owes a duty of reasonable care to third parties who may be endangered by the therapist's patient. Specifically, the court held:

> When a therapist determines, or pursuant to the standards of his profession should determine, that his patient presents a serious danger of violence to another, he incurs an obligation to use reasonable care to protect the intended victim against such danger. The discharge of this duty may require the therapist to take one or more of various steps, depending upon the nature of the case. Thus it may call for him to warn the intended victim or others likely to apprise the victim of the danger, to notify the police, or to

take whatever other steps are reasonably necessary under the circumstances.[3]

Several features of the *Tarasoff* rule warrant elaboration. First, by the explicit terms of the opinion, a therapist must act to protect a potential victim when the therapist in fact determines or even "should determine" that his or her patient poses a serious danger to another. Second, by its use of terms such as "intended"[4] victim and "foreseeable"[5] victim, the opinion seems to limit the therapist's duty to instances where the potential victim is identified or easily identifiable.[6] Third, a therapist's duty of reasonable care may be discharged by a broad array of actions, though actually alerting the would-be victim will expectedly constitute the standardized "safe" response to a patient's perceived dangerousness.[7] Finally, a nagging question remains regarding "the type of warning which must be given to those who already know at least to some extent that they are threatened."[8] Since *Tarasoff* assumes—perhaps incorrectly[9]—that therapists possess special professional expertise in gauging patient dangerousness, a mental health professional may be well advised to inform a potential victim of a seriously-regarded threat of violence even if the victim already knows of the threat. After all, given the assumption of therapeutic expertise, the fact that a patient reiterated the threat, and reiterated it to a trained therapist who took it seriously, might be information that would be regarded as particularly useful to a potential victim. If so, its divulgence might in many instances be deemed a necessary ingredient of due care.

Needless to say, *Tarasoff* was not warmly received by mental health professionals.[10] Clearly, the most elegant of its psychiatric and scholarly critiques was developed in an article in the *Harvard Law Review* written by Dr. Alan Stone,[11] former President of the American Psychiatric Association and Professor of Law and Psychiatry at Harvard University. Stone's position is that *Tarasoff* and its supporters fail to appreciate the "cardinal" point: "that the imposition of a duty to protect, which may take the form of a duty to warn threatened third parties, will imperil the therapeutic alliance and destroy the patient's expectation of confidentiality, thereby thwarting effective treatment and ultimately reducing public safety."[12]

To Stone, the "particularly destructive" nature of the *Tarasoff* duty becomes evident when one considers the type of illness and recommended treatment of the typical dangerous patient who voluntarily enters outpatient therapy.[13] First of all, such a patient is ordinarily not a "hardened criminal," but is a person whose violence, Stone claims, is the "product of passion or paranoia."[14] Usually, the passion or paranoia is directed at a person of "intense significance" to the patient.[15] In terms of treatment, therefore, the task of the therapist is to draw the patient into a "therapeutic alliance in which feelings are acknowledged at the same time that the impulses to act them out are discouraged."[16] If therapy is successful, "the patient whose feelings are accepted will come to trust the therapist and be able to explore and understand his violent impulses and consider meaningful alternatives to them."[17] *Tarasoff* is intolerably intrusive, therefore, because "given the special significance of the potential victim to those whose violence is the product of passion and paranoia, nothing could be more destructive of the tenuous therapeutic alliance than the patient's perception that there exists a significant relationship between the therapist and the potential victim."[18] The *Tarasoff* tension is perhaps most powerfully illustrated by Stone with respect to patients suffering from "morbid jealousy"—paranoid delusions of infidelity:[19]

> [O]ne typical pattern of violence involves male paranoid jealousy with profound ambivalence toward the potential female victim and suspicion of all her male relationships. If the male therapist must prevent violence, he will do better to seek the assistance of the police or invoke civil commitment rather than give the patient the idea that he, the therapist, has a relationship with the woman.[20]

As the above passage indicates, Stone's "solution" to the *Tarasoff* problem is not necessarily to have psychotherapists follow a course of nonintervention. He believes that if and when a psychotherapist in fact concludes that his or her patient poses a serious risk of violence, civil commitment is the appropriate route to follow.[21] Indeed, so long as a psychotherapist is judged by what he or she in fact believes—rather than by a standard of what a reasonable psychotherapist *should* believe— regarding the dangerousness of a particular patient, Stone would seemingly have no objection to recognizing a *legal duty* of a therapist to trigger civil commitment of a patient believed to pose a serious danger to another.[22]

While Stone's "solution" seems too pat—and in fact would, if workable,[23] virtually place psychotherapists in an enviable "no-lose" legal posture[24]—my purpose in the present chapter is only in part to criticize Stone's proposals. Principally, my purpose is to assert that the enmity of Stone and others toward *Tarasoff* is bottomed largely on their adherence to an "individual pathology" model of violent behavior[25] which, the literature strongly suggests, is theoretically and therapeutically unwarranted.[26] More important, what *is* apparently warranted, according to those who have seriously studied the type of interpersonal violence that is therapeutically preventable,[27] is an approach that focuses on troubled *relationships*.[28] Ideally, such an approach should involve both the patient and the potential victim and should therefore often take the form of "couple" or "family" therapy.[29] Finally, it is my thesis that, if taken seriously and followed widely, the *Tarasoff* decision, despite its many obvious drawbacks,[30] has the clear-cut potential of prompting and prodding practicing therapists to terminate their continued clinging to an outmoded "individual pathology" model of violence,[31] and to accept the paradigm of "interactional" or "couple" violence already endorsed by the professional literature.

The pertinent professional literature, though it technically spans a variety of the behavioral sciences,[32] is actually overwhelmingly "victimological" in nature. Victimology has distinguished itself internationally by focusing attention and study on the offender-victim relationship.[33] In the context of potentially violent voluntary outpatients, pertinent victimological subquestions include such matters (some of which were noted by Stone himself)[34] as the nature of the patient, the nature and identity of the potential victim, the role of the victim in promoting patient violence, and the sorts of therapeutic interventions that would naturally flow from knowledge about the patient, the potential victim, and the relationship between the two. The next section, then, will deal in some detail with the information now known, or nearly known, about the "victimological variables" likely to be apposite in *Tarasoff*-type situations.

THE VICTIMOLOGICAL VARIABLES

The Nature of the Patient

To date, no systematic study has been completed of the sorts of voluntary outpatients who make *Tarasoff*-type threats of violence.[35] Investigators have, however, studied hospitalized violent patients,[36] and the results of those studies are relevant to our current inquiry.

Skodol and Karusu, for example, studied 62 emergency room patients who had been admitted voluntarily or involuntarily and who had been categorized as violent because of violent action (42) or ideation (20).[37] Of that group of patients, only 65% suffered from a major mental disturbance such as psychosis or its equivalent.[38] The remainder were diagnosed as having assorted neuroses, character disorders, and the like.[39]

Clearly the most pertinent study for our purposes is MacDonald's Colorado investigation of hospitalized patients who had made homicidal threats.[40] A number of those patients had also assaulted their victims.[41]

Of the 100 consecutive "threat-to-kill" admissions to the Colorado Psychiatric Hospital in 1966 and 1967, only 23 were psychotic.[42] Fully 77% of those patients, therefore, fell into nonpsychotic diagnostic categories, almost always of a "character disorder" variety.[43] Of the 100 patients, only 7 had been committed, although several of the 93 voluntary admissions—presumably from the group who had committed physical assault rather than mere verbal threat—sought admission as an alternative to facing criminal charges.[44]

What is particularly significant about the above studies is the large percentage (in MacDonald's case, the overwhelming percentage) of hospitalized patients perceived to be violent but nonetheless diagnosed as nonpsychotic. Indeed, given the pressure to affix a serious psychiatric label on those who are hospitalized,[45] it may be that the percent of psychotic patients in those studies was even lower than indicated.

If psychosis is often absent even among patients whose homicidal threats or whose assaultive acts are deemed serious enough to warrant hospitalization, we must assume that the presence of psychosis is probably very low indeed in the typical *Tarasoff* situation, a situation which involves a *voluntary outpatient* who confides to his therapist violent thoughts or intentions.[46] Surely, for example, if "many offenders who murder their loved ones do so not under any insane belief, but in a sane awareness of the extent of their loss,"[47] many patients with homicidal intent of such a nature must similarly lack full-fledged mental disorder.

Significantly, since full-fledged mental disorder is emerging as an indispensable element in involuntary commitment,[48] Stone's suggestion of "solving" *Tarasoff* problems through commitment should, in the great bulk of instances, fail badly.[49] Interestingly, in an important and influential monograph,[50] Stone himself agrees that involuntary commitment should be available only in the face of "severe mental illness."[51]

Indeed, under the proposed "model" commitment criteria crafted by Stone in his monograph,[52] patients posing typical *Tarasoff* problems would, for a *variety* of reasons, fall without the realm of the commitment process. In addition to requiring a "severe mental illness," for example, Stone's scheme would require, among other elements,[53] a patient's "incapacity" to make treatment decisions,[54] and a showing of treatment availability and effectiveness.[55]

While the "severe mental illness" requirement alone should surely suffice to negate the committability of nonpsychotic patients, Stone's additional elements solidify the case for noncommittability. Under the "incapacity" requirement, for example, Stone admits that "only seriously psychotic—irrational—patients would be confined,"[56] for he properly concedes that "no patients with a personality disorder, neurosis, or behavior problem would be incompetent."[57] And to the extent that threatening patients suffer, as did the overwhelming bulk from MacDonald's sample, from some sort of "personality disorder," commitment would fail under the "treatment effectiveness" prong of Stone's formula. Stone asserts that "it is a truism in psychiatry that treatment success with personality disorders, particularly sociopaths, is quite limited."[58] Dangerous personality disorders, he claims, are amenable neither to chemotherapy nor to brief individual therapy.[59] If treatment is "unlikely to succeed, or will take years,"[60] a court endeavoring to apply honestly Stone's "treatability" element would disallow commitment. And short-term emergency commitment, where technical legal criteria may in practice be easily glossed over,[61] will by definition be of insufficient duration to treat a disorder that will assertedly respond at best to long-term treatment.

A later section of this chapter will question seriously the therapeutic recalcitrance of typical *Tarasoff*-type patients.[62] That section, however, will look to a "couple therapy" approach and will in no sense suggest that involuntary institutionalization of the patient is the preferred therapeutic path. Indeed, the important lesson to be learned from the instant section is that, to the extent the typical *Tarasoff* patient suffers at most from a mental malady short of psychosis, coerced commitment will, by statute and even by Stone's own criteria, be simply unavailable.

THE IDENTITY OF THE POTENTIAL VICTIM

Some investigators who have studied patients with homicidal thoughts have noted that a number of such patients possess violent urges not directed toward any particular target, but present instead with "diffusely directed"[63] violent urges or with the fear of "running amok."[64] Though patients with diffusely directed violent urges constitute an important category of therapeutic concern, they fall well without the scope of the present chapter.

First of all, a *Tarasoff* duty seems to be triggered only if and when a specific victim is identified or is easily identifiable.[65] A therapist, therefore, may well lack any legal obligation to exercise reasonable care to the unidentifiable potential victims of a patient with diffusely directed violent urges. Moreover, patients with diffusely directed violent urges typically experience intense anxiety.[66] The anxiety propels such patients into treatment,[67] and the patients generally request hospitalization or eagerly accept it when it is suggested to them.[68] Even if a therapist legally must take action, therefore, the therapist's task will, in the ordinary case, not be a difficult one.[69]

In any event, since diffusely directed violence cases lack by definition a specific victim, they fall without what seems to be Stone's principal objection to *Tarasoff:* that compliance with *Tarasoff* will lead a patient
to perceive the existence of "a significant relationship between the
therapist and the potential victim."[70] Equally, because diffusely directed
violence cases cannot, with or without *Tarasoff's* application, encourage
contact between a therapist and a particular potential victim, those cases
fall without my area of interest: the extent to which *Tarasoff* may precipitate the acceptance of therapeutic modalities involving potential victims
as well as patients with specifically directed violent ideation.

With regard to patients whose violent urges are in fact directed at a
specific target, Stone is correct in stating that the targeted individual is
typically a person of "intense significance"[71] to the patient. Clearly, it is
a criminological universal that consummated offenses of homicide or
assault very often involve relatives or close friends.[72] Women, for example, "are overwhelmingly killed in a family or lover relationship."[73] And
when women themselves kill, "they are more likely to kill their husbands than any other category of persons."[74]

The "familial" pattern of homicide and assault persists even among
offenders drawn from the "psychiatric sector." Lanzkron, for example,
studied patients charged with murder who had been committed to Matteawan State Hospital in New York. In reviewing 150 consecutive commitments of such patients, Lanzkron learned that a family member had
been victimized in fully 47% of the instances.[75] Working within the
setting of a psychiatric emergency room, other investigators have observed that, among a mainly male self-referred group of violent patients,
wives were the "common objects" of those patients with specifically
directed urges of violence.[76]

Noteworthy, too, is the examination by Skodol and Karusu of
emergency room patients deemed violent because of aggressive ideation
or actual assaultive behavior.[77] In cases of actual assault, slightly more
than half the victims were members of the patient's family.[78] Family
member "victims" rise to 58% when the focus is on patients with aggressive fantasies.[79] And, when assaultive behavior was preceded by a
"fermentation" period—a period of "prior conscious consideration of
violence"[80]—the rate of family member victims soared to 77%.[81] It
should be noted that aggressive fantasies and fermentation periods may
be particularly pertinent for *Tarasoff* purposes: patient acknowledgments
of fantasies or fermentation may trigger a therapist's *Tarasoff* obligation
to seek to prevent the very violence that the self-referred patient is
fearful of engaging in.

Again, the most pertinent reference (and perhaps the most refined categorization) for present purposes is MacDonald's identification of the potential victims against whom his patients had threatened homicide.[82] In MacDonald's study, 80% of the subject patients threatened family members and an additional 8% threatened persons (paramours, guardians, homosexual partners) falling just beyond the technical definition of a member of the family.[83]

To Stone, *Tarasoff* is particularly intolerable *because* the typical potential victim is someone close to the patient.[84] In his view, therapy is threatened by the patient's perception of the therapist's divided allegiance.[85] In my view, however, *Tarasoff* would be far more troubling if the typical target were unrelated to and relatively remote to the patient. To me, *Tarasoff* is rendered terribly tolerable—even, it will be argued, possibly advantageous—by the fact that in perhaps 88% of the cases, the prospective victim is someone potentially suitable for participation in a form of "couple," "conjoint," or "family" therapy.[86] The therapeutic benefit to be derived from the participation in the therapy by the potential victim becomes evident when an exploration is undertaken of the nature of the potential victim, of the patient–victim interpersonal relationship, and of the victim's possible role in a relationship involving actual or potential patient–victim violence.

The Nature and Role of the Potential Victim

Clearly the greatest contribution of "victimology" to behavioral science is its broadening of the basis of theoretical and empirical inquiry regarding criminal behavior and its causes. Instead of attending to the characteristics of the offender alone, the victimological perspective forces us to focus our attention as well on the characteristics of the victim and on the nature of the offender–victim relationship.[87]

The most startling, and significant, result derived from the reoriented research focus is that, to an appreciable extent, and especially with regard to crimes such as homicide[88] and assault,[89] "the stereotype of the innocent and unsuspecting victim has proved to be false."[90] The major studies support the assertion that victims often contribute to, precipitate, or even provoke the acts of violence directed against them.[91]

Victim precipitation is, of course, a vague concept, subject to varying interpretations and applications. Depending on one's definition, for example, the concept is capable of being stretched to cover a broad spectrum of situations or of being restricted in application to a fairly narrow range of behavior. In contrast to broad concepts of victim contribution, narrow definitions have the advantage of being rather easy to operationalize, and their relative clarity requires very little interpretation on the part of coders and therefore enhances the reliability of research findings.[92]

In the context of homicide, the narrowest and clearest definition of victim precipitation was employed in the seminal sociological study conducted by Marvin Wolfgang.[93] In Wolfgang's work the only cases included within the category of victim precipitated were "those in which the victim was the first to show and use a deadly weapon, [or] to strike a blow in an altercation."[94] Even employing that restrictive a definition, Wolfgang found 26% of Philadelphia homicides to have been victim precipitated.[95] Under that same definition, other investigators have found the rate of victim precipitated homicide to reach 38%.[96] Indeed, in domestic disturbances leading to the death of a husband, Wolfgang's research reveals that 60% of the cases fall within his victim precipitation definition.[97]

Despite its precision and consequent reliability for research puposes, Wolfgang's definition fails to capture a wide variety of provocative victim behavior (infidelity, name-calling, verbal altercations[98]) which may be critical clinically in devising an appropriate therapeutic strategy to reduce the risk of patient–victim interpersonal violence. It is of course beyond dispute (and virtually tautologically true) that if the definition of victim precipitation were to be significantly expanded, the rate of homicides and assaults attributed to victim precipitation would rise considerably.[99]

The rate of victim precipitated homicide rose to 49%, for example, where precipitation was defined as "any situation in which the provocative action of the victim played an important part in the perpetrator's decision to act."[100] Significantly, a Scottish study revealed that "in about two out of three cases of homicide, the victim had participated in some measure in a way which encouraged the interaction with the offender in a progression to violence."[101] Finally, when the focus is turned from homicide to nonlethal violence (such as intrafamilial aggravated assault) the victim's role remains an important and active one,[102] but the majority of provocative instances are likely to involve verbal, rather than physical, attacks by the victim against the person who ultimately becomes the assaultive offender.[103]

Investigators who have studied closely the phenomenon of interpersonal violence have concluded that the escalation of an altercation from the realm of the verbal to the realm of the violent often involves the behavioral contribution of both combatants.[104] Indeed, the reciprocal precipitation is sometimes so pervasive that, in a substantial number of the cases studied, "the offender and the victim had, until the last moment, almost interchangeable roles, and it seemed a matter of chance who lived and who died."[105]

The "interchangeability" of offender and victim roles, at least in cases of narrowly defined victim-precipitated criminal homicide, was most convincingly demonstrated by Wolfgang.[106] Comparing the prior arrest records (including arrest records for assault)[107] of offenders and victims of victim-precipitated (VP) and non–victim-precipitated homicide, Wolfgang concludes "that the victim of VP homicide is quite similar to the offender in non-VP homicide—and that the VP victim more closely resembles the non-VP offender than the non-VP victim."[108]

Even if the victim is not "interchangeable" with the offender, an examination of the clinical characteristics of victims of violence reveals the potential enormity of the extent of their contributory role in encouraging violent offender behavior. Homicide victims, for example, are very often known to have consumed alcohol immediately prior to their fatal confrontation with an offender.[109] Wolfgang noted that the extent of preconfrontation alcohol consumption was significantly greater (69% versus 47%) in victims of victim-precipitated homicide than it was in victims of non–victim-precipitated homicide.[110] Moreover, a recent study of the clinical states of homicide victims reveals that such persons were much more likely than were others living in their geographical vicinity to have been treated at a state-supported mental hospital or mental health center.[111] Of the victims suffering from diagnosed symptoms, alcoholism accounted for the largest category,[112] followed fairly closely by sociopathy.[113] There are even indications that certain sorts of victims actually commit or attempt suicide by provoking others— typically intimates—into acts of lethal assault.[114]

In any event, it seems evident, at least when victim precipitation is defined in a fairly broad—and therapeutically instrumental—fashion, that the incidence of victim precipitation in homicidal and assaultive behavior is quite prevalent. MacDonald, for example, recounts numerous instances where a victim's behavior provoked or contributed to the homicidal threat that became the predicate for a patient's hospitalization.[115] Even psychodynamically oriented therapists, including some cited by Stone,[116] admit to or detail the masochistic nature or provocative influence of the victims of violent threats, assaults, and homicides.[117] In short, the scientific, clinical, and empirical evidence from a wide variety of sources and disciplines calls for a firm conclusion that victims of violence or of violent threats often contribute in some meaningful manner to their own victimization.

THERAPEUTIC IMPLICATIONS OF VICTIMOLOGICAL THEORY

Despite the clear-cut conclusion that victims often contribute to violence, some commentators, fearful that a victimological perspective will work against improving the plight of battered wives, seek, in cavalier fashion, to cast aside the entire victim contribution perspective:

> [S]ome elaborate theories on provocation have developed out of the social sciences; they fall under the general heading of "victimology." Victims are treated as if they created the situation in which they find themselves and are held responsible for their own problems, irrespective of other contributing factors.[118]

Though the above quote is surely an overstatement of the victimological perspective, it is an important statement insofar as it recognizes that public policy implications abound in the fertile field of "applied" victimology.[119] In accommodating public policy to a victimological perspective, care must surely be taken to insure that we do not "overdo the emphasis on the role of the victim and reach the opposite conclusion, namely that the victim is the real criminal and the criminal a mere victim of his victim."[120]

There *are* potential dangers to important interests (feminist interests included)[121] in recognizing the possibility of provocative victims. The potential dangers are particularly evident in the realm of criminal law, which demands the application of morally loaded attribution labels such as "blame," "responsibility," and "desert." Articles by criminal law scholars in the United States[122] and Israel[123] have begun to address those important issues. The crucial point, however, is that an empirically solid theory ought not to be discarded simply because it will require us to unpack new notions, and to rethink old ones, regarding the legal status of the victim. Perhaps the matter can be better balanced by considering the significant fact that feminists have not hesitated to rally behind and profit from victimological evidence which demonstrates beyond doubt that victim precipitation runs rampant in *husband killings,* where "the usual course of events is that the husband lashes out and the wife responds in the extreme."[124] Indeed, fueled by factual data demonstrating the nature of the battering husband and the shortage of crisis centers available to battered wives, some have argued that the law, through use of the mitigating doctrine of manslaughter or the exculpating doctrine of self-defense, should be particularly responsive to battered wives who kill their husbands.[125]

Fortunately, the present chapter deals not with the nagging problems of victimological implications on the criminal law, but with a far less troubling matter. Its focus is on the *therapeutic implications* that flow from empirically supportable victimological theory and, in the following section, on the manner in which mental health law, through *Tarasoff*-type mandates, can operate to foster the clinical application of victimological principles.[126]

Whatever may be the case with respect to schools of psychiatric thought regarding the treatment of other problems, the literature regarding violence directed at specifically identified victims suggests overwhelmingly that the treatment of that particular "condition" should transcend an "intrapsychic" individual pathology approach. Ideally, the treatment should in many cases involve not only the self-referred violence-prone patient, but also the targeted victim (typically a family member) who may well contribute to a violence-prone ongoing pathological relationship with the potentially violent patient. In essence, then, when a patient in therapy speaks seriously of hostile acts or hostile urges directed at another, the patient and the potential victim should both be considered prime candidates for a type of "couple" or "family" therapy.

Surely, offering therapeutic assistance to the potential victim, and not simply to the identified patient, makes especially good sense in several frequently arising situations discussed in the previous section. Such treatment is plainly appropriate in its own right, for example, where the victim personally suffers from symptoms of psychiatric distress,[127] where a victim's excessive use of alcohol is associated with provocative action on his or her part,[128] and where a victim resorts to provocative action in order indirectly to attempt suicide.[129]

In still other instances, involvement of the potential victim in the therapeutic process should plainly profit the identified patient. After all, to the extent that the patient and the proposed victim have "interchangeable" roles, as they often do,[130] the hostile relationship, unless it is defused, could also result in serious harm to—or in the demise of—the *patient*. In any case, whenever an interpersonal relationship contains a meaningful amount of victim precipitation, a patient seeking assistance in avoiding argumentative, assaultive, or homicidal behavior will presumably be aided considerably if the victim learns to control or curtail behavioral patterns which contribute to the patient's aggressivity.[131] Sometimes, victim contribution to violence can be very subtle indeed, as when a violent spouse becomes assaultive principally when under the influence of alcohol, and when the victimized spouse tacitly encourages the former to drink.[132] Finally, even in the absence of ascertainable victim contribution, a victim's involvement and cooperation with the patient's therapist can be extremely instrumental in the success of the therapeutic endeavor. Such victims can be instructed in limit setting,[133] can learn to alter the patient's environment to reduce the risk of violence,[134] and can in other ways contribute favorably to the patient's recovery.[135]

Not surprisingly, then, a number of therapeutic modalities to deal with interpersonal violence have been developed which are derived from, or which are at least completely consistent with, victimological knowledge. Family therapy has, of course, from its conception taken the position that interpersonal *systems*, rather than isolated individuals, ought to be the focus of therapeutic attention,[136] and variations of family or couple therapy have arisen to ameliorate violent, combative, or argumentative intrafamilial conflicts.[137] Some commentators emphasize the importance of conjoint sessions with planned confrontation occurring in the presence of the therapist.[138] Others speak of feuding couples devising reciprocal agreements (therapeutic contracts) whereby both partners agree to alter certain behavioral traits.[139] Still others emphasize the need for couples to develop communicative skills in order to avoid the escalation of arguments into assaultive confrontations.[140] Combative, violence-prone couples may need to learn "fair fighting" techniques,[141] and they may need to learn that certain incendiary topics or provocative remarks (name calling, derogatory references to another's ethnicity) must simply become communicative taboos.[142]

Proponents of family type therapy for patients who act aggressively toward specified others feel the "interactionist" element is so potent that family therapy is recommended even when chemotherapy is also indicated,[143] and even when the patient may suffer from organic impairment.[144] Thus, one important psychiatric study found that socially aggressive chronic schizophrenic outpatients function markedly better with phenothiazine treatment if, and only if, the patients resided in low-conflict family settings.[145] In high-conflict families, however, where aggressivity is common and where reciprocal provocation is the pattern, chemotherapy was rather unsuccessful. Though chlorpromazine might, in such families, temporarily reduce the identified patient's aggressiveness, his reduced aggression would then be dissonant with the expected notions of family functioning. Other family members might then be prompted to escalate their own provocative behavior in order to return the patient to a fullfledged, and therefore aggressive, participant in family affairs. In order for a patient in such a family to improve, then, the family itself might have to undergo therapy to modify interactional patterns. Only if that is accomplished might the aggressive schizophrenic patient respond favorably to phenothiazines.[146] Similarly, a recent study dealing with seizure-related episodic dyscontrol in adolescents, noting that seizures are in part stress related, suggested that family therapy, rather than reliance on anticonvulsants alone, might be necessary for effective treatment of adolescent dyscontrol episodes.[147] In that therapist's experience, "family therapy is particularly indicated when the aggressive act is directed toward another family member."[148]

What is most compelling about "interactionist" therapeutic approaches to interpersonal violence is the near uniformity with which such approaches are endorsed by therapists seemingly belonging to divergent schools of psychological thought. The influence of the social structure in which both patient and victim reside is recognized, we have just seen, even by some who recognize as well the relevance of such crucial factors as a patient's possible organicity or receptivity to chemotherapy. Further, an interactionist perspective is clearly compatible with principles of behavioral psychology. Behaviorists, of course, would hold that a person's aggressivity is in large part learned, maintained, and altered by the extent to which the person's aggressive behaviors are attended to and reinforced by others in the patient's environment.[149] Accordingly, a behavioral model would recognize the importance of dealing with the family as a social system and with the importance of victim-prone family members as therapeutic "change agents."[150] Indeed, a behaviorist such as Gerald Patterson has noted the similarity of his area of interest to the area of interest of family therapists such as Jay Haley and Salvador Minuchin,[151] and Haley, recounting the development of the family therapy field, has noted that the 1960s witnessed the entrance into the field of the "conditioning therapists."[152]

Even psychotherapists who seem typically to employ traditional psychiatric nomenclature and techniques have been forced, when dealing with patients harboring hostility toward specific victims, to recognize the role of the victim in the therapeutic process. Some, when dealing with violent marital relationships, have supplemented individual psychotherapy with a period of conjoint sessions.[153] In treating patients who had made homicidal threats, MacDonald often turned to a family therapy approach. In his words, "as eight out of ten patients in this study threatened members of their family, it was possible to involve many of the victims in the treatment situation."[154] At the least, MacDonald asserts in his chapter on psychiatric treatment, "the victim should always be interviewed."[155] Likewise, Drs. Lion, Bach-Y-Rita, and Ervin,[156] cited prominently by Stone in the course of hammering home his "cardinal point" that "a duty to warn threatened third parties will imperil the therapeutic alliance,"[157] themselves state that, when treating patients with specifically directed violent urges (urges which they found were typically directed against one's spouse), "it was just as necessary a therapeutic maneuver to instruct the spouse to contact us as it was to teach the patient to come to the hospital when he felt anxious or impulsive."[158]

Indeed, even in the treatment of "morbid jealousy," which Stone sets forth as illustrating most vividly the terrors inherent in a *Tarasoff*-type requirement that a potential victim be alerted of the possibility of patient violence,[159] the authorities cited by Stone[160] do not condone a therapeutic enterprise which ignores the potential victim and involves only the patient and his therapist. Indeed, to the extent that they address the issue, even those authorities seem to cut the other way.

In his discussion of morbid jealousy, Stone cites Mowat, a British authority who studied morbidly jealous murderers and attempted murderers committed to the Broadmoor Institution,[161] Lanzkron, an American who studied murderers (including morbidly jealous ones) committed to Matteawan State Hospital,[162] and Shepherd, a British psychiatrist who undertook a careful clinical and social study of morbid jealousy.[163] A careful reading of those studies, however, suggests that, even in the concededly tricky treatment of morbid jealousy, a skillfully executed scheme for notification of the victim is clinically indicated.

Mowat's study is itself purely descriptive. His description, however, presents a number of interesting and significant facts. For example, a morbidly jealous person who turns to violence will almost invariably assault or kill his or her own spouse or lover.[164] Rarely will anyone other than the accused spouse or lover (*e.g.*, a sex rival) be attacked.[165] Further, the potential victim is typically abundantly aware of the morbidly jealous partner's anger and accusations.[166] In keeping with his descriptive task, Mowat specifically states that "it is not within the scope of this study to discuss the treatment of morbid jealousy."[167]

Lanzkron, the second source cited by Stone, actually discusses morbid jealousy and delusions of infidelity in only perfunctory fashion. His study deals with all murderers committed to Matteawan, not just with morbidly jealous murderers. After stating that 20% of Matteawan murderers suffered from morbid jealousy or a like condition, Lanzkron simply cited Shepherd's British study and remarked that "our survey confirms some of the assertions of other investigators in England."[168]

Shepherd, Stone's final authority, *does* discuss the clinical side of morbid jealousy. His discussion of the clinical aspects is interesting indeed. His focus, moreover, is very much on "interpersonal relations,"[169] "ruptured marital relations,"[170] and the sometimes apparent feigned

indifference or even "deliberate provocation"[171] of the nonpatient partner. Building on that interactionist framework, Shepherd states asser-
tively that

> the interplay of both partners therefore entered into and modified the symp-
> toms and the manifestations of behaviour to such a degree that the signifi-
> cance of the phenomena in an individual case could not be assessed without
> an understanding of the relationship between them.[172]

> In particular some understanding must be acquired of the character and
> likely reactions of the patient's marital partner who may also be in need of
> help and support. Without this knowledge the physician will be handi-
> capped in the practical advice which he can provide about domiciliary manage-
> ment.[173]

Even in the troubling situations involving morbid jealousy, then,
contact with the potential victim seems possible and highly desirable.
And whether we speak of morbid jealousy or of very different diagnostic
conditions, in virtually all clinical situations of violence directed at a
specific target, the literature seems, contrary to Stone, to call for an
interactionist therapeutic perspective.

Stone's anti-*Tarasoff* stance, it will be recalled, is for a therapist to
see a potentially violent patient alone, to avoid contact with the potential
victim, and, if necessary, to seek the involuntary hospitalization of a
patient perceived to be dangerous. At the therapeutic polar extreme
from Stone, but seemingly more in keeping with the emerging
victimological evidence, stands the solution posited by Dr. Frank
Pittman and associates.[174] While Stone advocates seeing the patient
alone and, if necessary, hospitalizing him or her, Pittman, in an important article entitled *Family Therapy as an Alternative to Psychiatric Hospitalization,*[175] proposes seeing the patient together with other family
members and avoiding hospitalization (even voluntary hospitalization)
at all costs.

Pittman's Family Treatment Unit (FTU) sees only patients who present themselves for psychiatric hospitalization and who are deemed by
the staff to require immediate hospitalization. Instead of being admitted,
however, some patients, who are obviously diagnostically comparable
to the inpatients, are randomly assigned to the FTU. The FTU staff will
immediately see the family as a whole, draw up a treatment plan,
schedule a home visit within 24 hours, and perhaps prescribe medication for one or more family members.[176]

Relatives, in Pittman's experience, are surprisingly willing to
understand how their behavior may contribute to the patient's problems
and are equally willing to participate in the therapeutic process.[177]
Pittman's preliminary results, reported in the published study, were

impressive indeed: "of the twenty-five cases seen during the first six months, only one was hospitalized."[178]

Perhaps most important for present purposes is the fact that Pittman's approach has been applied successfully even to violent patients. It is worth reporting in full Pittman's description of what he calls a "typical example"—the case of a "Mr. D," who was seen in a family, outpatient setting despite the fact that the patient initially requested hospitalization out of fear that he would kill his wife, his family, and himself:

> The nominal patient was Mr. D, a 34 year old unemployed house painter. He had been referred to Colorado Psychopathic Hospital by a social worker, who had seen him and his driving and capable wife in regard to the school failure of one of their six children. The admitting physician recommended admission because of his "paranoid jealousy bordering on the delusional," homicidal threats, and severe depression. Mrs. D had already left him after a violent fight at the cafe where she worked. A divorce was planned. The family's difficulties were intensified the year before, during the sixth pregnancy, when Mrs. D refused her husband sexual intercourse and he had an affair which he then told her about. She retaliated by moving the family into the house formerly occupied by the other woman, then taking a job as a nighttime waitress, something which her husband had always forbidden her to do. Within a few weeks, Mr. D lost his job and was having jealous rages; the 14 year old daughter who was left with the care of her siblings, had attempted suicide and was contemplating marriage; the 10 year old boy began bedwetting; the 9 year old son was suddenly failing in school; the 5 year old girl was also bedwetting; the 3 year old girl was becoming very withdrawn; and the year old baby ceased attempts at ambulation.
>
> All eight were seen at once and then the attention was focused on the couple. They were encouraged to live together again. Mr. D was placed on Thorazine. He confessed his guilt over the affair and the entire family was made aware that his difficulties were in part a response to other factors in the family. Mrs. D recognized her involvement and the family began begging her to make adjustments for the common good. When her strong need to socialize through her work was discussed, she became anxious and was also placed on medications. After a week of vigorous wrangling, she recognized that she had punished him long enough. Compromises were worked out between the adults, and a reasonable family equilibrium was reached. She quit her job, he went back to work, plans were made to move, and her needs for more social outlets were respected. Therapy was terminated after seven visits in two weeks. At the six month follow-up, all eight were symptom free and the family functioned as well as it had before the crisis.[179]

Pittman's procedure avoids the liberty-threatening and stigmatizing act of hospitalization and seems to be therapeutically successful. Of course, we are at present lacking, with respect to patients threatening violence against specific others, a controlled study of the comparative effectiveness of other therapeutic methods (individual psychotherapy, hospitalization, etc.) against a "family" or "couple" method of outpatient therapy.[180] Yet, outpatient interactionist therapy promotes liberty interests, seems preliminarily to be successful, and meshes well with our knowledge of victimology and with the clinical experience and intuitions of those commentators who have seriously studied violent patients.[181] In light of those factors, a family or couple approach to treating interpersonal violence seems deserving at least of presumptive validity for purposes of formulating present public policy. What Stone has said about a somewhat different matter seems highly appropriate in the context of the current problem: "In the absence of a reliable empirical study, a judgment based on clinical experience is obviously perferable to a judgment that contradicts such experience."[182]

TARASOFF'S VICTIMOLOGICAL VIRTUES

The available information from scholarly sources and from clinicians who have written on the subject suggests strongly that a "couple" or "family" approach to therapy is often warranted when a mental health professional seeks to treat a patient who has seriously threatened violence against a specified other—at least when, as is typically the case, that "specified other" is himself or herself a member (or virtually a member) of the patient's family. The evidence is equally strong, however, that, contrary to the recommendations in the literature, practitioners have thus far eschewed the emerging "interactionist" therapeutic models and have clung, even with respect to treating interpersonal violence, to the "individual pathology" models in which they were originally schooled.[183] Interestingly, however, constant compliance with perceived *Tarasoff* problems may prompt practitioners to shift away from an intrapsychic model and may propel them increasingly toward a presumably preferable interactionist model of treating violence-prone self-referred outpatients. Ironically, then, *Tarasoff,* despite its potential for impeding treatment in certain instances, might ultimately have the effect of generally *enhancing,* rather than hindering, the efficacy of therapy provided to violence-prone patients.

In light of the discussion in previous portions of this article, the mechanism by which *Tarasoff* might serve as a catalyst in a victimological revolution is probably by now fairly apparent. And when the prior discussion is coupled with the conclusions reached by some post-*Tarasoff* empirical endeavors to ascertain the impact of *Tarasoff,*[184] the role of *Tarasoff* as such a catalytic agent may be made even more explicit.

Though *Tarasoff* is understandably disliked by therapists who cling closely to psychoanalytic techniques of treatment,[185] a *Stanford Law Review* survey of mental health professionals in California reveals that *Tarasoff* is widely—perhaps almost universally—known among therapists practicing in the jurisdiction in which the case is binding authority.[186] Moreover, the decision has actually affected the behavior of those psychotherapists. The Stanford study concludes that, since *Tarasoff*, therapists have lowered the threshold at which they will view a patient as dangerous and at which they will presumably warn others of the patient's potential for violence.[187] Further, the study cautiously concludes (too cautiously, it would seem) that the frequency of warnings has increased since *Tarasoff*.[188] Finally, the study asserts conclusively that *when* warnings are given, the potential *victim* is much more likely post-*Tarasoff* than pre-*Tarasoff* to be included among the various persons notified of the patient's violent proclivities.[189]

Though the *Stanford Law Review* study views the impact of *Tarasoff* to be detrimental to the practice of psychotherapy, that conclusion is based, as is Stone's, on an "individual pathology" model of violence and its treatment. *Tarasoff* may be far from detrimental, however, if it serves to transform the model for treating violent persons to a more efficacious one. It is time, then, to specify explicitly how such a transformation might occur.

Increasingly, when a patient threatens violence against a specified other, the post-*Tarasoff* scenario may begin to take shape along the following lines:

1. After *Tarasoff*, a typical therapist, despite intrapsychic therapeutic inclinations, is likely to focus far more than before on the potential victim and on the extent to which harm to the victim can be averted.

2. For fear of *Tarasoff* liability in the event he or she takes no action and a threatened victim is later seriously injured or killed by a patient, the therapist will presumably be induced, even in fairly borderline cases, to seek some acceptable means of alerting the potential victim of a patient's serious or possibly serious threat.

3. Ideally, of course, the therapist would wish to act in a manner acceptable to the patient—in a manner, that is, not disruptive of their on-going therapeutic relationship.

4. Fortunately, since the typical potential victim is a family member who presumably knows the patient is in therapy and who also typically knows at least to some extent of the patient's hostility toward the victim,[190] a skillful therapist ought often to be able to secure the patient's consent to notify the potential victim.[191]

5. If the patient's consent to the divulgence is obtained, *Tarasoff* can of course be satisfied without sacrificing the patient's trust and without

the therapist running the risk of violating ethical or legal obligations to keep a patient's confidences.[192]

6. When the victim is contacted, the therapist may first learn, as some therapists are apparently now first learning post-*Tarasoff*, of the victim's contributory or provocative role in the patient's potential violence.[193]

7. In addition or alternatively, the therapist may learn from the victim certain significant facts about the patient's behavior.[194]

8. If the therapist ascertains a meaningful presence of victim precipitation, he may seek—and obtain—the patient's consent to have additional contact with the potential victim,[195] and the potential victim, particularly if he or she is a member of the patient's family, may be very willing to cooperate.[196]

9. Even if victim contribution is not apparent, if the potential victim provides the therapist with important information about the patient,[197] that information may be used to enhance therapy. Often, too, the patient may have an explanation that will lead the therapist to seek additional dialogue with the potential victim, and which may then provide evidence of victim contribution.[198]

10. In any event, if the above chain of events begins to occur with any regularity, the typical therapist treating a potentially violent patient will find him- or herself, because of the pressure of *Tarasoff*, transformed from a practitioner of "intrapsychic" psychotherapy to a practitioner of a presumably preferable "interactionist" model of treating interpersonal violence.

In *The Structure of Scientific Revolutions*,[199] Thomas Kuhn teaches that the toppling of old scientific paradigms, and their replacement by new ones, is often far from a tidy process.[200] If a *Tarasoff*-type obligation is widely recognized[201] and adhered to seriously, we may experience a particularly unusual process where a *rule of law* prompts a paradigmatic (or at least a pragmatic) shift in the treatment of interpersonal violence from an intrapsychic model to a model more interactionist in perspective. Perhaps more precisely, *Tarasoff* may lead mental health professionals to practice the paradigm currently resisted but already accepted and preached by the bulk of the scientific and clinical literature. In terms of its overall impact, then, *Tarasoff* may help rather than hinder therapy, and may well constitute a major victimological victory.[202]

NOTES

[1]17 Cal. 3d 425,551 P.2d 334, 131 Cal. Rptr. 14 (1976) (*Tarasoff II*), *vacating* 13 Cal. 3d 117, 529 P.2d 553, 118 Cal. Rptr. 129 (1974) (*Tarasoff I*).

[2]*See* references in note 1 *supra*. Following the first *Tarasoff* decision, the American Psychiatric Association and several local associations of psychotherapists filed a brief

amici curiae successfully urging the California court to rehear the case. On rehearing, however, the court largely reaffirmed its decision with respect to the responsibilities of psychotherapists.

³17 Cal. 3d at 431, 551 P.2d at 340, 131 Cal. Rptr. at 20.

⁴*Id.*

⁵17 Cal. 3d at 439, 551 P.2d at 345, 131 Cal. Rptr. at 25.

⁶*See particularly id.* at n.11: "Defendant therapists and amicus also argue that warnings must be given only in those cases in which the therapist knows the identity of the victim. We recognize that in some cases it would be unreasonable to require the therapist to interrogate his patient to discover the victim's identity, or to conduct an independent investigation. But there may also be cases in which a moment's reflection will reveal the victim's identity. The matter thus is one which depends upon the circumstances of each case, and should not be governed by any hard and fast rule."

⁷*Tarasoff I* was in fact cast specifically in terms of a duty to warn. *Tarasoff II*, however, following a pattern more in keeping with typical concepts of tort law, spoke in terms of a general—and more flexible—duty of due care. Even under *Tarasoff II*, though, it is likely that therapists will seek to comply with the case by warning the victim rather than by resorting to other possible avenues of protecting the victim (increasing the patient's medication, etc.). Roth & Meisel, *Dangerousness, Confidentiality, and the Duty to Warn*, 134 AMER. J. PSYCHIATRY 508, 509 (1977); Note, *Where the Public Peril Begins: A Survey of Psychotherapists to Determine the Effects of* Tarasoff, 31 STANFORD L. REV. 165 (1978) (hereinafter cited as Stanford Law Review Note).

⁸Brief Amicus Curiae of the American Psychiatric Association *et al.* at 5 (filed on 1/7/1974 in response to *Tarasoff I*).

⁹*E.g.*, Cocozza & Steadman, *The Failure of Psychiatric Predictions of Dangerousness: Clear and Convincing Evidence*, 29 RUTGERS L. REV. 1048 (1976). Research is lacking, however, regarding the capabilities of psychotherapists to predict violence in short-range, emergency situations. Monahan, *Strategies for an Empirical Analysis of the Prediction of Violence in Emergency Civil Commitment*, 1 LAW AND HUMAN BEHAVIOR 363 (1977). If what is at stake in predicting violence is not the deprivation of a patient's liberty, but only the warning of a potential victim, perhaps a lower threshold probability of violence will suffice to trigger a therapist's obligation to warn. At the same time, it is obvious that the lower the threshold probability of violence, the easier it is for therapists accurately to predict that low-level probability. On a closely related matter, *see* Chapter 3, this volume.

¹⁰*E.g.*, Stone, *The* Tarasoff *Decisions: Suing Psychotherapists to Safeguard Society*, 90 HARVARD L. REV. 358 (1976); Gurevitz, Tarasoff: *Protective Privilege Versus Public Peril*, 134 AMER. J. PSYCHIATRY 289 (1977); Brief Amicus Curiae of the American Psychiatric Association *et al.*, *supra* note 8.

¹¹*Supra* note 10.

¹²*Id.* at 368.

¹³*Id.*

¹⁴*Id.* at 369.

¹⁵*Id.*

¹⁶*Id.*

¹⁷*Id.*

¹⁸*Id.*

¹⁹R. MOWAT, MORBID JEALOUSY AND MURDER 21 (1966).

²⁰Stone, *supra* note 10, at 371.

²¹*Id.* at 374–375.

²²*Id.* at 375.

[23] *See* notes 48–62 *infra* and accompanying text.

[24] If a therapist acts to trigger commitment, that action will satisfy the legal obligation. If a therapist takes no action, that would presumably buttress the therapist's assertion that he or she did not in fact regard the patient as dangerous, in which case the therapist would, under Stone's proposal, be under no legal duty to take action.

[25] As applied to violent behavior, the "individual pathology" model seems to assume that a patient, because of passion or paranoia, is likely to be violent to another, and that the proper path to recovery lies in a series of one-to-one confidential sessions with a skilled psychotherapist in whom the patient places complete trust.

[26] *See* section on therapeutic implications (p. 167) in this chapter.

[27] Of course, most violence, whether between intimates or not, is not *therapeutically preventable* for the obvious reason that the great bulk of potentially violent persons do not participate in therapy. Tardiff, *A Survey of Psychiatrists in Boston and Their Work with Violent Patients*, 131 AMER. J. PSYCHIATRY 1008, 1009–1010 (1974) (few persons from high-crime areas seen as patients). *See also* J. MACDONALD, HOMICIDAL THREATS 12–13 (1968) (most homicide offenders are young, black males). MacDonald's book is largely a synthesis of two previously published articles: MacDonald, *The Threat to Kill*, 120 AMER. J. PSYCHIATRY 125 (1963); MacDonald, *Homicidal Threats*, 124 AMER. J. PSYCHIATRY 475 (1967). Future references to MacDonald pertain to his book rather than to the articles.

[28] *See* section on therapeutic implications (p. 167) in this chapter.

[29] *Id.*

[30] I surely do not wish to minimize *Tarasoff's* potential detrimental impact, much of which is detailed in Justice Clark's dissenting opinion in *Tarasoff*. Therapists, for example, are rather poor predictors of violence and, even without the added impetus provided by *Tarasoff*, are likely to overpredict dangerousness. Therapists, too, may be placed in an anxious situation where they fear liability for breach of confidentiality if they disclose a patient's threat, and where they fear *Tarasoff*-type liability if they fail to disclose the threat. And although a failure to disclose is technically supposed to be measured by what was "reasonable" professional behavior at the time the threat was made, therapists are understandably fearful of juror use of hindsight in finding therapist negligence. *See generally* Fischhoff, *Hindsight ≠ Foresight: The Effect of Outcome Knowledge on Judgment Under Uncertainty*, 1 J. EXP. PSYCH.: HUMAN PERCEPTION AND PERFORMANCE 228 (1975). Further, patients may terminate treatment if and when they learn of an unconsented-to breach of confidentiality. Indeed, to the extent patients or would-be patients know of the limits on confidentiality, they may avoid disclosure of sensitive topics or may even avoid therapy altogether.

Whether therapists ought to inform patients of the limits on confidentiality is an emerging, hotly contested question. If the operative test is what the professionals themselves regard as reasonable behavior, the failure so to inform patients would seemingly not constitute negligence. See Stanford Law Review Note, *supra* note 7 (California practitioners typically do not discuss such matters with their patients, even though the patients seemingly assume incorrectly that confidentiality is absolute). If, however, a therapist is mandated by tort law principles to disclose risks that a patient would regard as "material" to the patient's decision to accept or to forego therapy, a more compelling case can be made for requiring therapists to disclose the limits of confidentiality. *Cobbs* v. *Grant*, 8 Cal. 3d 229, 502 P.2d 1, 104 Cal. Rptr. 505 (1972). It is unclear, though, whether a doctrine such as *Cobbs* v. *Grant*, which now conceptualizes informed consent in terms of negligence rather than in terms of battery, will be readily applied to cover a class of professionals, such as psychotherapists, who were never really jeopardized by the law of battery.

[31]The relative reluctance of psychiatrists to treat violent-prone persons according to a paradigm that centers on troubled interpersonal relationships is documented in Tardiff, *supra* note 27, at 1010–1011. Indeed, family therapy in general is practiced by only a rather small proportion of therapists. Marcus, *The Benefits of an Incomplete Education (A Sketch of Salvador Minuchin)*, PSYCHOLOGY TODAY (January, 1977) at 68; Stanton, *Psychology and Family Therapy*, PROFESSIONAL PSYCHOLOGY (February, 1975) at 45 (psychologists have curiously not played a major role in family therapy).

[32]Relevant disciplines include criminology, sociology, psychology, psychiatry, speech communication, etc.

[33]Although victimology has been defined as "the study of the criminal– victim relation," R. GELLES, THE VIOLENT HOME: A STUDY OF PHYSICAL AGGRESSION BETWEEN HUSBANDS AND WIVES 156 (1972), and although the study of the offender–victim relationship clearly constitutes the core of much interesting victimological work, the dimensions of the discipline are actually considerably broader than that. For a broader focus, *see generally* Wolfgang & Singer, *Victim Categories of Crime*, 69 J. CRIM. LAW CRIMINOL. 379 (1978). The discipline, which from its inception captured the interest of a number of scholars internationally, now boasts its own journal entitled VICTIMOLOGY: AN INTERNATIONAL JOURNAL.

[34]Stone, *supra* note 10, at 368–369.

[35]The only genuine empirical study to be conducted post-*Tarasoff* is the Stanford Law Review Note, *supra* note 7, and that survey relates only to therapists, not to their patients.

[36]MACDONALD, *supra* note 27; Skodol & Karusu, *Emergency Psychiatry and the Assaultive Patient*, 135 AMER. J. PSYCHIATRY 202 (1978). *See also* Lion, Bach-Y-Rita, & Ervin, *Violent Patients in the Emergency Room*, 125 AMER. J. PSYCHIATRY 1706 (1969).

[37]Skodol & Karusu, *supra* note 36, at 203.

[38]*Id.*

[39]*Id.*

[40]MACDONALD, *supra* note 27. Actually, MacDonald studied two separate groups of "homicidal threat" patients, each group consisting of 100 members. His study embraced 100 such patients admitted to a psychiatric facility in 1961–62 and another 100 patients admitted in 1966–67. MacDonald himself interviewed all patients in the 1966–67 group, but he did not personally interview each member of the 1961–62 group. *Id.* at 31.

[41]*Id.* at 26, 32.

[42]*Id.* at 32. Of the psychotic patients, all but 2 were schizophrenic. *Id.*

[43]*Id.* at 32–33. Of the total admissions, 70% constituted character or personality disorders. *Id.* at 33. The precise diagnostic breakdown is as follows (*id.*):

Schizophrenia	21
Chronic Brain Syndrome	1
Acute Brain Syndrome	1
Passive-aggressive personality	31
Sociopathic personality	30
Hysterical personality	5
Obsessional personality	2
Borderline character	2
Neurotic depression	1
Adjustment reaction of adolescence	6
	100

[44]*Id.* at 32. In 1961–62, however, 44 of the 100 had been committed. *Id.* at 26. There are certain other interesting differences between the earlier and the later group. In 1966–67, 87 were males and only 13 were females, *id.* at 32, whereas in 1961–62, nearly half (45%)

were females. *Id.* at 26. Further, in 1961-62, although a majority of the patients were nonpsychotic (52%), and 48% had character disorders, there was a considerably larger number of psychotic patients (48%) than in 1966-67. *Id.*

[45]Rosenhan, *On Being Sane in Insane Places*, 179 SCIENCE 250 (1973), *reprinted in* 13 SANTA CLARA LAWYER 379 (1973).

[46]The "typical *Tarasoff*" situation may occur with some frequency. Stone, *supra* note 10, at 369 n.52 ("violent thoughts and ideas are not uncommon among patients coming to psychotherapy").

[47]Arison, *Victims of Homicide*, in 4 VICTIMOLOGY: A NEW FOCUS 55, 62 (I. Drapkin & E. Viano eds. 1975) (Scottish study). (Volume 4 of this multivolume victimology set, carrying papers presented at the first International Symposium on Victimology and held in Jerusalem in 1973, is devoted to the topic of "Violence and its Victims.")

[48]Commentators have urged that a major mental illness should constitutionally be required for commitment under the paternalistic or the police power of the state. Note, *Developments in the Law—Civil Commitment of the Mentally Ill*, 87 HARVARD L. R. 1190 (1974). As a matter of policy, too, it seems wise to invoke the public mental health system only when serious mental disorder is at issue. When state statutes define "mental disorder," as does the Arizona statute (ARIZ. REV. STAT. § 36-501 (18)), as "a substantial disorder of the person's emotional processes, thought, cognition or memory," such a definition translates in practice to the rough equivalent of psychosis. *See* Chapter 6, this volume. *See also* A. STONE, MENTAL HEALTH AND LAW: A SYSTEM IN TRANSITION 66 (1975).

[49]And, of course, Stone's alternative suggestion of alerting the police, Stone, *supra* note 10, at 374, would be equally empty if the patient has not assaulted or personally threatened the proposed victim but has only disclosed to the therapist an intention to harm a specified individual. Of course, despite the unavailability of commitment, many patients may be persuaded to sign themselves into a hospital voluntarily. If that is true, however, therapists should not in those cases fear *Tarasoff*. In any case, less liberty-sacrificing therapeutic measures seem generally to be both available and more efficacious than hospitalization. *See* notes 174-182 *infra* and accompanying text.

[50]A. STONE, *supra* note 48.

[51]*Id.* at 66. The Arizona commitment statute specifically excludes from its definition of "mental disorder" conditions relating primarily to alcoholism and "character and personality disorders characterized by lifelong and deeply ingrained antisocial behavior patterns." ARIZ. REV. STAT. § 36-501 (18) (c).

[52]A. STONE, *supra* note 48, at 66-70.

[53]Those other elements include a finding of major distress and a determination whether a reasonable person might reject the proffered treatment. *Id.* at 67.

[54]*Id.* at 67-69.

[55]*Id.* at 67-68.

[56]*Id.* at 69.

[57]*Id.*

[58]*Id.* at 36.

[59]*Id.*

[60]*Id.* at 37.

[61]*Id.* at 47-48. In his *Harvard Law Review* article, Stone sometimes asserts that emergency commitment, rather than long-term commitment, is what he has in mind for dealing with dangerous patients. Stone, *supra* note 10, at 374. In his monograph, however, Stone criticizes even the emergency commitment system for its failure to embrace his suggested model (severe mental illness entailing incapacity, etc.) A. STONE, *supra* note 48, at 47-48.

[62]*See* section on therapeutic implications (p. 167) of this chapter.

[63]Lion, *Developing a Violence Clinic,* in VIOLENCE AND VICTIMS 71, 72(S. Pasternack ed. 1975).

[64]Lion, Bach-Y-Rita, & Ervin, *supra* note 36.

[65]See notes 4–6 *supra* and accompanying text.

[66]Lion, *supra* note 63, at 72.

[67]*Id.* at 72–73.

[68]Lion, Bach-Y-Rita, & Ervin, *supra* note 36.

[69]Therapeutic action in such cases might involve prescribing or increasing medication, continuing outpatient therapy, recommending hospitalization, or, if legally available, *see* pp. 160–162 *supra,* triggering commitment. *See generally* Comment, *A Therapist's Duty to Potential Victims: A Nonthreatening View of Tarasoff,* 1 LAW AND HUMAN BEH. 309 (1977).

[70]Stone, *supra* note 10, at 369.

[71]*Id.*

[72]National (U.S.) Commission on the Causes and Prevention of Violence, *To Establish Justice, To Insure Domestic Tranquility* 25 (1969) (victim-offender survey conducted by the Commission reveals that, when the relationship between the offender and the victim is known, two-thirds to three-fourths of homicides and assaults occur between relatives, friends, or acquaintances); Svalastoga, *Homicide and Social Contact in Denmark,* 62 AMER. J. Soc. 37 (1956); Horoszowski, *Homicide of Passion and its Motives,* in 4 VICTIMOLOGY: A NEW FOCUS 3 (I. Drapkin & E. Viano eds. 1975) (Polish study); Sessar, *The Familiar Character of Criminal Homicide,* in *id.* at 29 (German study).

[73]Goode, *Violence Among Intimates,* in D. MULVIHILL & M. TUMIN, CRIMES OF VIOLENCE 941, 954 (1969) (volume 13 of a staff report to the National Commission on the Causes and Prevention of Violence).

[74]*Id.*

[75]Lanzkron, *Murder and Insanity: A Survey,* 19 AMER. J. PSYCHIATRY 754, 755–756 (1963).

[76]Lion, Bach-Y-Rita, & Ervin, *supra* note 36, at 1708.

[77]Skodol & Karusu, *supra* note 36.

[78]*Id.* at 203.

[79]*Id.*

[80]*Id.*

[81]*Id.*

[82]MACDONALD, *supra* note 27.

[83]*Id.* at 43.

[84]Stone, *supra* note 10, at 369.

[85]*Id.*

[86]Over half of the intrafamily threats in MacDonald's study involved a spouse threatening his or her spouse. MACDONALD, *supra* note 27, at 43. Fifteen percent of the intrafamily threats involved parents threatening children. MacDonald does not indicate the ages of the children victims. To the extent that the children are themselves adults, as they were in Lanzkron's Matteawan study, *supra* note 75, at 755 (1.9% of the homicide victims were adult children; no young children appeared to be involved), they may of course be suitable subjects for participation in family therapy. Adolescents, too, might profitably participate in family therapy. *Cf.* J. HALEY & L. HOFFMAN, TECHNIQUES OF FAMILY THERAPY 265–289 (1967); Patterson, *The Aggressive Child: Victim and Architect of a Coercive System,* in BEHAVIOR MODIFICATION WITH FAMILIES 267 (E. Mash, L. Hamerlynck, & E. Handy eds. 1976); Harbin, *Episodic Dyscontrol and Family Dynamics,* 134 AMER. J. PSYCHIATRY 1113 (1977) (the adolescents in the above cited studies, however, were aggressors or threateners, not victims). *See also* MACDONALD, *supra* note 27, at 33 (6% of MacDonald's homicidal threat patients suffered from "adolescent adjustment reaction").

Only if the threatened victims were infants or very young children would their involvement in family therapy be unsuitable. Moreover, threats directed at infants and young children can, under *Tarasoff*, pose ticklish problems for therapists. Warning the victim would obviously be inappropriate and ineffective. If the parent-patient does not suffer from a serious mental illness, commitment should be technically unavailable. *See* pp. 160–162 *supra*. Perhaps the appropriate action, if any is required, is to contact the police or a child protective service agency. Fortunately, however, to the extent that our concern is with a parent-patient who seeks therapy because of fear that loss of control will lead to injury to his or her young child, coercive action may be unnecessary. Some mental health professionals, *see* J. Lieb, I. Lipsitch, & A. Slaby, The Crisis Team: A Handbook for the Mental Health Professional 66 (1973), have summed up the matter as follows:

> Homicidal ideation of an obsessive nature is common, particularly in mothers who fear that they might harm their children. If the patient denies a conscious wish to harm the children, is very anxious about her thoughts, has good impulse control—and if there is evidence of an underlying obsessive-compulsive character disorder identifiable through undoing, reaction formation, rationalization, denial and displacement—then there is generally no need to be concerned about homicidal potential, and this should be communicated to her.

It may just be, therefore, that those voluntary patients who fear killing their young children predictably *do not* kill their children, so that *Tarasoff* ought not to require a therapist confronted with such a situation to take drastic action. Perhaps those persons who *do* kill their young children are persons who do not fear losing control and who do not seek therapy. With or without *Tarasoff*, therefore, *those* deaths would not be therapeutically preventable. *See* note 27 *supra* (discussing therapeutically preventable violence).

[87]With varying degrees of success, recent attempts have been made to categorize and even to diagram various offender–victim relationships. Simon, *Type A, AB, B Murderers: Their Relationship to the Victims and to the Criminal Justice System*, 5 Bull. Amer. Acad. Psychiatry and the Law 344 (1977); Weber, *On the Psychodiagnosis of the Offender–Victim Relationship: An Approach to the Quantifying Description*, in 1 Victimology: A New Focus 155 I. Drapkin & E. Viano eds. 1974) (volume 1 of this multivolume work relates to "Theoretical Issues in Victimology").

Some investigators and theoreticians have broadened the discussion beyond the offender–victim "dyad" and have studied as well the role of the bystander in promoting or inhibiting altercations and assaults. Sheleff, *The Criminal Triad: Bystander, Victim, and Criminal*, in *id.* at 111. If an "involved" bystander is closely associated with the "penal couple," as seems often to be the case, *id.* at 111–112, there are implications flowing from that fact for family-type therapy. *See* pp. 167–174, this chapter.

[88]Wolfgang, *Victim Precipitated Criminal Homicide*, 48 J. Crim. Law, Criminology, and Police Science 1, 11 (1957).

[89]R. Gelles, *supra* note 33.

[90]Anttila, *Victimology: A New Territory in Criminology*, in 1 Victimology: A New Focus 5, 6 (I. Drapkin & E. Viano eds. 1974).

[91]*E.g.*, Wolfgang, *supra* note 88; R. Gelles, *supra* note 33. *See also* Silverman, *Victim Precipitation: An Examination of the Concept*, in 1 Victimology: A New Focus 99 (I. Drapkin & E. Viano eds. 1974).

[92]On narrow versus broad definitions of victim contribution, *see* Silverman, *supra* note 91. *See also* Arison, *supra* note 47, at 58. When stretched to its broadest, the concept would view *every* victim as a contributor simply because the existence of a victim is by definition a necessary condition for the occurrence of given crimes (assault, homicide, rob-

bery, rape etc.). Silverman, *supra* note 91, at 101. Stretching the coverage of victim contribution to that extent, however, would render the concept meaningless. On the methodological advantages of narrow definitions, *see id.* at 102–103.

[93]Wolfgang, *supra* note 88.

[94]*Id.* at 2.

[95]*Id.* at 4.

[96]Silverman, *supra* note 91, at 102 (referring to a Chicago study). *See also* MacDonald, *supra* note 27, at 44 (referring to Baltimore study which, under Wolfgang's narrow definition, revealed that 32% of homicides were victim precipitated).

[97]Wolfgang, *Suicide by Means of Victim-Precipitated Homicide*, 20 J. Clin. Exp. Psychopathol. 335, 344 (1959) (data derived from Table V: of 47 husbands killed, 28 of them—or 60%—precipitated their own killing). When wives were killed, there was, as expected, a much lower proportion (approximately 10%) of victim precipitation under the narrow definition. *Id.* Under a broader definition, however, the amount of victim precipitation may be considerable. *See* note 103 *infra* and accompanying text.

[98]Wolfgang, *supra* note 88, at 2. Note that what Wolfgang *does* view as victim precipitation is roughly the equivalent of what the law of homicide views as sufficient provocation to reduce murder to manslaughter. *Id.*

[99]"If he [Wolfgang] had been able to include serious psychological provocation, the percentage of victim-precipitated cases would undoubtedly have been considerably higher." Palmer, *Family Members as Murder Victims*, in Violence in the Family 91, 93 (S. Steinmetz & M. Straus eds. 1974).

[100]Silverman, *supra* note 91, at 103.

[101]Arison, *supra* note 47, at 64.

[102]R. Gelles, *supra* note 33, at 155.

[103]*Id.* at 156.

[104]Goode, *supra* note 73, at 955, 960.

[105]Arison, *supra* note 47, at 65. In fact, "not uncommonly, victim and offender were taken to the same hospital, where one remained to be autopsied and the other transferred to a police station after treatment." *Id. See also* Wolfgang, *supra* note 88, at 11: "In many cases the victim has most of the major characteristics of an offender; in some cases two potential offenders come together in a homicide situation and it is probably often only chance which results in one becoming a victim and the other an offender."

[106]*Id.*

[107]*Id.* at 9–10.

[108]*Id.* at 10. In fact, although the difference falls short of statistical significance, Wolfgang found that in victim-precipitated homicides, the victim was more likely than the offender to have a previous arrest record. *Id.* at 9.

[109]*Id.* at 8–9.

[110]*Id.* at 9.

[111]Herjanic & Meyer, *Psychiatric Illness in Homicide Victims*, 133 Amer. J. Psychiatry 691 (1976). Indeed, since the study ignored the question of victims who went untreated or who were treated in private settings, *id.* at 693, the amount of psychiatric illness in homicide victims (and, of course, in others in the community) may have been underestimated.

[112]*Id.* at 692 (34% were alcoholic).

[113]*Id.* (22% were sociopaths). The high proportion of sociopaths seconds Wolfgang's assertion, *see* notes 106–108 *supra* and accompanying text, that many victims are far from innocent, passive persons who happen to stray into an assaultive setting.

In the Herjanic and Meyer study, *supra* note 111, although it was found that "fewer victims with a history of psychiatric care had been killed by members of their own family and more were killed on the street or in their cars than victims without previous psychiatric treatment," *id.* at 693, the authors admonish that "in view of the small numbers in each subgroup and the low levels of significance obtained," those patterns "should be viewed as trends at best." *Id.*

[114]Wolfgang, *supra* note 97. A vivid illustration of a likely suicide masquerading as an instance of victim-precipitated homicide is portrayed in MACDONALD, *supra* note 27, at 6–7.

[115]*Id.* at 44–48.

[116]Shepherd, *Morbid Jealousy: Some Clinical and Social Aspects of a Psychiatric Symptom,* 107 J. MENTAL SCI. 687, 698 (1961) (spouse of a patient suffering from morbid jealousy may exacerbate the situation by feigning indifference or by deliberate provocation), *cited by* Stone, *supra* note 10, at 371 n.57; Lion, Bach-Y-Rita, & Ervin, *supra* note 36, at 1708 (masochistic traits of victims), *cited by* Stone, *supra* note 10, at 369 n.48. *See also* Lion, *supra* note 63, at 72, where Dr. Lion concludes that "the sadomasochistic interaction of patient and victim are obvious and the pathological and provocative role of the victim is also apparent."

[117]*See* sources cited in note 116 *supra.* The American Psychiatric Association admitted as much in its *Tarasoff* amicus brief. *See* Brief, *supra* note 8, at 13 n.6: "In the vast majority of violent crimes, the victim plays an active role in provoking the violence, normally during the course of a complex, mutually frustrating relationship with the perpetrator." *See also id.* at 23: "Very often, the threatened person will be one deeply involved in a psychologically unhealthy relationship with the patient."

[118]D. MARTIN, BATTERED WIVES 156 (1977).

[119]*See* Anttila, *supra* note 90, at 6:

> This reorientation—deliberately exaggerated here—has also influenced policy-making. In earlier times, the emphasis was on deterrence designed to influence the motivation of potential criminals: the threat of punishment and the risk of getting caught were considered the primary means of preventing crime. Victim-centered research has pointed to new alternatives. Once the stereotype of the innocent and unsuspecting victim has proved to be false, it has seemed natural to plan measures that are supposed to change the behavior of the victims, rather than that of the offenders.

[120]*Preface* to 1 VICTIMOLOGY: A NEW FOCUS xv (I. Drapkin & E. Viano eds. 1974) (remarks of Professor Israel Drapkin).

[121]R. GELLES, *supra* note 33, puts one of the dangers well: "Wives often accept being struck. They feel that they deserved to be hit because they precipitated the attack by badgering or nagging their husbands. *Victim-precipitated violence often is normalized by the wife, who states that because she caused it, she deserved to be hit.*" *Id.* at 59 (emphasis supplied).

[122]Gobert, *Victim Precipitation,* 77 COLUM. L. R. 511 (1977).

[123]Bein, *The Impact of the Victim's Behavior on the Severity of the Offender's Sentence (With Special Reference to Israeli Law),* in 3 VICTIMOLOGY: A NEW FOCUS 49 (I. Drapkin & E. Viano eds. 1975) (volume 3 of this multivolume work is devoted to "Crimes, Victims, and Justice").

[124]R. GELLES, *supra* note 33, at 156. Recall that even under Wolfgang's restrictive definition, 60% of husbands killed by their wives had precipitated their own demise. *See* note 97 *supra.* Consequently, Wolfgang recommends that when a woman kills a man, and particularly when a wife kills her husband, the police investigate carefully the possibility of provocation. Wolfgang, *supra* note 88, at 86.

[125]Comment, *Battered Wives Who Kill: Double Standard Out of Court, Single Standard In?,* 2 LAW AND HUMAN BEH. 133 (1978).

[126]Ultimately, however, a victimological perspective will raise controversial questions even in mental health law. In the area of mental health law, where interpersonal tensions and frictions frequently lead to the emotional distress or commitment of one of the partners, commitment courts are not presently authorized to require the nonpatient partner to submit to counseling or to cooperate in the recovery of the patient. Will a growing acceptance of the victimological perspective lead to pressure on the legal system to depart from its present restrictive posture? *See* Chapter 2, this volume.

[127]Herjanic & Meyer, *supra* note 111.

[128]Wolfgang, *supra* note 88, at 8–9.

[129]Wolfgang, *supra* note 97. *See also* MacDonald, *supra* note 27, at 6–7.

[130]*See* notes 105–108 *supra* and accompanying text.

[131]*See* J. Lieb, I. Lipsitch, & A. Slaby, *supra* note 86, at 65: "At times an assault is brought on in an overt or more often covert way by the victim; the concept of the role of victims in inviting assault suggests a new approach to violence which may prove fruitful in the management and prevention of assaultive behavior." Note that the potential victim also serves to profit from an alteration in behavior, for the available evidence indicates that in those cases where a patient who threatens violence against a particular victim ultimately turns to homicide, the person killed is likely to be the person previously threatened. MacDonald, *supra* note 27, at 29.

[132]J. Haley, Uncommon Therapy: The Psychiatric Techniques of Milton H. Erickson, M.D. 240 (1973). In such cases, Erickson finds it necessary to see the spouses *together*. Conjoint sessions enable the couple to get a handle on how the alcohol-inducing spouse will attempt to change and will allow the alcohol-consuming "patient" to monitor whether the other party is in fact changing. *Id.*

[133]Lion, Bach-Y-Rita, & Ervin, *supra* note 36, at 1708 ("it was just as necessary a therapeutic maneuver to instruct the spouse to contact us as it was to teach the patient to come to the hospital when he felt anxious or impulsive"); Harbin, *supra* note 86, at 1115 (even in the face of episodic dyscontrol fostered by organicity, "one of the most immediate and primary interventions that a therapist should make with these families is to clarify and systemitize the steps to be taken if another violent episode occurs").

[134]In one instance reported by MacDonald, for example, "whenever [a violence-prone] husband announced his intention of selling the shotgun, his [victimized] wife would insist on his keeping it." MacDonald, *supra* note 27, at 47. Therapists of violent patients typically advise such patients to sell their firearms. *Id.* at 69, 107. In the type of situation presented above, however, a therapist could be helpful indeed in persuading the victim to acquiesce in the patient's sale of the weapon.

[135]*E.g.,* J. Haley & L. Hoffman, *supra* note 86, at 265–289 (cooperation of F, the father-victim, was seen as essential to a family therapist seeking to terminate the violent behavior of S, a 17-year-old boy against F; seemingly, S and M, his mother, were actually allied in having S take out, against F, their collective hostilities); Harbin, *supra* note 86, at 1115 ("seizures... are triggered by emotional conflicts and stress and... everyone in the family can work on coping with this stress in ways that will decrease the likelihood of a violent episode").

[136]S. Minuchin, Families and Family Therapy (1974); Changing Families: A Family Therapy Reader (J. Haley ed. 1971). Minuchin, *supra* at 7, even discusses how the presence or absence of a third-party family member can arouse other family members in a manner measurable biochemically by the concentration of free fatty acids in the body. Minuchin, therefore, provides some biochemical evidence of the role of what Sheleff, *supra* note 87, terms the "involved bystander." For a behavioral explanation of a similar phenomenon, *see* Patterson, *supra* note 86, at 273.

[137]E.g., J. HALEY, supra note 132 (discussing Milton Erickson's techniques); G. BACH & P. WYDEN, THE INTIMATE ENEMY: HOW TO FIGHT FAIR IN LOVE AND MARRIAGE (1969); Pittman, Langsley, Kaplan, Flomenhaft, & De Young, Family Therapy as an Alternative to Psychiatric Hospitalization, in FAMILY STRUCTURE, DYNAMICS AND THERAPY 188 (I. Cohen ed. 1966) (hereinafter cited as Pittman et al).

[138]J. Haley, supra note 132, at 249 (discussing Erickson); Pittman et al., supra note 137, at 190; Grosser & Paul, Ethical Issues in Family Group Therapy, 34 AM. J. ORTHOPSYCHIATRY 875 (1964).

[139]C. Sager, MARRIAGE CONTRACTS AND COUPLE THERAPY: HIDDEN FORCES IN INTIMATE RELATIONSHIPS (1976).

[140]G. BACH & P. WYDEN, supra note 137; D. LANGSLEY & D. KAPLAN, THE TREATMENT OF FAMILIES IN CRISIS 47 (1968); Minuchin, Conflict-Resolution Family Therapy, 28 PSYCHIATRY 278 (1965). See also Goode, supra note 73, at 960–962 (unlike other types of conversations, there are no clear-cut social rules for peacefully terminating an argument; the bedroom is a likely place of violence because neither feuding partner can easily manufacture an adequate excuse to exit or to end the conversation).

[141]Scratton, Violence in the Family, in D. MADDEN & J. LION, RAGE-HATE-ASSAULT AND OTHER FORMS OF VIOLENCE 22, 25 (1976); G. BACH & Y. BERNHARD, AGGRESSION LAB: THE FAIR FIGHT TRAINING MANUAL (1971); G. BACH & P. WYDEN, supra note 137, at 111, 337; Minuchin, supra note 140; Charny, Marital Love and Hate, in VIOLENCE IN THE FAMILY 52 (S. Steinmetz & M. Straus eds. 1974) (discussion by marriage counselor); Sprey, On the Management of Conflict in Families, 33 J. MARRIAGE FAMILY 722 (1971). In an editors' introduction, Steinmetz and Straus, commenting on the work of Sprey and on the work of Bach and Wyden, make the following interesting statement, VIOLENCE IN THE FAMILY, supra, at 49:

> Although the principles set forth in Sprey's article also have not been tested by research, our confidence in both his conclusions and those of Bach and Wyden is strengthened by the convergence of the two articles. Bach and Wyden base their work on clinical experience and theory. Sprey bases his on ethology and sociology. Thus, they draw on very different scientific traditions. Yet they come to some quite similar conclusions, notably an emphasis on learning to fight constructively (which these authors all feel can strengthen a marital relationship) rather than fighting violently and destructively.

[142]R. GELLES, supra note 33, at 165; Gilbert, Self-Disclosure, Intimacy and Communication in Families, THE FAMILY COORDINATOR 221, 224, 226 (July, 1976).

[143]Cohen, Freedman, Englehardt, & Margolis, Family Interaction Patterns, Drug Treatment, and Change in Social Aggression, 19 ARCH. GEN. PSYCHIATRY 50 (1958) (hereinafter cited as Cohen et al.). See also Pittman et al., supra note 137.

[144]Harbin, supra note 86.

[145]Cohen et al., supra note 143.

[146]Id. Note that chemotherapy may be warranted even for family members other than the "presenting" or "identified" patient. Pittmen et al., supra note 137, at 189.

[147]Harbin, supra note 86. On the possible relationship between violence and brain damage, see V. MARK & F. ERVIN, VIOLENCE AND THE BRAIN (1970). See generally Chapter 8, this volume.

[148]Harbin, supra note 86, at 1115.

[149]A. BANDURA, AGGRESSION: A SOCIAL LEARNING ANALYSIS 245 (1973) ("since aggression is largely under situational, cognitive, and reinforcement control, these are the events to which treatment addresses itself, rather than to traits, to presumptive drive forces, or to historical causes"); Patterson, supra note 86, at 273; Patterson & Cobb, A Dyadic Analysis

of "Aggressive" Behavior, in 5 MINNESOTA SYMPOSIA ON CHILD PSYCHOLOGY 72 (J. Hill ed. 1971) ("the victim's behavior provides the cues which produce the attack and, paradoxically, also the reinforcer which increases the probability that in the future he will be assaulted again"). Note that Patterson and Cobb explain even the *victim* role in terms of behaviorist principles.

150BANDURA, *supra* note 149, at 246, has said that "the most fundamental and enduring changes in aggression are accomplished by altering the social instigators and reinforcement practices prevailing in the deviant subculture." Accordingly, drawing upon that notion, Dr. Bandura, *id.* at 247, is able to provide some guidance as to who should participate in therapy: "The most effective treatments are generally carried out under close professional supervision by persons who have intensive contact with the aggressor and can therefore serve as powerful change agents." *See also* Patterson, *supra* note 86, at 291 (advantages of teaching "parenting skills" to parent-victims of aggressive boys and adolescent males); Benassi & Larson, *Modification of Family Interaction with the Child as the Behavior Change Agent,* in BEHAVIOR MODIFICATION AND FAMILIES 331 (E. Mash, L. Hamerlynck, & L. Handy eds. 1976) (child as change agent); Greer & D'Zurilla, *Behavioral Approaches to Marital Discord and Conflict,* in 4 ANN. REV. BEH. THERAPY: THEORY AND PRACTICE 793 (C. Franks & T. Wilson eds. 1976).

Legal analyses of behavior modification have thus far been restricted principally to discussions of the regulation of behavior modification in total institutions. *See* Friedman, *Legal Regulation of Applied Behavior Analysis in Mental Institutions and Prisons,* 17 ARIZ. L. REV. 39 (1975). *See generally* Chapters 9 and 10, this volume.

151Patterson, *supra* note 86, at 287–288.

152Haley, *A Review of the Family Therapy Field,* in CHANGING FAMILIES: A FAMILY THERAPY READER 1, 6 (J. Haley ed. 1971). *See also* Stanton, *supra* note 31, at 45 (family therapy is consistent with behavioral and even psychoanalytic ideologies).

153Pinderhughes, *Managing Paranoia in Violent Relationships,* in PERSPECTIVES ON VIOLENCE 109, 116 (G. Usdin ed. 1972) ("rage reactions with paranoid views and fantasies of violence continued until the paranoid mechanisms of both partners were demonstrated to them in conjoint sessions").

154MACDONALD, *supra* note 27, at 103.

155*Id.* at 97.

156*Supra* note 36.

157Stone, *supra* note 10, at 368. In *id.* at 369 n.48, Stone cites Lion, Bach-Y-Rita, & Ervin, *supra* note 36.

158Lion, Bach-Y-Rita, & Ervin, *supra* note 36, at 1708.

159Stone, *supra* note 10, at 371.

160*Id.* at 371 n.57, *citing* R. MOWAT, *supra* note 19, Lanzkron, *supra* note 75, and Shepherd, *supra* note 116.

161R. MOWAT, *supra* note 19.

162Lanzkron, *supra* note 75.

163Shepherd, *supra* note 116.

164R. MOWAT, *supra* note 19, at 63–64.

165*Id.*

166*Id.* at 80–81.

167*Id.* at 116.

168Lanzkron, *supra* note 75, at 757.

169Shepherd, *supra* note 116, at 698.

170*Id.*

[171]*Id.*

[172]*Id.* at 698–699.

[173]*Id.* at 702. Presumably, since the potential victim is already aware of the patient's anger and accusations, *see text accompanying* note 166 *supra*, it may be easy enough for a therapist to secure the patient's consent to involve the spouse. *See also* J. HALEY, *supra* note 132, at 236 ("When you have a husband and wife who are extremely suspicious as well as angry at one another, you need to see them together") (discussion of Milton Erickson's therapeutic advice).

[174]Pittman *et al, supra* note 137. *See also* J. HALEY & L. HOFFMAN, *supra* note 86, at 361, 362 (published interview with Dr. Pittman).

[175]*Supra* note 137.

[176]*Id.* at 189.

[177]*Id.* at 191.

[178]*Id.*

[179]*Id.* at 190–191.

[180]Tardiff, *supra* note 27, at 1011.

[181]"[I]n light of evidence of the breakdown in close interpersonal relationships between the perpetrator of violence and his victim," *id.*, Tardiff was surprised that family and couple therapy were not more widely practiced in the treatment of violent patients. *Id.* In his survey, however, Tardiff learned that hospitalization of violent patients was overwhelmingly avoided. Eighty-four percent of them were treated as outpatients. *Id.* at 1009.

[182]Stone, *supra* note 10, at 370. Stone's comment was made in connection with the possible adverse impact on patient disclosures of a therapist's admonition to a patient that confidentiality is not absolute. *See discussion in* note 30 *supra*.

[183]Tardiff, *supra* note 27, at 1011. *See also* Stanton, *supra* note 31; Marcus, *supra* note 31, at 69 (published interview with Salvador Minuchin).

[184]Stanford Law Review Note, *supra* note 7; Gurevitz, *The Tarasoff Decision Revisited* (unpublished, unabridged version of a paper later condensed for presentation at the American Psychiatric Association Annual Convention on May 11, 1978); Roth & Meisel, *supra* note 7; Roth, *Clinical and Legal Considerations in the Therapy of Violence-Prone Patients*, in CURRENT PSYCHIATRIC THERAPIES (J. Masserman ed. 1978).

[185]Stanford Law Review Note, *supra* note 7 (most—60%—of the psychotherapists who responded to the Stanford survey regarded themselves as falling within the psychoanalytic tradition, and most respondents viewed the *Tarasoff* decision as unhelpful).

[186]*Id.* In fact, 96.1% of the respondents were familiar with the *Tarasoff* case. It may be, of course, that self-selection factors led those familiar with the case to respond to the survey and led others to disregard (and discard) the survey instrument.

[187]*Id.*

[188]*Id.* Although the percent of respondents reporting that they gave warnings after *Tarasoff* did not vary appreciably from the percent who reported giving pre-*Tarasoff* warnings, the fact that the typical respondent practiced for 13 years before *Tarasoff* and, at the time of the survey, for only *one year* after *Tarasoff*, suggests to me the likelihood of a genuine post-*Tarasoff* increase in the frequency of warning third parties. Surely, that interpretation seems to me more sensible than does the alternative hypercautious conclusion, suggested in the Stanford study, that the recent memory of therapists regarding warning-giving is vivid and that the long-term memory regarding the same is dim.

[189]*Id.*

[190]Brief, *supra* note 8, at 13; MacDonald, *supra* note 27, at 43, 48 (many patients had threatened or assaulted the victim on multiple occasions); Grosser & Paul, *supra* note 138 (family members are typically aware of hostility toward them harbored by other members of the family); Mowat, *supra* note 19, at 80–81; Gurevitz, *supra* note 10, at 290; Gurevitz, *supra* note 184, at 10 (when, post-*Tarasoff*, victims were alerted by therapists of patient threats, the victims typically knew of the threats and often had been previously threatened by the same patient).

Despite the likely knowledge on the part of the victim, a therapist seeking cautiously to comply with *Tarasoff* would be well advised to seek to warn a victim of a patient threat because (1) the therapist might have more complete knowledge or details of the threat than does the victim, and (2) in any event, a warning coming from a *therapist* may be regarded by a victim as important in its own right. *See text accompanying notes 8–10 supra.* Similarly, if a warning is to be given the victim, it ideally should be given by the therapist personally rather than by some other party (the patient, etc.) acting at the therapist's suggestion.

[191]Roth & Meisel, *supra* note 7, at 510, give a case example of securing a patient's consent to warn a potential victim, and note that "in no instance have we directly warned the potential victim without first obtaining the patient's permission." *Id.* Also, *id.*, at 511, "some patients . . . are willing to warn potential victims or permit others to warn them about the patient's fears, anger, and recent turmoil." Consented-to disclosures regarding the patient should be revealed to others while the patient is present. *Id.* In typical *Tarasoff*-type situations, where a therapist is confronted with a voluntary outpatient who is seeking help, a cooperative attitude on the part of the patient should not be at all surprising.

Note that even before *Tarasoff*, a therapist could always have sought (often successfully) to obtain a patient's consent to warn a potential victim. *Tarasoff* may now be inducing therapists to do some things that they could have done, and should have done, but probably were not typically doing, before the *Tarasoff* case was decided.

[192]Note, *Psychotherapists' Liability for Extrajudicial Breaches of Confidentiality*, 18 Ariz. L. Rev. 1061 (1976). Even in the absence of seeking the patient's consent, note that in the typical case, where the victim (ordinarily a relative) seemingly knows the patient is in therapy and knows at least sketchily of the threat, it ought not in any objective sense to be deemed a major breach of confidentiality for a therapist to tell a victim that which the victim more or less already knows. Note, too, that if the victim is someone close to the patient and if a therapist seeks the patient's consent to alert the victim but is unsuccessful in securing consent, the typical reasons for a patient withholding consent are likely to be either that (1) the patient did not really intend to carry out the threat, in which case, if that is the conclusion reached by the therapist, it may be reasonable for the therapy to continue without alerting the victim, or (2) the patient is so intent on executing the threat that he does not want the victim alerted, in which case, if that conclusion is reached by the therapist, *Tarasoff* would clearly require action whether or not the patient consents.

[193]Gurevitz, *supra* note 184, at 10, discusses how, acting post-*Tarasoff* on the advice of counsel to warn threatened victims, the staff of a crisis prevention hotline "learned of the victim's interaction, often of a very provocative nature, in the stimulation and perpetuation of the violent threats." Presumably, pre-*Tarasoff*, the crisis prevention staff lacked contact with potential victims and were unaware of the important role sometimes played by victim precipitation.

[194]*For example:* "True, I (the father and potential victim) never let my 19 year old son X (the

patient) have the car and I often let his twin brother Y take it, but that is because Y always returns home at an appropriate hour, and X usually stays out all night and returns drunk."

[195]Roth & Meisel, *supra* note 7, at 510–511; Roth, *supra* note 184 (other persons, including potential victims, can be brought into the therapy).

[196]Pittman *et al.*, *supra* note 137, at 191. *See also* MacDonald, *supra* note 27, at 103; *sources cited* note 195 *supra*.

[197]*See* note 194 *supra* and accompanying text.

[198]*For example*, "I only kept the car out all night twice, and on both occasions I was agitated because my father had lost all his money gambling and took out his anger by slapping my mother."

[199]T. Kuhn, The Structure of Scientific Revolutions (1962).

[200]Legal scholarship surely follows no more predictable an intellectual path than does scientific scholarship. The progression of my own thinking in connection with the thesis presented here is perhaps illustrative. Initially, I was terribly troubled by *Tarasoff* and by its potential for undermining the therapeutic relationship. As I began to undertake a serious study of the problem, my interest in the case apparently became known to certain members of the psychiatric community. One psychiatrist engaged me in a discussion of available options in dealing with the apparently common type of patient who believes his wife is having several affairs and who warns his therapist that "unless she cuts it out, there's going to be big trouble." Seeking a solution that would satisfy possible *Tarasoff* requirements without violating confidentiality, *see* note 192 *supra* and accompanying text, I inquired of the psychiatrist how such a patient would react if asked, "Mr. P, if you're so agitated about this, what would you think of my calling your wife now, telling her of your agitation, and finding out what she has to say for herself?" When the psychiatrist responded that he thought such a patient would typically consent to having the therapist contact the spouse, our discussion terminated with mutual satisfaction. As I pursued my research, however, that conversation kept reentering— and interrupting—my train of thought. Then, as I reviewed the victimological literature and the literature on marital jealousy, I realized that my proposed "solution," initially devised solely to finesse the legal dilemma, might have been good psychiatry as well as good law. Finally, when I recognized that involvement of the spouse in such a case seemed therapeutically warranted but presumably, at least with traditional practitioners of psychotherapy, would not come about absent the pressure generated by *Tarasoff*, my present thesis reached fruition.

[201]*See* McIntosh v. Milano, 168 N.J. Super. 466, 403 A.2d 500 (1979) (*Tarasoff* rule in New Jersey).

[202]For more on this and on victimology and mental health law generally, *see* Wexler, *Victimology and Mental Health Law: An Agenda*, 66 Va. L. Rev. 681 (1980).

Part Two
LAW AND THERAPY

B. Institutional Therapy

8

Psychosurgery and the
Kaimowitz Case

INTRODUCTION

Though it was argued in the preceding chapter that the *Tarasoff* case may, in the long run, generally enhance therapy, some current critics of the controversial decision believe *Tarasoff* will curtail effective treatment and thus lead to increased violence. Some critics believe, too, that the case will motivate mental health professionals, anxious to protect themselves from *Tarasoff*-type liability, to outdo their previous efforts in overpredicting violence and in triggering the commitment of patients who utter violent threats.

Regardless of the impact of *Tarasoff*, however, therapy with confined patients bristles with legal difficulties regarding the rights of institutionalized patients to receive and to refuse treatment, and the remainder of this book therefore concentrates on the major legal bristles of institutional therapy. In terms of treatment technologies, the biggest bristle of them all is psychosurgery—a highly instrusive but infrequently invoked procedure designed to diminish violent propensities in patients. The present chapter, which deals with psychosurgery and the law, is itself divided into two sections. The first section will lay the factual foundation underlying psychosurgery and other possible legal and medical mechanisms for controlling violent behavior. The foundation is laid principally by a discussion and analysis of the leading book in the field, *Violence and the Brain*, a controversial and provocative work authored by neurologist Vernon Mark and psychiatrist Frank Ervin. The neurological model of violence presented here contrasts rather sharply with the "interpersonal" model and even with the "intrapsychic" model presented in the previous chapter. As the reader progresses through the present chapter, it will become apparent, too, how the neurological model contrasts sharply with a prevalent sociological explanation of deviance as a product of societal labeling. The second section of the present chapter will discuss and analyze the *Kaimowitz* case, the leading judicial decision in the area of psychosurgical procedures.

THE FACTUAL FOUNDATION AND POTENTIAL LEGAL PROBLEMS

Increasingly, profound scientific advances are being received not simply with awe, but also with ambivalence, alarm, and even outright dispair. Concerned reactions are especially prevalent when scientific insights threaten to alter the very nature of our customary beliefs. Developments in behavioral theory are, of course, prime candidates for generating controversy, as evidenced by the stir caused by B. F. Skinner's thesis that freedom and dignity are outmoded and illusory psychological concepts.[1]

Now, scientists are beginning to offer genuine hope that violence, crime, and deviance may be capable of effective control and correction, but their discoveries have led concerned commentators to warn of the coming of the "therapeutic state," where matters of the liberty and treatment of deviants—matters basic to our social and legal order—may be left largely to the almost unchecked discretion of behavioral specialists.[2] These behavioral specialists include sociologists, psychologists, psychiatrists, and, as the book *Violence and the Brain*[3] tells us, an emerging class of neurological experts.

Recent contributions to our understanding of crime and deviance have been overwhelmingly sociological. Much of mainstream sociological thought, however, is not actively concerned with explaining the causes of initial or primary rule-breaking behavior. Instead, much of modern sociology attaches far greater significance to the societal reaction to deviant behavior and to the consequences that follow when an individual has been labeled deviant by society. Principal matters of sociological interest, therefore, include "societal reaction" or "labeling" theory (which concerns itself, for example, with the circumstances under which society will invoke its law enforcement machinery against particular types of deviant conduct) and "secondary" deviance (which includes, for example, the effect that the official labeling processes of arrest and conviction will have on the deviant's self-concept and the extent to which institutionalization and its accompanying social stigma operate to encourage a person to follow a long-range deviant career).[4]

Though labeling theory has been very much in vogue, particularly since the mid-sixties, its popularity has probably now peaked, and, in any event, it never commanded respect from all criminological quarters. Don Gibbons, for example, lamented the fact that the detour from the study of deviance causation has resulted in freezing our etiological knowledge at about the 1950 level.[5] Clearly, one of the most forceful critiques has come from Walter Gove,[6] who condemned the absence of systematic evaluation or empirical verification of labeling theory[7] and then indicated how the existing sparse evidence actually cuts against the importance of secondary deviance.

Focusing particularly on societal reaction theory in the context of mental illness, but with insights at least partly pertinent to deviance in general, Gove suggests that society is actually quite reluctant to confer a deviant label on rule breakers, and even when it does so, the ensuing consequences of institutionalization and social stigma are probably insufficient to induce the labeled individual to assume a permanent deviant role. In any event, Gove concludes that "the societal reaction theorists have generally treated their framework as a sufficient explanatory system. In doing so, they have underemphasized the importance of acts of primary deviance and overemphasized the importance of the forces promoting secondary deviance."[8]

If Gove is calling for a redress of the balance, *Violence and the Brain* by Vernon H. Mark and Frank R. Ervin (respectively a neurosurgeon and a psychiatrist) should provide a powerful jolt to the scales. As its title suggests, the book deals with the "primary" causes of deviant violent behavior, and seeks to attribute much of that behavior to no less "primary" a source than the human brain. Moreover, the Mark and Ervin thesis—that violence is often rooted in structural or functional impairment of the limbic (emotional) region of man's brain—may have considerable sociological as well as biological significance. And the sociological significance is by no means restricted to underscoring the futility of rehabilitating biologically impaired deviants by purely social techniques. Indeed, many possible causes of limbic brain disease (birth injuries, viral infections, severe malnutrition, lack of maternal care,[9] and head injuries resulting from fights and accidents) may well be closely associated with socioeconomic conditions, including poor obstetrical and medical attention. Thus, although Mark and Ervin do not themselves make the point, their work suggests that, in an epidemiological sense, social forces may be vitally important causal factors in violent behavior, though those forces may operate in a manner strikingly different from that assumed by the conventional criminological wisdom.

But the value of *Violence and the Brain* is not that it is masked sociology. Simply stated, the authors' thesis is that the neural mechanism for self-preservation (for "fight or flight" behavior) can be thrown out of kilter by acquired or inherited[10] abnormalities of brain structure or function. The resulting pathology—which is typified by temporal lobe epilepsy and related conditions—leads, in the authors' view, to repeated violent conduct by an appreciable percentage of the fifteen million persons in this country afflicted with obvious or hidden brain disease.

From animal research and clinical work with human patients, various scientists, the authors included, have been able to map out which specific areas of the brain regulate certain types of behavior. Be recording brain wave activity that accompanies pertinent conduct, by observing behavioral changes following surgical removal of portions of the brain, and by inducing changes in conduct by stimulating particular areas of the brain electrically and chemically, investigators are developing what might be termed a science of neurogeography.

Most important for present purposes is that neurologists are now beginning to locate specific portions of the brain which serve as triggers and brakes for violent action. Thus, through brain stimulation, the authors have been able both to initiate and to terminate assaultive behavior in humans. Based on their research and the research of others, Mark and Ervin conclude that abnormal electrical discharges in pertinent regions of the brain produce the same type of violent activity as that produced by artificial stimulation of the brain.

In most cases, limbic brain disease can apparently be controlled by antiseizure medication (such as Dilantin) and other drug combinations. Sometimes, however, surgery is required. The traditional surgical procedure has been lobectomy, the removal of the front portion of the diseased temporal lobe. A more modern technique, however, is stereotactic surgery, which involves, through the use of a surgical drill and other special instruments, implanting electrodes in the brain, determining through stimulation and recording procedures which brain cells are misfiring, and destroying a small number of cells in a precisely determined area by passing a heat-generating current through the appropriate electrode.

Many of the legal implications of the Mark and Ervin book are self-evident. Matters such as the criminal responsibility of persons with limbic brain dysfunction,[11] the possible committability of persons previously thought to be without mental impairment,[12] the right of persons so committed to appropriate treatment,[13] and the question of the right to refuse unwanted treatment,[14] all come readily to mind. The most important of those, the legal issues regarding treatment, are discussed in detail in the second section of this chapter. But other legal and social ramifications may not be quite so apparent. In cases of "hidden" brain disease, for example, Mark and Ervin note that violent or irrational behavior may be the only outward symptom of pathology, particularly when the abnormality is deep within the brain and is beyond detection by X-ray, brain wave examination, and other ordinary neurological diagnostic techniques. To what extent should civil commitment be authorized by a neurological prediction of such "hidden" brain disease?[15] Moreover, although ordinary neurological diagnostic devices are often incapable of confirming deep brain pathology, stereotactic surgical procedures may well lead to the discovery of abnormal electrical activity. To what extent, then, should compulsory stereotactic surgery emerge as an investigative tool in the administration of our mental health laws?[16]

Further, it may not be long before a telemetered device is perfected that will enable clinicians, stationed at great distances from their patients, to record and stimulate points within their patients' brains. By analogy, Dr. Ralph Schwitzgebel has already developed an electronic tracking device which is currently capable of tracking a wearer's location and monitoring his pulse rate within a radius of a few blocks. Present technology could apparently modify the machine to enable it to monitor, and perhaps assist, persons with diabetes, epilepsy, or cardiac conditions.[17] More to the point, perhaps, is that Dr. Jose Delgado has pioneered the clinical use of a "stimoceiver," which enables the brain to be recorded and stimulated from a distance of 100 feet without resort to connecting wires.

If electronic developments eventually permit stimoceivers to function over substantial distances, it is easy to anticipate their practical employment both to record electrical misfirings in the brain and to offset impending violence. Indeed, even with existing technology, Mark and Ervin were able to keep one exceptionally violent patient free from rage for nearly three months by periodically stimulating a relaxation center within his brain.[18] If stimoceivers are further developed, prolonged stimulation, either electrical or chemical, may become a very realistic possibility.[19] They may thus provide an alternative to institutionalization for many persons now housed in our prisons and mental hospitals. Needless to say, however, such a use would usher in a host of knotty legal questions (concerning a range of topics from invasion of privacy to cruel and unusual punishment), most of which have been explored in a legal analysis of Dr. Schwitzgebel's tracking machine.[20]

Of all the possible practical applications of the Mark and Ervin findings, however, the one (apart from psychosurgery) most likely to generate controversy—insofar as it is capable of rapid implementation—deals with the legal and social control of what the authors refer to as "the dyscontrol syndrome." By comparing the social histories and symptoms of a group of patients known to have limbic brain disease, a group of self-referred patients with impulse control complaints, and a group of violent prisoners, the authors found striking similarities of impulse dyscontrol among the three groups.[21] The syndrome is said to consist of four characteristic symptoms, which, however, are not always present:

> (1) a history of physical assault, especially wife and child beating; (2) the symptom of pathological intoxication—that is, drinking even a small amount of alcohol triggers acts of senseless brutality; (3) a history of impulsive sexual behavior, at times including sexual assaults; and (4) a history (in those who drove cars) of many traffic violations and automobile accidents.[22]

Mark and Ervin are not totally alone in their findings. Research by others in analogous areas lends inferential support to their claim. Thus, in an empirical study of serious motoring offenders in Great Britain, T. C. Willett, a British criminologist, shattered the myth that the typical serious motoring offender is an otherwise respectable, middle-class citizen who will not again become involved in a comparable motoring violation.[23] Instead, Willett found that 60% of his sampled offenders came from the manual classes, 23% had additional convictions for nonmotoring offenses (the figure rises to 32% if offenders "known to the police as suspects" are included), and a relatively large number of offenders, having once been found guilty and punished for a serious motoring offense, repeated the same or an equally serious offense.[24] And in this country, research has demonstrated that persons with certain chronic medical conditions, such as epilepsy, are involved in twice the number of accidents per unit of driving exposure as are drivers of like age without those medical conditions.[25]

Societal recognition of a dyscontrol syndrome could lead to widespread changes in policies and procedures regarding enforcement and punishment. Wife beating, for example, traditionally dismissed by the police as a matter of purely domestic concern, could come to be viewed as a serious offense calling for decisive public intervention.[26] Likewise, traffic violators may find themselves subject to considerably more than the traditional slap on the wrist they now receive. Consider, by analogy, Justice Blackmun's stinging language in Tate v. Short,[27] where he concurred in the Court's opinion holding unconstitutional the practice of imprisoning indigents who are unable to pay their fines:

The Court's opinion is couched in terms of being constitutionally protective of the indigent defendant. I merely add the observation that the reversal of this . . . judgment may well encourage state and municipal legislatures to do away with the fine and to have the jail term as the only punishment for a broad range of traffic offenses. Eliminating the fine whenever it is prescribed as alternative punishment avoids the equal protection issue that indigency occasions and leaves only possible Eighth Amendment considerations. If, as a nation, we ever reach that happy point where we are willing to set our personal convenience to one side and we are really serious about resolving the problems of traffic irresponsibility and the frightful carnage it spews upon our highways, a development of that kind may not be at all undesirable.[28]

Thus, in direct contravention to the labeling theorists, who might argue that in many instances "a concerted policy of doing nothing may be more helpful than active intervention, if the long-range goal is to reduce the probability of repetition of the acts,"[29] the dyscontrol syndrome theorists may press for early and swift intervention, even for deviant conduct currently regarded by society as rather innocuous or acceptable. Moreover, since pathology is said to be the root of the difficulty, "special" treatment, perhaps patterned along the lines of indefinite sexual psychopath commitment, may be urged in instances when an offender, because of his social history or abnormal electroencephalogram (EEG) reading, is thought to suffer from a neurological problem of impulse dyscontrol.

With respect to persons convicted of truly violent crimes, some members of the medical profession have already proposed schemes for hinging liberty on EEG results. Dr. William Feeman, Jr., in a published letter to the editor of the *New England Journal of Medicine*, thought for sure he had found the answer: "A person positive for such a criterion [abnormal electrical activity] should be removed from society until the EEG becomes normal after psychiatric therapy. The alternative would be capital punishment for a person whose EEG did not become normal within a given period (such as five years)."[30] Feeman's solution, moreover, trimmed of its capital punishment alternative, was cited as an excellent idea in a syndicated newspaper column written by Dr. Walter Alvarez, emeritus consultant in medicine at the Mayo Clinic and emeritus professor of medicine at the Mayo Foundation.[31] And if an individual with an abnormal EEG has not committed a major violent crime but has instead engaged in a series of other acts (such as wife beating, serious motoring offenses, etc.) indicative of dyscontrol, it is not difficult to anticipate doctors of the Feeman–Alvarez bent proposing, for therapeutic and preventive detention purposes, the indefinite confinement of that type of person as well.

Whatever the precise direction taken by society to control those who assumedly suffer from impulse dyscontrol, it is evident from the developments outlined in *Violence and the Brain* that neurologists will become increasingly familiar faces in legal proceedings relating to crime and mental illness. Moreover, because of its credible stature as a technical biological science, it is likely that neurology will be even more influential with commitment courts—if any science can be more influential[32]—than is its "softer" sister science of psychiatry.

But the failure of the law and lawyers to grapple properly with psychiatrists in the civil commitment arena[33] can hopefully serve as an important lesson as we begin to confront neurological testimony. Although some psychiatrists are still "amazed" at the assertion that violent behavior is not readily predictable,[34] anyone who bothers to study the literature will conclude, as did Professor Dershowitz,[35] that psychiatric predictions of antisocial conduct are surprisingly inaccurate and are particularly prone to overestimating the likelihood of future deviant conduct.

Whether neurology is or will be a better predictive science than psychiatry is a question that should be of considerable interest to the legal system. Whatever its relative predictive position, however, it is clear from *Violence and the Brain* itself that much neurological evidence should be reviewed with extreme caution. Thus, while some physicians seem already prepared to rely on EEG recordings to determine matters of liberty and even life, Mark and Ervin commendably illustrate the "diversity of results in [EEG] studies" and conclude that "EEG interpretation is a subject neglected in the literature," and that "there is an obvious need for . . . techniques in evaluating tracings from subject and control populations."[36]

One published study relating to brain wave patterns of violent and nonviolent prisoners, for example, revealed the same proportion of abnormal EEGs (30%) in both the violent and the nonviolent group.[37] Even more striking is the fact, presented by Mark and Ervin, that some EEG research has revealed the same incidence of EEG abnormality (20%) in a group of prisoners and in a group of college-age nonprisoner volunteers.[38] And as a final admonition against drawing inferences too readily from EEG research, the authors warn that the fact that many violent patients and prisoners show abnormal brain waves and suffer from epileptic-like phenomena does not necessarily justify a causal nexus between brain dysfunction and violence: many such persons, because they were violent, had sustained frequent head injuries; thus, "abnormal brain waves, may be a result of, rather than a contributor to, their violent behavior."[39]

Violence and the Brain both discusses the provocative possibility that brain research will make giant strides in contributing to our understanding of deviant behavior and at the same time candidly concedes some limitations of present neurological knowledge. If the legal system hopes to take advantage of neurology's advances without being bullied by its overstatements—if, in short, the legal system hopes to avoid with neurology the mistakes it has already made with psychiatry—there will be a constant need for works that discuss, lucidly and without unnecessary scientific jargon, the internal rifts within the discipline of neurology. Perhaps the result in the *Kaimowitz* case, discussed in the next section, can best be explained not on conceptual grounds but on the basis of our lack of neurological knowledge.

AN ANALYSIS OF THE *KAIMOWITZ* CASE

Because psychosurgery is so intrusive, irreversible, and uncertain, it was a prime candidate to receive a court challenge. As we will see, the easiest legal handle for challenging the procedure entails the doctrine of informed consent. That doctrine was in fact the basis of the case of *Kaimowitz v. Department of Mental Health.*[40] In *Kaimowitz*, a Michigan three-judge trial court held that, as a matter of law, involuntarily confined patients cannot give legally adequate consent to experimental psychosurgery. The *Kaimowitz* court concluded that "the three basic elements of informed consent—competency, knowledge, and voluntariness—cannot be ascertained with a degree of reliability warranting resort to use of such an invasive procedure."[41]

In finding confined patients incompetent to consent, the court did not make the mistake, often made in the past, of concluding that committable patients are automatically legally incompetent.[42] Rather, the court found that the process of institutionalization and the dependency that typically accompanies hospitalization lead to an atrophying of patients' decision-making powers and render them incapable of making decisions as serious and complex as whether to undergo experimental psychosurgery. With respect to the element of knowledge, the court viewed the risks of psychosurgery as profoundly uncertain and held that consent thereto cannot be truly informed. Finally, the court concluded that no consent given by a confined patient is voluntary. The lure of release, which might be made possible by successful psychosurgery, is so powerful that it would be virtually impossible for a patient to refuse consent.

The conclusion in *Kaimowitz* that the current level of scientific knowledge makes psychosurgery an unacceptable treatment for institutionalized patients may be sound, but the court's reasoning is unsatisfactory. Though the court was careful to confine its holding to the facts before it, the court's reliance on the consent concept makes it analytically difficult to distinguish *Kaimowitz* from other situations in which consent perhaps should be deemed effective.

If institutionalization leads to the deterioration of decision-making abilities and renders a patient incompetent to elect to undergo experimental psychosurgery, it would seem that the same deterioration must render the person incompetent to make other important and complex decisions (to submit to other operations, to other therapies, to dispose of property, etc.). But any real extension of the concept beyond the area of psychosurgery would be unacceptable because it would virtually resurrect the rule that mental patient status per se establishes legal incompetence, a rule which the law has been dismantling rather successfully for some time.[43] Note that the new rule also rests on a doubtful premise in assuming that the syndrome of institutionalization will operate on confined patients *immediately*, rather than only after a prolonged period of hospitalization.

The *Kaimowitz* court's remarks regarding knowledge and informed consent are likewise difficult to confine logically to the facts of the case. For instance, if the risks of psychosurgery are so uncertain that a committed patient cannot render truly informed consent to the operation, informed consent should be similarly unobtainable from noninstitutionalized subjects, for the risks of the experimental operation are equally unknown with respect to them.

Some will surely argue, however, that, whatever the risks, nonconfined persons ought to be able to participate in psychosurgery and other experimental research, so long as they recognize the wholly speculative and perhaps irreversible nature of the venture.

Finally, the conception of coercion in *Kaimowitz* is difficult to contain, and, if the courts allowed its expansion, the result would be ironic indeed. Theoretically, if the carrot of release is viewed as coercing confined patients into psychosurgery, it should also be viewed as "coercing" them into electroconvulsive therapy, chemotherapy, group therapy, and so forth. Involuntary confinement could therefore be considered to coerce all decisions to engage in therapy. The absurdity of such an extension can be easily demonstrated by considering its application in a legal system which, as elaborated in the accompanying note, already widely recognizes a committed patient's right to treatment[44] and which is well on its way to recognizing as well a right not to be treated in the absence of consent (see also Chapter 10). If involuntary confinement itself creates coercion, administering any therapy to the patient violates his or her right not to be treated without free consent, which obviously vitiates entirely the right *to* treatment.

Surely, the courts would not extend the concept of coercion to cover more conventional types of therapy, even though the inducement to submit to such therapies may be identical to the inducement to submit to psychosurgery. What this indicates, then, is that this area of the law, like many others, uses the concept of coercion not simply to invalidate choices made under impermissible pressure, but rather invokes the concept as camouflage when condemning choices the consequences of which are unacceptable. Choices deemed beneficial are typically sustained despite the presence of indisputable, and perhaps overwhelming, pressure to select a particular option. "Voluntary" acceptance of a program of outpatient mental health treatment in lieu of criminal prosecution is one clear example, as is "voluntary" agreement to comply with reasonable conditions of probation and parole. In both examples, the strong desire to avoid incarceration must overwhelmingly shape a person's decision to consent to the conditions of release; yet, precisely because those conditions are regarded as reasonable, the consent is not legally condemned as being coerced.[45]

In light of these difficulties in applying the reasoning of *Kaimowitz*, the "coercion" holding may simply mean that psychosurgery, because it is experimental, drastic, and irreversible, with no known lasting benefits and many possible unknown side effects, is at present an inappropriate and impermissible treatment or research choice for involuntarily confined patients.[46] In other words, inducing involuntary patients to submit to therapy may be regarded as reasonable, but inducing them to submit to no-benefit or low-benefit high-risk experimentation is unreasonable. (As often as not, patients induced to submit to such a procedure would probably be *misinformed* rather than uninformed. In any event, it is probably unwise public policy for the government to involve itself—and its resources—in low-benefit, high-risk experimentation on confined subjects).

If that is all the *Kaimowitz* court intended to hold, it should have been more explicit and should not have used such broad language regarding the concepts of knowledge, competency, and coercion. Actually, a careful reading of *Kaimowitz* indicates that, despite its conceptual confusion and ambiguity, its holding should *not* be read as turning either on the question of incompetence or on the question of coercion by inducement of possible cure and release.

At the close of its opinion, the *Kaimowitz* court took pains to emphasize that its conclusion was based on the state of existing medical knowledge and that, if and when psychosurgery sheds its experimental status and becomes an accepted neurosurgical procedure, involuntarily confined patients might be able to consent to such a procedure.[47] Indeed, the court specifically held that committed patients can today give adequate consent to conventional neurosurgery,[48] even though the lure of release might be equally influential whether the surgical procedure proposed be deemed conventional or experimental, and even though conventional neurosurgery is very serious and should require a rather high level of competence.

The *Kaimowitz* holding should therefore not be read as premised on the incapacity of committed patients to give legal consent to experimental psychosurgery, nor on the coercion inherent in the desire to be released from the institution, but rather on the almost total absence of knowledge about the procedure (which perhaps precludes its performance on any human subjects) or on the impropriety of inducing (misleading?) committed patients to submit to such a low-benefit, high-risk research procedure.[49] Although this interpretation of *Kaimowitz* may be regarded as the more reasonable, the conceptual confusion generated by the case indicates that as the law moves steadily toward a model of consensual therapy, it will be critical that the elements of competence, knowledge, and coercion be kept analytically distinct.[50]

A careful analysis of the decision to undergo a particular procedure is especially important because the legal status of that decision may depend on whether the procedure provides some real prospect of therapeutic benefit. It may, for example, be constitutionally impermissible for a court or legislature to deny a patient access to even a drastic therapeutic technique and, in effect, mandate continued confinement if the technique, while possibly injurious, offers a likelihood of freedom.[51]

If their spirit is followed, the Supreme Court abortion cases[52] suggest that certain medical decisions made by a patient in consultation with a physician may be protected from state interference, absent a compelling state interest, by a Fourteenth Amendment right to privacy. In *Roe* v. *Wade* and *Doe* v. *Bolton,* the physician–patient decision regarding abortion was held to be protected from noncompelling and unnecessary governmental interference, and, given a sympathetic Court, there is ample theoretical room for extending those cases beyond the context of the decision to abort. For example, in according fundamental status to a woman's decision to terminate her pregnancy and in deeming that decision to fall within the Fourteenth Amendment right to privacy, the Court in *Roe* was concerned particularly with "[t]he detriment that the State would impose upon the [patient] by denying this choice altogether."[53] Specifically, the Court mentioned the taxing of mental and physical health and, more generally, forcing on the person "a distressful life and future."[54] If considerations of detriment and distress weigh heavily in determining whether the right to privacy embraces particular physician–patient decisions, many medical procedures other than abortion ought to receive substantial protection against state interference.

Thus, if psychosurgery, despite its serious risks and severely distasteful side effects, were also to present a real prospect of lasting and beneficial behavioral change, it might be constitutionally offensive for a state, by statute or otherwise, to preclude its performance on a patient when the patient and his or her physician conclude it is the most promising treatment alternative. For instance, a severely aggressive patient, confined indefinitely because of his or her violence and unresponsiveness to conventional and less drastic therapies, might agree with the physician that only psychosurgery might subdue the violence and effect release. In such a situation, if the patient is willing to assume the risk of the operation and can be found competent to make such a decision, the state's interest in "safeguarding health and maintaining medical standards"[55] might not, on balance, be sufficiently compelling to require the patient to forego the operation and lead a distressful, violent life behind the walls of an institution. Indeed, the state seemingly has no interest in protecting a patient from even "an inherently hazardous procedure" when "it would be equally dangerous . . . to forego it,"[56] and the concept of "danger" can reasonably be read to include factors (such as a distressful life and mental anguish) beyond purely physical risks.

In the mental health field, restrictions on governmental interference with voluntary treatment decisions made by physician and patient can extend well beyond the area of psychosurgery. Not long ago, for example, a Denver man awaiting trial on 14 counts of child molestation admitted to molesting, during his lifetime, between 400 and 500 girls under 12 years of age and agreed to castration as the only medically feasible means of accommodating society's protective interest and his own interest in leading a productive life in his home community.[57] The disclosure caused a stir among Colorado's psychiatric community, and the medical society was asked to conduct an ethical inquiry.[58] If the medical propriety of the procedure is assumed, however, attempted state regulation of it may well raise *Roe* problems. Indeed, *Roe* arguments are now flourishing even with respect to highly unconventional medical treatments such as laetrile use.[59]

Because they are drastic devices, medical measures such as psychosurgery and castration surely raise sharply the competing concerns regarding rights to receive and to refuse treatment. These drastic procedures, however, probably largely *because* they are so drastic, are rather infrequently employed. It is important to recognize, though, that "law and therapy" issues abound in the institutional context even with routine, day-to-day type therapeutic measures such as behavior modification based on the principles of operant conditioning. That is the content of the next chapter.

NOTES

[1]B.F. SKINNER, BEYOND FREEDOM AND DIGNITY (1971). Skinner has been attacked by persons as diverse as Noam Chomsky and Spiro Agnew. *See* Chomsky, *The Case Against B.F. Skinner*, NEW YORK REVIEW OF BOOKS, Dec. 30, 1971, at 19; *Agnew's Blast at Behaviorism*, PSYCHOLOGY TODAY, Jan., 1972, at 4 (reprint of speech to National Farm Bureau).

[2]*E.g.*, N. KITTRIE, THE RIGHT TO BE DIFFERENT: DEVIANCE AND ENFORCED THERAPY (1971). *See generally* Chapter 2.

[3]V. MARK & F. ERVIN, VIOLENCE AND THE BRAIN (1970).

[4]Lemert has defined "secondary deviation" as a "means of defense, attack, or adaptation to the overt and covert problems created by the societal reaction to primary deviation." E. LEMERT, HUMAN DEVIANCE, SOCIAL PROBLEMS, AND SOCIAL CONTROL 17 (1967). A critical review of the literature of labeling theory may be found in Schur, *Reactions to Deviance: A Critical Assessment*, 75 AM. J. SOCIOL. 309 (1969). *See also* E. SCHUR, LABELING DEVIANT BEHAVIOR: ITS SOCIOLOGICAL IMPLICATIONS (1971).

[5]Gibbons, *Observations on the Study of Crime Causation*, 77 AM. J. SOCIOL. 262 (1971). For other "etiologically" oriented sociological works, *see* J. GIBBS, CRIME, PUNISHMENT AND DETERRENCE (1975); T. HIRSCHI, CAUSES OF DELINQUENCY (1969). Even Howard Becker, one of the pioneer labeling theorists, has somewhat softened his stance. Becker, *Labelling Theory Reconsidered*, in THE ALDINE CRIME AND JUSTICE ANNUAL (S. Messinger *et al.* eds. 1973).

[6]Gove, *Societal Reaction as an Explanation of Mental Illness: An Evaluation*, 35 AM. SOCIOL. REV. 873 (1970).

[7]One notable exception—not mentioned by Gove—is the experimental work performed by two social psychologists with a group of normal students who were supposedly solicited to take a "personality" test. J. FREEDMAN & A. DOOB, DEVIANCY: THE PSYCHOLOGY OF BEING DIFFERENT (1968). Freedman and Doob experimentally induced a feeling of deviance in some of the subjects by informing a random group that they had received personality test scores far from the "average." Then, other experiments were performed to assess the impact of the deviant label. Interestingly, the investigators learned that when the personality test results were not made public, the "deviants," in an apparent attempt to conceal their deviancy, preferred to work alone. The desire to avoid close contact with others disappeared, however, when the test results were made public, but the deviants then preferred to associate with the other experimentally manufactured deviants rather than with the nondeviant subjects. The latter finding may shed some light on the social-psychological origins of deviant subcultures. For a summary of the Freedman and Doob labeling experiments, see Doob, *Deviance: Society's Side Show*, PSYCHOLOGY TODAY, Oct., 1971 at 47.

[8]Gove, *supra* note 6, at 882-83.

[9]The authors cite monkey research to demonstrate the proposition that environmental factors, such as maternal deprivation, may cause actual brain dysfunction. MARK & ERVIN, *supra* note 3, at 143.

[10]The book notes that the XYY chromosome configuration—which is purportedly associated with antisocial behavior—may well be related to brain disease. Indeed, chromosomes cannot themselves "cause" criminal behavior; they can do so only by altering brain function, perhaps by producing in the blood that bathes the brain an abnormally high ("supermale") hormonal level. *Id.* at 49–50. For a clear introduction to the area, *see* Baumiller, *XYY Chromosome Genetics*, 14 J. FORENSIC SCIENCES 411 (1969). An early review of the literature of cytogenetic developments relating to the XYY syndrome appears in Court Brown, *Males with an XYY Sex Chromosome Complement*, 5 J. MED. GENET. 341 (1968). Later, more critical studies include Witkin *et al.*, *Criminality in XYY and XXY Men*, 193 SCIENCE 547 (Aug., 1976); Hook, *Behavioral Implications of the Human XYY Genotype*, 179 SCIENCE 139 (1973); Owen, *The 47 XYY Male: A Review*, 78 PSYCH. BULL. 209 (1972).

[11]The work done in the XYY area is highly relevant here. *See* Note, *The XYY Chromosome Defense*, 57 GEO. L.J. 892 (1969); *Cf.* Murphy, *Involuntary Acts and Criminal Liability*, 81 ETHICS 332, 340 (1971) (legal philosopher proposes rather broad negation of *actus reus* by defining act as involuntary when it "is explainable by factors which causally prevent the exercise of normal capacities of control or eliminate such capacities entirely").

[12]For a discussion of the "mentally healthy and dangerous," *see* Postel, *Civil Commitment: A Functional Analysis*, 38 BKLYN. L. REV. I, 60–76 (1971).

[13]Rouse v. Cameron, 373 F.2d 451 (D.C. Cir. 1966) (person involuntarily committed to mental hospital on being acquitted of an offense by reason of insanity has cognizable right to treatment). *See generally* note 44 *infra*. For an exhaustive analysis, *see* Spece, *Preserving the Right to Treatment: A Critical Assessment and Constructive Development of Constitutional Right to Treatment Theories*, 20 ARIZ. L. REV. 1 (1978).

[14]*See generally* Plotkin, *Limiting the Therapeutic Orgy: Mental Patients' Right to Refuse Treatment*, 72 NW.L. REV. 461 (1977).

[15]*Cf.* Dershowitz, *The Psychiatrist's Power in Civil Commitment: A Knife That Cuts Both Ways*, PSYCHOLOGY TODAY, Feb., 1969, at 43, 47.

[16]*Cf.* Davis v. Mississippi, 394 U.S. 721 (1969) (detention for sole purpose of obtaining fingerprints subject to Fourth Amendment constraints); Schmerber v. California, 384 U.S. 757 (1966) (Fourth and Fifth Amendment rights not violated by doctor's taking blood sample from nonconsenting defendant).

[17]*See generally* Note, *Anthropotelemetry: Dr. Schwitzgebel's Machine*, 80 HARV. L. REV. 403, 404–05 (1966).

[18]The authors also discuss the neurological (though not the legal or ethical) implications of the fact that the patient agreed to major brain surgery while relaxed through brain stimulation, but became enraged at the idea of surgery after the effect of stimulation had worn off (he finally consented to it after several weeks of explanation). MARK & ERVIN, *supra* note 3, at 96–97.

[19]In fact, Dr. Kenneth B. Clark, former president of the American Psychological Association, once called for the development of psychotechnological medication to be taken by world leaders in order to "control the animalistic, barbaric, and primitive propensities in man." PSYCHIATRIC NEWS, Oct. 6, 1971, at 3, col. 1.

[20]Note, *supra* note 17. *See also* Schwitzgebel, *Electronic Innovation in the Behavioral Sciences: A Call to Responsibility*, 22 AM. PSYCHOLOGIST 364 (1967).

[21]*Cf.* H. EYSENCK, CRIME AND PERSONALITY (1964) (discussing genetic factors leading to poor conditionability and to impulsive personalities).

[22]MARK & ERVIN, *supra* note 3, at 126.

[23]T. C. WILLETT, CRIMINAL ON THE ROAD (1964).

[24]*Id.* at 299–307.

[25]Waller, *Chronic Medical Conditions and Traffic Safety*, 273 NEW ENG. J. MED. 1413, 1420

(1965). *See generally* Waller, *Medical Impairment and Highway Crashes,* 208 J.A.M.A. 2293 (1969).

[26]With or without a neurological nexus, wife beating is now being viewed far more seriously than it was in the past. *See* Comment, *Battered Wives Who Kill: Double Standard Out of Court, Single Standard In?* 2 Law & Hum. Behav. 133 (1978). *See generally* D. Martin, Battered Wives (1977).

[27]401 U.S. 395 (1971).

[28]*Id.* at 401. In light of post-*Tate* developments, a legislature seeking to follow Blackmun's advice, and to require jail sentences for traffic offenders, would have to provide counsel for indigent traffic court defendants. Argersinger v. Hamlin, 407 U.S. 25 (1972); Scott v. Illinois, 99 S.Ct. 1158 (1979).

[29]S. Wheeler & L. Cottrell, Juvenile Delinquency: Its Prevention and Control 23 (1966).

[30]203 New Eng. J. Med. 603 (1970).

[31]*Doctor Alvarez,* Tucson Daily Citizen, Nov. 16, 1970, at 16, col. I.

[32]For a discussion of the extent to which the courts follow psychiatric recommendations in civil commitment cases, *see* Chapter 4 (empirical study indicating recommendations followed in approximately 98% of the cases).

[33]*See generally id.*

[34]Letter to the Editor, *Psychiatric News,* Dec. 15, 1971, at 2, col. 4 ("I was amazed to read in *Psychiatric News* of September 15, 1971, that Dr. Seymour L. Halleck states that violent behavior is not predictable").

[35]Dershowitz, *supra* note 15, at 47.

[36]Mark & Ervin, *supra* note 3, at 136–137.

[37]Levy & Kennard, *A Study of the Electroencephalogram as Related to Personality Structure in a Group of Inmates in a State Penitentiary,* 109 Am. J. Psychiatry 832 (1953).

[38]Mark & Ervin, *supra* note 3, at 136.

[39]*Id.* at 131.

[40]No. 73-19434-AW (Cir. Ct. of Wayne County, Mich., July 10, 1973), *abstracted* in 13 Crim. L. Rep. 2452 (1973), and reprinted in A. Brooks, Law, Psychiatry, and the Mental Health System 902 (1974).

[41]*Id.,* slip opinion at 31–32.

[42]*See* Chapter 4.

[43]The old rule, which has fallen into disrepute, equated committability itself (not the later fact of hospitalization) with incompetence, and assumed that if a person was sufficiently mentally ill to warrant commitment, the person should also be stripped of the right to perform other legal functions. But both the old rule and the resurrected version discussed in the text, relying on the effects of hospitalization rather than on mental status at the time of commitment, would achieve the same result—automatic incompetence—if applied to populations of involuntarily confined patients.

[44]*E.g.,* Rouse v. Cameron, 373 F.2d 451 (D.C. Cir. 1966) (statutory basis); Wyatt v. Stickney, 344 F. Supp. 373 (M.D. Ala. 1972), aff'd in part, rev'd in part, remanded in part *sub nom.* Wyatt v. Aderholt, 503 F.2d 1305 (5th Cir. 1974) (constitutional basis). *See generally* Spece, *supra* note 13, at 1.

In terms of Supreme Court pronouncements, the question whether there is a constitutionally prescribed right to treatment remains unresolved. Many observers had expected the question to be resolved by the Court in the case of O'Connor v. Donaldson, 422 U.S. 563 (1976), but the Court decided that case on narrow grounds and left open the right-to-treatment question. The Court ruled simply that it is inappropriate to confine without treatment nondangerous persons capable of adequate community adjustment.

But the Court did not consider whether such persons *could* be confined if treatment were forthcoming or whether persons confined because of *dangerousness* have a right to treatment.

Regardless of the Court's ultimate verdict on the existence of a constitutionally grounded right to treatment and its contours, the right, or at least some semblance of it, is now so firmly embedded in lower court decisions, modern statutory enactments, and legal commentary (*supra*) that its continued existence, with or without a Supreme Court imprimatur, is almost assured. The right may have a different theoretical basis and scope, however, when applied to patients committed pursuant to the state's paternalistic power (*parens patriae* patients) than when applied to patients committed pursuant to the police power of the state (police power patients) (*see* Chapter 2).

The "core" recipients of a right to treatment are presumably those *parens patriae* patients who are committed because they are mentally ill, legally incompetent to make hospitalization and treatment decisions, and *in need of treatment*. To the extent that a need for treatment is part of the rationale for commitment, confinement without treatment would be legally unwarranted. Note, *Developments in the Law: Civil Commitment of the Mentally Ill*, 87 HARV. L. REV. 1190, 1326–1327 (1974). Apparently, the only instance in which a *parens patriae* patient could be retained without treatment is where an "untreatable" patient is committed because of the need for *humane custodial care*, rather than for treatment. *Id.* at 1327. (The Harvard Note argues, however, that even with regard to *parens patriae* patients committed because of a clear-cut need for treatment, "due process does not require that the treatment given be effective," for "the possibility that treatments actually given will not benefit a patient are to be taken into consideration in the initial commitment hearing." *Id.* at n.43. If the Note is suggesting that need-for-treatment patients can be continually confined even after it is ascertained that efficacious treatment cannot be provided them, the Note's reasoning is faulty. It is of course proper at the initial commitment hearing, in order to balance competing interests and to decide whether commitment is in the patient's best interest, to take testimony regarding estimates of therapeutic success. But while that estimate, even if incorrect, can legitimate the initial act of commitment, it should not, at least if the need for humane custodial care is not present, legitimate continued confinement after therapy proves ineffective and firmly undercuts the validity of the original estimate of therapeutic efficacy.)

Police power patients are also generally thought to enjoy a right to treatment, but the scope and theoretical base for this assumption is far shakier than in the case of *parens patriae* patients. Courts have often accorded police power patients a right to treatment on the theory that detention is ordinarily appropriate only for a finite period, following a trial with many procedural protections, and after a finding that the subject has committed a specifically defined offense. Since police power commitments deviate substantially from that criminal model, the quid pro quo or "trade-off" for the departure ought, according to the theory, to result in a right to treatment even for police power patients. *Id.* at 1325 n.39. The theory has, however, been sharply criticized on a number of grounds. (First, it has been contended that, contrary to the implications of the theory, there perhaps ought to be a constitutional right to treatment *even if* full-blown procedural protections are adopted in the commitment process. Furthermore, the theory might allow for the acceptance of an argument to the effect that since treatment is available, there is no constitutional need for procedural protections. Finally, police power commitments ought, in theory at least, to be available on a finding of future dangerousness, regardless of whether the subject has manifested his dangerousness through the commission of a specific overt act. *Id.*) Two other bases for a police power right to treatment, less subject to criticism than the quid pro quo rationale, have recently been advanced:

In order to prove that the societal benefit of the commitment outweighs the detriment to the confined person, the state might introduce evidence concerning the nature and amount of any treatment that could reduce the predicted duration of the detention and which would be available to the patient if he desired it. A police power commitment following the presentation of such evidence is thus justified, in part, by the promise of treatment, and a person committed under these circumstances would have a due process right to its provision. In other cases, the dangerousness of an individual may be so great that potentially permanent confinement would be warranted; thus mere custody under humane conditions would not be arbitrary or irrational. Nevertheless, failure to provide available treatments would violate the constitutional requirement that deprivations of fundamental liberties be the least restrictive necessary to accomplish valid state objectives.

Id. at 1327–1328. The last basis is thoroughly examined in Spece, *supra* n.13. Spece, in fact, exhaustively analyzes the entire conceptual morass surrounding the right to treatment. Additional bibliographic references may be found in A. Brooks, Law, Psychiatry and the Mental Health System 185–186 (Supp. 1980).

[45]Similarly, although it is axiomatic that a guilty plea must be given voluntarily in order to be binding, pleas resulting from bargains entered into in the hope of avoiding incarceration (or even death) have been upheld. *See, e.g.,* Parker v. North Carolina, 397 U.S. 790 (1970); Brady v. United States, 397 U.S. 742 (1970). Justice Brennen's combined *Parker* dissent and *Brady* concurrence, 397 U.S. at 800–812, in which he was joined by Justices Douglas and Marshall, provides an excellent analysis of voluntariness as an ambiguous and abstract legal concept. Brennan notes that "the concept has been employed to analyze a variety of pressures to surrender constitutional rights, which are not all equally coercive or obvious in their coercive effect." *Id.* at 801. As such, the concept embraces not only situations of literally overborne wills, but also "situations in which an individual, while perfectly capable of rational choice, has been confronted with factors which the government may not constitutionally inject into the decision-making process." *Id.* at 802. *See also* Schneckloth v. Bustamonte, 412 U.S. 218, 224 (1973) (voluntariness reflects a "complex of values"). *Bustamonte* also recognizes that, except in extremely rare instances, most decisions are "voluntary" in the sense of representing a choice between alternatives, even though one or both of the alternatives may be disagreeable. *Id.* at 224, and n.7. The law, however, may deem a decision involuntary when it regards the choice as an unfair or unacceptable one, such as a choice between the rack and a confession. *Id.* Perhaps the clearest example of the use of voluntariness as a notion of fairness rather than of coercion is provided by cases involving plea bargains broken by prosecutors. A plea induced by a prosecutive promise (such as to recommend leniency in sentencing) will, despite the inducement, be upheld as voluntary so long as the prosecutive promise is kept, but if the prosecutor should renege on the bargain, many courts will upset the plea on the grounds that it was involuntarily obtained. *See* Santobello v. New York, 404 U.S. 257, 266 (1971) (Douglas J., concurring).

[46]*Cf.* Fortner v. Koch, 272 Mich. 273, 261 N.W. 762 (1935).

> We recognize the fact that, if the general practice of medicine and surgery is to progress, there must be a certain amount of experimentation carried on; but such experiments must be done with the knowledge and consent of the patient or those responsible for him, *and must not vary too radically from the accepted method of procedure.*

Id. at 282, 261 N.W. at 765 (emphasis added).

An exhaustive review of the psychosurgery literature from 1971 to 1976, undertaken by Dr. Elliot Valenstein under contract from a national commission, concludes that the scientific merit of the literature is low and that there is considerable controversy, even among its proponents, regarding the efficacy of psychosurgery for violent patients, schizophrenics, and sexual offenders. The report contains an excellent bibliography.

National Commission for the Protection of Human Subjects of Biomedical and Behavioral Research, Appendix on Psychosurgery (1977). A recent book rather sympathetic to psychosurgery is S. Shuman, Psychosurgery and the Medical Control of Violence (1977). The commission itself was rather sympathetic to the continuation of psychosurgery under controlled circumstances. National Commission for the Protection of Human Subjects of Biomedical and Behavioral Research, Report and Recommendations: Psychosurgery (1977).

[47]No. 73-1943-AW (Cir. Ct. of Wayne County, Mich., July 10, 1973), *abstracted in* Crim. L. Rep. 2452 (1973), slip opinion at 40.

[48]*Id.*

[49]This analysis seems consistent with (and, indeed, might help to explain) the otherwise curious statement in *Kaimowitz* that a guardian's consent to experimental psychosurgery would be legally insufficient: "Although guardian or parental consent may be legally adequate when arising out of traditional circumstances, it is legally ineffective in the psychosurgery situation. The guardian or parent cannot do that which the patient, absent a guardian, would be legally unable to do." *Id.*, slip opinion at 26.

By prohibiting substituted judgment in the psychosurgery situation, the *Kaimowitz* court could not be relying on the legal incompetence of institutionalized patients or on the distortion of capacity that may flow from the lure of possible release. Those are paradigm cases of problems that can be readily overcome by the substituted judgment of a competent and detached guardian. If, however, *Kaimowitz* is simply suggesting that knowledge about psychosurgery is so wholly inadequate that a patient could not make a legally informed judgment to undergo it, then surely a guardian would be in no better position to make such a judgment. Similarly, if *Kaimowitz* is suggesting that experimental psychosurgery is a no-benefit, high-risk procedure to which patients should not be induced to submit, the preclusion of guardian consent would follow from the proposition that guardians may not subject their wards to harmful or nontherapeutic experimentation.

[50]For an excellent analysis of *Kaimowitz* by a legal philosopher, *see* Murphy, *Total Institutions and the Possibility of Consent to Organic Therapies*, 5 Human Rights 25 (1975).

[51]With respect to psychosurgery, the American Orthopsychiatric Association noted:

> [S]uch judicial action [precluding psychosurgery on committed patients] would *not* deny to involuntary mental patients access to a procedure which would give them a substantial chance of prompt release to the community. This would be a more difficult case if involuntarily confined patients were given a stark choice between continued confinement, on the one hand, and the likelihood of freedom with a possibility of injury, on the other. Such a choice could exist if some disease entity had been defined, and if there were a clear likelihood that psychosurgery would treat the disease, ameliorating behavior and allowing mental patients to obtain release from the institution. But this is *not* such a situation.

Brief for American Orthopsychiatric Association as Amicus Curiae at 74, Kaimowitz v. Dep't of Mental Health, *supra* note 40 (italics in original). The Association then noted (and the court agreed):

> [T]he benefits of psychosurgery to the research subject are highly uncertain *at best.* There is no assurance that any behavior changes will remain effective in the long run, thereby justifying the subject's release. Moreover, there are substantial risks of harm—both known and unknown. And these harms... threaten the individual's autonomy and personality, in addition to posing a danger to physical well-being and possibly causing pain.

Id. at 74–75.

[52]Roe v. Wade, 410 U.S. 113 (1973); Doe v. Bolton, 410 U.S. 179 (1973).

[53]410 U.S. at 153.

[54]*Id.*

[55]*Id.* at 154. As an original proposition, it could of course be argued that the state has no legitimate interest in safeguarding an individual's health and in protecting him or her from risky medical procedures, but in practice that argument has been squarely rejected—even in *Roe* itself. *Id.*

[56]*Id.* at 149. Thus, even when, prior to the perfection of antiseptic techniques, abortion was considered medically hazardous and mortality rates from the operation were high, the state's interest in forbidding abortion to protect the mother gave way when pregnancy itself posed a threat to the mother's life. *Id.* at 148–149. In the psychosurgery context, *see* the related argument and discussion in Aden v. Younger, 129 Cal. Rptr. 535 (Ct. App. 1976).

[57]ARIZONA DAILY STAR, April 18, 1972, at 9A, col. 1.

[58]*Id.*

[59]*Compare* People v. Privitera, 153 Cal. Rptr. 431 (1979) *with* Rutherford v. United States, 438 F. Supp. 1287 (D. Okla. 1977), remanded 582 F.2d 1234 (10th Cir. 1978), rev'd and remanded 99 S.Ct. 2470 (1979). *See generally* Comment, *Laetrile: Statutory and Constitutional Limitations on the Regulation of Ineffective Drugs*, 127 U. PA. L. Rev. 233 (1978). On a related matter, *see* Shapiro, *The Right of Privacy and Heroin Use for Painkilling Purposes by the Terminally Ill Cancer Patient*, 21 ARIZ. L. REV. 41 (1979).

9

Behavior Modification

LEGAL RESTRICTIONS ON TOKEN ECONOMIES

INTRODUCTION

Commentators and authorities have recently directed attention not only to important procedural problems in the administration of therapeutic justice[1] but also to the legal issues presented by various methods of institutional therapy. Legal restrictions on a hospital's right to subject unwilling patients to electroconvulsive therapy[2] and psychosurgery[3] are developing rapidly, and close scrutiny is also now being given to "aversive" techniques of behavior modification and control[4]—such as procedures for suppressing transvestism by administering painful electric shocks to the patient while he is dressed in women's clothing, and procedures for controlling alcoholism or narcotics addiction by arranging medically for severe nausea or even temporary paralysis (including respiratory arrest) to follow ingestion of the habituating substance.[5] It is likely that certain treatments may be deemed so offensive, frightening, or risky that the law may eventually preclude them altogether,[6] or at least restrict them by requiring the patient's informed consent.[7]

Though aversive therapeutic techniques are receiving close attention, schemes of "positive" behavior control[8] (whereby appropriate, nondeviant behavioral responses are encouraged by rewarding their occurrence) have not been subjected to any careful study. It is perhaps assumed that when rewards rather than punishments are employed, no grave legal, social, or ethical questions are involved.[9] To a great extent, that is unquestionably true: few would have their ire aroused, for exam-

213

ple, by praising a child and offering him candy for correctly spelling or reading a word,[10] nor would many be upset over a scheme that encouraged scholastic achievement of institutionalized juvenile delinquents by offering them, contingent on academic success, private rooms, a wider choice of food, and selections of items from a mail-order catalogue.[11] But, as will be seen in the following section, many techniques of positive control are far more troubling. Most troubling of all seem to be the use of token economies with chronic psychotic mental patients.

PSYCHOLOGY AND TOKEN ECONOMIES

GENERAL CONSIDERATIONS

Many behavior modification practitioners apply clinically the learning theory principles of Skinnerian operant conditioning. Operant theory is based on the principle, amply demonstrated by empirical data, that behavior is strengthened or weakened by its consequences.[12] The frequency of a behavior increases if it is followed by desirable consequences, whereas it will be extinguished if the positive consequences are discontinued or if the consequences are aversive.[13]

The application of operant conditioning to humans has come a long way since 1949, when a severely regressed person was taught to raise his arm by a procedure that rewarded appropriate arm motions by the subsequent squirting of a sugar–milk solution into his mouth.[14] Now, a multitude of therapeutic behavior modification systems are in operation on ward-wide and institution-wide scales. By and large, these programs seek to shape[15] and maintain appropriate behavior patterns (designated as "target behaviors" or "target responses") by rewarding or "reinforcing" the desired responses. Usually, rewards are dispensed in the form of tokens or points (known as "secondary" or "generalized" reinforcers) which can then be converted, pursuant to a specific economic schedule, to "primary reinforcers" such as snacks, mail-order catalogue items, and the like.

These "token economies" have flourished since their development in the sixties[16] and are currently employed in a variety of clinical settings.[17] This chapter will be confined almost exclusively to a discussion of the application of the token system to chronic psychotics.

There are two reasons for this limitation in scope: first, despite mammoth advances in psychopharmacology[18] and a burgeoning community mental health movement,[19] which have combined to reduce drastically mental hospital enrollment, almost all chronic psychotics are still hospitalized.[20] If other clinical categories are increasingly diverted from institutions while the chronics continue to accumulate, the treatment of the chronic psychotic may soon constitute the major therapeutic concern of mental hospitals. Second, because the behavior patterns of chronic psychotics are by definition particularly resistant to therapy, more drastic methods of behavior modification have been applied to them. These therapeutic methods will raise important legal questions.

Token Economies

Teodoro Ayllon and Nathan Azrin pioneered the token economy concept on a ward of chronically psychotic female patients at the Anna State Hospital in Illinois.[21] Because of their adaptation to long periods of stagnant hospitalization, chronic patients typically suffer from extreme apathy and dependency. That condition, known as institutionalization,[22] impedes the chronic's chances for improvement or release. To overcome the problem, Ayllon and Azrin rewarded target behaviors that would reverse the institutionalization syndrome. Work assignments within the hospital and various self-care behaviors were rewarded with tokens. The self-care category included grooming, bathing, toothbrushing, bed making, and the like.[23] Work assignments included kitchen chores, serving in the dining room, assisting in the laundry, janitorial work, and related tasks.[24]

For the token economy to succeed, it is necessary to insure that the items or events purchasable with the tokens are effective reinforcers—in lay terms, that they would in fact be desired by the patients. To assess reinforcer efficacy, the Anna State Hospital psychologists applied the "Premack Principle":[25] if certain behaviors occur naturally with a high frequency, then the opportunity to engage in those behaviors can be used as effective reinforcers to strengthen a low-frequency behavior. The psychologists determined the high frequency-behaviors empirically:

It was noted that certain patients often hoarded various items under their mattresses. The activity in this case, in a general sense, consisted of concealing private property in such a manner that it would be inaccessible to other patients and the staff. Since this event seemed to be highly probable, it was formally scheduled as a reinforcer. Keys to a locked cabinet in which they could conceal their private possessions just as they had been doing with the mattresses were made available to patients.

Another activity that was observed to be highly probable was the attempt of patients to conceal themselves in several locations on the ward in an effort to enjoy some degree of privacy. A procedure was therefore instituted whereby a patient could obtain a portable screen to put in front of her bed or access to a bedroom with a door. Another event that had a high probability of occurrence for some patients was a visit with the social worker or psychologist. This was used as a reinforcer by arranging appointments with either of these staff members.[26]

Ground privileges and supervised walks by the staff were also established as reinforcers by application of the Premack Principle, since patients were frequently observed to "stay at the exit to the ward and try to leave."[27] The opportunity to attend religious services was also used as a reinforcer since several patients attended frequently when they were allowed to freely.[28]

Thus, personal cabinets, room dividers, visits with the professional staff, ground privileges, supervised walks, and religious services were all made contingently available to the patients: they could be purchased if the patient had performed a sufficient number of target responses to have earned the requisite tokens to purchase the reinforcers. They were otherwise unavailable. Other reinforcers in the Anna State Hospital program included a personal chair, writing materials and stationery, movies, television programs, and various commissary items.[29]

By using these "strong, albeit untapped"[30] sources of motivation, the Ayllon and Azrin economy produced rather impressive results, at least when measured by standards of work performance. They compared the work output of their patients during a specified period of the token economy with a subsequent experimental period during which the various reinforcers were freely available without tokens—a situation which "approximated the usual conduct of a mental hospital ward."[31] Ayllon and Azrin found that patient performance during the experimental period plummeted to less than one-fourth the token economy level. Hence, they concluded that "the performance on a usual ward would be increased fourfold by instituting this motivating environment."[32]

Nonetheless, the Anna State Hospital program did not change the behavior of 8 out of the 44 patients[33] involved:

> Eight patients, who expended fewer than 50 tokens within 20 days, all earned by self-care rather than from job assignments, were relatively unaffected by the reinforcement procedure. Statistical comparison of them with the other patients revealed no difference in diagnosis or age. It appears that their failure to modify behavior appreciably stemmed from the relative absence of any strong behavior patterns that could be used as reinforcers. The only two behaviors that existed in strength were sleeping and eating. The present program did not attempt to control the availability of food. This action may have to be considered in future research in order to rehabilitate patients with such an extreme loss of behavior.[34]

Many token economy programs have been patterned after the Ayllon and Azrin model.[35] In Atthowe's program for chronic patients at the

Palo Alto Veterans Administration Hospital, for example, patients earned points not only for their industrial therapy job assignments, but also for participating in group activities, in recreational therapy, and for attending weekend movies.[36] And reinforcers in various programs include later wake-up times,[37] passes,[38] clothing,[39] clothing maintenance,[40] reading materials,[41] dances,[42] and even release.[43] Moreover, several programs have taken the step recommended but not taken by Ayllon and Azrin and have made food and beds available only on a contingent basis.[44] Indeed, those programs have exceeded the Ayllon and Azrin recommendation by using beds and meals as reinforcers on a ward-wide basis, even for patients who have not failed under a system where food and sleeping facilities were noncontingently available.

One of the token economies that hinges food and beds on appropriate behavioral responses, a chronic ward at the Patton State Hospital in San Bernardino, California, may be "willing to let a patient go for as long as five days without food, or until he has been reduced to 80% of his previous body weight."[45] The Patton program is one of several token economies[46] that follows a "phase" or "tier" system, where at least certain privileges are dependent on the patient's place in the hierarchy of tiers.

At Patton, for example, newly admitted patients are, according to the literature, placed in the orientation group, where living conditions are exceedingly drab and where a subsistence-level existence can be purchased for a small number of tokens. After a patient has adapted well to the orientation group, he or she is elevated to the middle group, where conditions are better but are considerably more expensive. Patients in the middle group are given five months to be promoted to the rather luxurious ready-to-leave group, but if after three months in the middle group a patient is not adequately facing the eventual prospect of life on the outside, he or she will be returned to the orientation group.[47] Margaret Bruce, a psychiatric technician at the Patton State Hospital, described the orientation group in these words:

> This group sleeps in a relatively unattractive dormitory which conforms to bare minimums set by the state department of mental hygiene. There are no draperies at the windows or spreads on the beds, and the beds themselves are of the simplest kind. In the dining room the patient sits with many other patients at a long table, crowded in somewhat uncomfortably. The only eating utensil given him is a large spoon. The food is served in unattractive, sectioned plastic dishes. So long as he is in this group, he is not allowed to wear his own clothes and cannot go to activities which other patients are free to attend off the unit. He may not have permission for off-the-ground visits, and the number of visitors who can see him is restricted.
>
> During this time, the patient learns that his meals, his bed, his toilet

articles, and his clothes no longer are freely given him. He must pay for these with tokens. These tokens pay for all those things normally furnished and often taken for granted. In the orientation group most of the things the patient wants are cheap; for example, it costs one token to be permitted to go to bed, one token for a meal. Patients find it easy enough to earn the few tokens necessary for bare subsistence.[48]

Before leaving the description of token economies, we should find it instructive to discuss in some detail a token environment established at the Richmond State Hospital in Indiana.[49] This particular system, although involving a population of civilly committed alcoholics rather than chronic psychotics, is particularly worthy of note because it suggests just how easily the Ayllon and Azrin token economy model can be extended to other clinical categories of patients.[50]

Prior to the inception of the token economy, legally committed alcoholics at Richmond State were first admitted to the Receiving Unit, where they were provided with rest and medical care. Within one or two weeks the patient was usually assigned to an open ward, with a work assignment within the hospital and all the available privileges.[51] When the token system was introduced, certain alcoholic patients without intellectual, organic, or psychotic impairments were inducted into the program.[52] Work in the hospital labor force, compensated by points, was deemed the target behavior. The reinforcers included a broad range of patient needs and privileges:

> The motivational power of the points was derived from allowing their exchange for every possible purchase within the hospital; thus, room and board, clothing maintenance, canteen purchases, Alcoholics Anonymous meetings, short leaves of absence, disulfiram treatment, different kinds of psychotherapy, and special instruction could all be freely selected, if paid for out of earnings.[53]

Points were also needed to purchase advancement through the five-tier system used at Richmond. The five tiers consisted of two closed wards, a semiclosed ward where ground privileges were available by purchase, and two open wards with pass privileges. Patients could purchase promotion only at weekly intervals.

The program was considered aversive by prospective members,[54] as well as by the inducted members who requested weekly group meetings which became, mainly, "a grievance session centering around project rules."[55] No doubt the grievances were in part attributable to the fact that "a deprivation situation was established by starting patients in a closed ward of low status, substandard material and social comfort, and curtailed freedom, relative to other wards in the hospital."[56] The legal issues raised by the token economies may be apparent by now and they will be considered in the next section.

LAW AND TOKEN ECONOMIES

To speak at the moment of a specific "law of token economies" is of course out of the question. Until fairly recently, the judicially manufactured "hands-off" doctrine enabled the courts to duck important questions regarding the limits of administrative discretion in the operation of prisons and mental institutions.[57] Accordingly, the correctional and therapeutic establishments were in effect given, by default, the legal nod to manage their institutions—and to conduct their therapy[58]—as they saw fit. But the last decade has witnessed a remarkable turnabout in the willingness of courts to scrutinize living conditions in total institutions.

Some bold and far-reaching decisions have been rendered,[59] and there is the further possibility of widespread legislative action.[60] From the still sparse legal precedents, one can detect a rather clear trend, and the emerging law bears rather directly on the rights of patients subjected to a token economy.

The encouragement of certain target responses (such as proper personal hygiene and self-care) surely seems beyond legal question,[61] but it will be recalled that the principal target response of most token economies is adequate functioning on an institutional work assignment. Many persons both within and without the legal profession, however, find it objectionable to require patients, especially involuntarily committed patients, in effect to work for mental institutions, particularly without standard compensation. Though the work assignments are often cast in such therapeutic terms as overcoming apathy and institutionalization, the critics view the jobs as simple laborsaving devices which exploit patients[62] and, indeed, which sometimes make hospital retention of particular patients almost indispensable to the functioning of the institution.[63]

That patient job assignments are, in fact, often laborsaving is beyond question, as is the fact that work output will increase substantially when work is contingently reinforced by the standard reinforcers employed by token economies. Indeed, it will be recalled that at Anna State Hospital in Illinois, Ayllon and Azrin concluded that ward efficiency soared astronomically (fourfold[64]) because of a token system involving job performance, and they noted further that unsatisfactory job performance resulted in administrative disruption.[65] During a patient vacation period "the additional work required to keep the ward functioning . . . had to be made up by paid employees whose hours almost doubled."[66]

It seems clear that the law will not tolerate forced patient labor that is devoid of therapeutic purpose and which is required solely as a laborsaving technique. The Second Circuit, invoking a Thirteenth Amendment involuntary servitude rationale, so held in 1966.[67] Since then, recognition that there is not always a sharp line dividing therapeutic and nontherapeutic assignments has led to varying legal theories for dealing with, or for avoiding, the problem.

One rule is suggested by Bruce Ennis, a leading mental health lawyer who is keenly aware of the disparate per diem cost between private and state hospitalization and of the cost-saving devices resorted to by state hospitals. He would adopt the following as a legal rule of thumb in deciding whether work assignments have therapeutic value: "If a given type of labor *is* therapeutic, we would expect to find patients in private facilities performing that type of labor. Conversely, labor which is not generally performed in private facilities should be presumed . . . to be cost-saving rather than therapeutic."[68]

The "avoidance" approach is exemplified by the elaborate decision in *Wyatt* v. *Stickney*,[69] in which the court barred all involuntary patient labor involving hospital operation and maintenance, whether therapeutic or not, but permitted voluntary institutional work of either a therapeutic or a nontherapeutic nature, so long as the labor is compensated pursuant to the federal minimum wage law.[70] To insure the voluntary nature of any institutional work assignment undertaken, the *Wyatt* court specified further that "privileges or release from the hospital shall not be conditioned upon the performance of labor"[71] involving hospital maintenance.[72]

The approach taken by the landmark *Wyatt* decision, if widely followed, would have an immense impact on traditional token economies. Patients could not be forced in any way to perform institutional labor assignments—and force could also not legitimately be exerted indirectly by making basic reinforcers "contingent" on appropriate performance. Further, if patients should decide voluntarily to undertake institutional tasks, the minimum wage would be the legally required "reinforcer." Under *Wyatt*, therapeutic assignments unrelated to hospital operations can constitute legitimate target responses that can be rewarded without regard to the minimum wage. But, perhaps most significant for token economies, *Wyatt* and related legal developments seem to have a great deal to say regarding the definition of legally acceptable reinforcers. *Wyatt*, together with steadily increasing pieces of proposed[73] or enacted[74] legislation, has begun the process of enumerating the rights guaranteed to hospitalized mental patients. The crux of the problem, from the viewpoint of behavior modification, is that the items and activities that are emerging as seemingly absolute rights are the very same items and activities that the behavioral psychologists would employ as reinforcers—that is, as "contingent rights."

According to the *Wyatt* court, for example, a residence unit with screens or curtains to insure privacy, together with a "comfortable bed, . . . a closet or locker for [the patient's] personal belongings, a chair, and a bedside table are all constitutionally required."[75] Under *Wyatt*, patients are also insured nutritionally adequate meals with a diet that will provide "at a minimum the Recommended Daily Dietary Allowances as developed by the National Academy of Sciences."[76] (One instance of the extent to which behavior therapists are seeking to avoid the requirements of *Wyatt* might be mentioned. Now that, under *Wyatt* at least, nutritious meals are required to be provided patients as a matter of right, a therapist who previously used the contingent availability of meals as reinforcers is grudgingly complying with *Wyatt* and offering all his patients nutritious food by taking all the courses, blending them together in an electric blender, and serving the mush-like product at mealtime! The "mush meal" is freely available to all patients, but those patients desiring more flavorful meals, and segregated course offerings, must still pay for them with earned tokens.)

Wyatt further enunciates a general right to have visitors,[77] to attend religious services,[78] to wear one's own clothes[79] (or, for those without adequate clothes, to be provided with a selection of suitable clothing), and to have clothing laundered.[80] With respect to recreation, *Wyatt* speaks of a right to exercise physically several times weekly and to be outdoors regularly and frequently,[81] a right to interact with members of the other sex,[82] and even a right to have a television set in the day room.[83] Finally, apparently borrowing from Judge Bazelon's opinion for the District of Columbia Circuit in *Covington* v. *Harris*,[84] Judge Johnson recognized in *Wyatt* that "patients have a right to the least restrictive conditions necessary to achieve the purposes of commitment"[85]— presumably including, if clinically acceptable, ground privileges and an open ward.

Thus, the usual target behaviors for token economies would be disallowed and the usual reinforcers will be legally unavailable. The emerging law appears to vindicate the assertions of the patients who, at the inception of the Patton State Hospital token economy, "pointed out to the nurses that the state had an obligation to feed them and that the nurses were acting illegally in denying them entrance to the dining room."[86] Chronic patients at Anna State Hospital who had to work for screens and personal lockers to insure privacy would, under *Wyatt*, have those items provided noncontingently. According to the "least restrictive conditions" rationale of *Covington* and *Wyatt*, it would seemingly be impermissible to house on closed wards those patients clinically capable of exercising ground privileges, such as Richmond State Hospital's admittedly nonpsychotic alcoholic patients who, before the onset of the token economy program, would have quickly been placed on an open ward.[87] The identical "least restrictive conditions" rationale would presumably also invalidate programs, such as the one at Anna State Hospital,[88] in which ground privileges or supervised walks are available only by purchase, and programs in which outright release from the institution is conditioned on the accumulation of a set number of tokens or points.[89]

Wyatt is obviously a decision of extraordinary detail and specification, perhaps because of comprehensive stipulation among the parties and amici.[90] Nonetheless, the case[91] is fully consistent with the trend of legal thought.[92] Because the distinct direction of legal thinking bears so heavily on traditional tactics for the behavior modification of chronically psychotic behavior, it is important to examine closely certain particulars of the psycholegal conflict and their implications and to point, if possible, to a proper path for future legal and therapeutic development.

ANALYSIS AND IMPLICATIONS

The important question of the therapeutic or nontherapeutic nature of institutional labor is unfortunately far more complex than would be indicated by the black or white treatment it has received from both legal and psychological quarters. For instance, Ennis's initially attractive and easy-to-apply rule of thumb—that types of patient labor performed at public but not at private hospitals should be presumed cost-saving rather than therapeutic[93]—simply cannot withstand close scrutiny. Ennis's formula is undermined by the clinical and socioeconomic differences between private and public hospital patients. Private hospital patients are typically skilled, of adequate means, and in the hospital for a short stay. Chronic psychotics at state institutions are almost invariably persons who have been hospitalized and unemployed for long periods of time; they are overwhelmingly poor, unskilled, of advanced age, and likely to suffer considerable stigmatization on release from the hospital.[94]

Given this characterization of chronic mental patients, combined of course with apathy, dependency, and institutionalization, ambitious employment opportunities for released chronics are virtually out of the question.[95] Indeed, when viewed from that perspective, together with the fact that work of almost any kind is probably superior to idleness in offsetting apathy, a wide range of institutional work activities both have therapeutic value and realistically approximate future employment goals. For example, Ayllon and Azrin noted about their patients at Anna State Hospital:

> Almost all of the patients in the programmed environment were from rural or lower-class communities. They were all females. Most were housewives prior to admission and presumably would continue to be so after discharge. Their advanced age and their limited formal education indicated that if they were to be employed, they could hold only non-skilled positions. The target behaviors for these individuals seemed, therefore, to be the various performances involved in housekeeping and in unskilled employment.[96]

Further evidence that the motivation behind establishing such target behaviors is indeed therapeutic rather than simply cost-saving can be gleaned from several facts and from examples where cost-saving was not in issue. One Veterans Administration program for discharged chronics, for instance, provides patients with token-earning formal classes in shopping, washing, ironing and mending clothing, and related tasks.[97] Moreover, in one of the few reported instances where released chronics managed to adjust successfully to a form of community life and to remain employed—George Fairweather's project where released patients lived and worked together in a semiautonomous community lodge[98]—the nature of the employment was perfectly consistent with training provided by standard institutional tasks.

When the group of patients in Fairweather's project was about to leave the hospital for the community, for example, it originally planned on opening a restaurant, the bulk of positions to consist of "cook, assistant cook, dishwasher, busboys, waiters and cashier."[99] Eventually, however, the men settled on janitorial work and gardening as their source of income, but even those jobs were performed inadequately[100] until the men received specific training for the work.[101] And in a successful project conducted by one of Fairweather's associates and patterned after that model, but involving both sexes, community employment followed a strikingly similar course: "Men worked at golf courses and other such places in teams doing gardening, landscaping, and groundskeeping work. The women worked in groups at several nursing homes, as well as in motels and restaurants in the local area."[102]

From these examples, it should be apparent that many forms of institutional labor, even though concededly cost-saving, prevent apathy and prepare patients for life, however marginal,[103] on the outside. If the performance of therapeutic institutional labor by patients is to be encouraged, however, certain safeguards should perhaps be required to insure that no patient becomes indispensable to his or her supervisor, a possibility which might result in the patient's continuation on the job becoming more important to the staff than his or her welfare, treatment, or even discharge. Administrative precautions taken in the Anna State Hospital program may prove instructive as legal guidelines: Ayllon and Azrin insisted on periodic job rotation[104] and, moreover, established a firm rule that "no patient was ever allowed to obtain a position for which she alone was qualified."[105] Instead, "a position was established only when several patients were known to be capable of filling that position."[106]

If, given certain safeguards, voluntary[107] institutional labor by chronic patients is to be encouraged, what of *Wyatt*'s minimum wage mandate? Such a mandate, besides vitiating any cost-saving benefits of patient performance, might cause serious complications. First, it will inevitably divert scarce legislative appropriations away from other hospital and therapeutic uses. Second, a minimum wage requirement could encourage a hospital—and, indeed, the encouragement could be compounded by union and community pressure—to fill its institutional positions with permanent outsiders instead of with patients, perhaps leaving the patients to pursue less therapeutic activities.[108] In other words, a minimum wage requirement could possibly result in greater expenditures for less effective therapy.

Thus, although compensating all institutional tasks with the minimum wage appears to be an attractive goal, it is clear that several major problems might be created by that requirement.[109] It is clear, too, that various safeguards short of the minimum wage can be invoked to prevent patient peonage, and that voluntary patient labor can probably be encouraged either by monetary rewards somewhat below the minimum wage or by whatever other reinforcers satisfy the *Wyatt* test.

But in many respects the work and wage question is secondary to the question of legally acceptable and psychologically effective reinforcers. If adequate appropriations were available, if community residents did not threaten to displace patients in the institutional labor force, and if certain other kinks could be ironed out,[110] few objections would be raised to specifying the minimum wage as a legally required reinforcer for patient-performed hospital work assignments. Indeed, if monetary rewards, whether of minimum wage proportions or not, were sufficient to induce patient performance of therapeutically sound activities, that would be a small price to pay to strengthen target behaviors.

The major problem faced by the token economy is the current trend toward expansion of the category of protected inmate interests. The law, relying on concepts such as freedom and dignity, would require, for example, that all patients be accorded minimal levels of privacy and comfort. To the behavioral psychologist, however, who operates from the premise of determinism, philosophical notions of "freedom" and "dignity" are irrelevant.[111] Rather, the psychologist views privacy or comfort as no more than useful tools to manipulate to make a psychotic's behavior more appropriate and socially adaptive, a goal which presumably all agree is in the best interest of both the patient and society. In the psychologist's view, it would surely be an ironic tragedy if, in the name of an illusory ideal such as freedom, the law were to deny the therapist the only effective tools known to restore the chronic psychotic to health and to a place in the community.

Wyatt thus poses a painful dilemma. The behavior modifier suggests that chronic psychotics respond initially to only the most primitive reinforcers, and, therefore, only the contingent availability of those reinforcers can motivate development of socially adaptive behavior.[112] It follows, the behaviorists claim, that if the basics are made freely available as rights rather than as reinforcers, chronic psychotics may be destined to spend their lives functioning poorly in an institutional setting, whereas if those basic rights are converted into contingent reinforcers, there may be a real prospect of clinical improvement and discharge.[113]

If the empirical evidence supported the claim that token economies relying on primitive reinforcers worked very well with chronic patients—that, for example, virtually all patients improved dramatically and were able to earn the reinforcers required for a decent existence, or if the evidence demonstrated that no less drastic means could accomplish similar results—a reevaluation of the emerging law might very well be in order. But a review of the pertinent literature suggests that behavior modification proponents may have difficulty sustaining a burden of proof with respect to those matters.

First of all, while most token economy outcome studies report favorable results,[114] the successes are far from overwhelming. Even in a project as dramatic as the Anna State Hospital study, eight of the 44 subject patients were basically unresponsive to the program,[115] and success for the remaining patients was measured solely by their work output.[116] When judged by release data rather than by measures of work output, decreased apathy,[117] or improved clinical state,[118] results of token economy systems with chronic psychotics have not been encouraging. Even in the Atthowe and Krasner project at the Palo Alto Veterans Administration Hospital, which reported a doubling of the discharge rate, 11 of the 24 released patients returned to the hospital within 9 months,[119] a more rapid relapse than is normally found in studies of chronic patients.[120]

We must also consider whether the results achieved by token economies—whatever they may be—could be matched or surpassed by less drastic means.[121] Information is wanting, perhaps in part because behavior modifiers have not employed reinforcers other than the basics in standard use. It may be, for example, that creative observation of patient behavior preferences would reveal frequent behavior patterns, other than basic behaviors, which could be utilized as reinforcers. Also, although it is an impure technique according to orthodox behaviorism, another practical approach is simply to ask the patients what they would like to possess or to do. [122]

By exploring creatively for reinforcers, it is likely that therapists could construct a list of idiosyncratic objects and activities (mail order catalogue items, [123] soft-boiled rather than standard hard-boiled eggs, [124] and feeding kittens [125] are actual clinical examples) that could be made available contingently in order to strengthen appropriate target responses. Moreover, to the extent that effective reinforcers are in fact *idiosyncratic*, it follows almost by definition that their contingent availability could not conflict with the legally emerging absolute *general* rights of patients.

A system of positive behavior modification based heavily on idiosyncratic reinforcers might be clinically as well as legally superior. Psychologists employing such systems [126] have been able to devise individual treatment plans assuring each patient independent diagnostic and therapeutic attention. [127]

But individualized treatment plans, required by *Wyatt* [128] and perhaps part of the emerging right to treatment, [129] are not incompatible with the operation of ward-wide or hospital-wide general treatment systems designed to overcome general patient problems such as indecisiveness, dependency, or apathy. In fact, the most fruitful combination might be to combine individualized treatment programs with an efficient, easy-to-administer general therapeutic system. [130] If, however, the criterion for a successful system is efficacy with the least drastic deprivations possible, it appears that token economies for chronic psychotics may well finish no better than second best. [131]

Specifically, although it may not be determinative, the work of George Fairweather is highly relevant here. [132] Though he speaks the language of social psychology and of small group theory rather than the language of behaviorism and learning theory, Fairweather relies in part on principles of behavior modification, and his work is discussed prominently in texts on that subject. [133] But his study was bottomed on the belief that chronics, to survive outside, must acquire problem-solving and decision-making skills, and on the knowledge that small cohesive groups can effectively control the behavior of their members. [134] Patients were divided into small task groups with monetary and pass privileges awarded according to the level of responsibility each individual attained.

The money privileges for the most part came from personal funds of the patients who participated in the programs. The amounts of money and number of passes were set up in advance for each of four progressive levels of achievement. The task group as a unit became responsible for the progress of its individual members through the four designated steps. Step one involved personal care, punctuality on assignments, and cooperation in the orientation of new members. Step two required, in addition, acceptable work on the job assignment. Requirements in step three were individualized, with patients responsible for recommending the level of their own rewards. In step four the patient had responsibility for his departure plans and had unlimited rights to withdrawal of money and passes. In step one the patient received ten dollars and a one-day pass each week, in step two, fifteen dollars per week and an overnight pass every other week.[135]

The task group was responsible for dealing with patient problems and for recommending to the staff the level of pass and monetary privileges deserved by each patient member. Patient task group recommendations were considered weekly by a staff committee.[136] To establish cohesive and well-functioning groups, Fairweather would at times advance or demote the group as a unit.[137]

Fairweather found that over time pride in group achievement appeared to become a more important motivator than money or passes.[138] Leaders emerged in the chronic psychotic groups as well as in other clinical categories,[139] and the program was a therapeutic success: As compared with a control group subjected to traditional hospital therapy (not a token economy), the small group patients showed significantly less pathological behavior,[140] greater social interaction,[141] and greater participation during meetings.[142] Moreover, the small group program substantially reduced hospitalization.[143] When combined with an aftercare program involving a voluntary living arrangement in a semiautonomous (and eventually autonomous) community lodge, the Fairweather system achieved the long-awaited goal of adequate employment and community adjustment for discharged chronic psychotics.[144] Fairweather thus produced impressive results with chronic psychotics in an environment clearly "less drastic" in deprivation than any of the traditional token economies. Obviously, Fairweather's patients were provided with food and beds. Further, the ward was open and patients had complete access to the hospital grounds.[145] The ward was equipped with a television set, table games, magazines, and the like,[146] and freely available activities included library reading, movies, dances, and bowling.[147]

Most of these privileges were available only by purchase in the token economy programs. Yet a patient at the bottom of Fairweather's hierarchy was provided, without a work assignment, not only with these privileges, but also with ten dollars and a one day pass each week. Indeed, life at the lowest level of Fairweather's ladder compares favorably with the conditions at advanced levels in some token systems. [148]

Fairweather's approach, then, seems preferable to token economies on several counts. First and foremost, his small group system has yielded impressive results which are unmatched by token systems. Second, while token systems deprive patients of basic comforts in their reliance on primitive reinforcers, Fairweather employs only money and passes. [149] Third, Fairweather's approach is thoroughly oriented toward release and community adjustment, and he recognizes that once cohesive groups have been formed in the hospital, "an immediate move to the community is essential." [150] Finally, Fairweather's behavior modification model emphasizes the development of confidence and decision-making ability rather than performance of assignments. For whatever it is worth, Fairweather's system may be ethically, or at least emotionally, more palatable than the manipulative techniques of the token economies.

CONCLUSION

Fairweather's small group model, with its rich results and rather minor deprivations, poses a serious threat to token economies. If further studies continue to indicate that, except in extreme circumstances, token economies for chronic psychotics resort to more drastic deprivations than other therapies without producing better results, [151] it is likely that token systems will soon find themselves subject to both legal and behavioral extinction.

Indeed, if the law's general direction in the patient rights area proceeds uninterrupted, token economies may well become legally unavailable even if they are therapeutically *superior* to other approaches. That is because the developing law is creating new patient rights unaware that these rights will undermine a basic behavior modification technique. On the other hand, the behavior modifiers seem busy constructing token economies unaware that legal developments may soon call for their demolition.

Forcing these disparate disciplines to take note of each other—obviously the principal object of this chapter—should be helpful to both of them. Behavior modification proponents, convinced of the therapeutic indispensability of token economies for chronic patients, may have reservations about the Fairweather model. But unless systematic comparative studies of alternative therapies are performed soon,[152] the law will be unable to incorporate the results in developing a sensible package of patient rights, and expected legal developments may ultimately preclude such studies.[153]

NOTES

[1]*See* Chapter 4.

[2]CAL. WELF. & INST'NS CODE §§ 5325(f) & 5326.7.

[3]Breggin, *The Return of Lobotomy and Psychosurgery*, 118 CONG. REC. E1602 (daily ed. Feb. 24. 1972). *See* Chapter 8 for a discussion of psychosurgery and the *Kaimowitz* case.

[4]R. SCHWITZGEBEL, DEVELOPMENT AND LEGAL REGULATION OF COERCIVE BEHAVIOR MODIFICATION TECHNIQUES WITH OFFENDERS (1971). Schwitzgebel's work has been condensed to article form in Schwitzgebel, *Limitations on the Coercive Treatment of Offenders*, 8 CRIM. L. BULL. 267 (1972). On aversion therapy generally, *see* S. RACHMAN & J. TEASDALE, AVERSION THERAPY AND BEHAVIOR DISORDERS (1969); A. BANDURA, PRINCIPLES OF BEHAVIOR MODIFICATION 293–354 (1969) (hereinafter cited as BANDURA). *See* Note, *Aversion Therapy: Punishment as Treatment and Treatment as Cruel and Unusual Punishment*, 49 SO. CALIF. L. REV. 880 (1976).

[5]*See* Schwitzgebel, *supra* note 4, at 267, 285–86. Anectine, a drug that induces temporary paralysis and respiratory arrest, has been used for behavior control in some California institutions. *See* Note, *Conditioning and Other Technologies Used to "Treat?" "Rehabilitate?" "Demolish?" Prisoners and Mental Patients*, 45 SO. CALIF. L. REV. 616, 633–40 (1972).

[6]Dr. Peter Breggin argues that psychosurgery should be precluded on these grounds. *See generally* Breggin, *supra* note 3. *Compare* NATIONAL COMMISSION FOR THE PROTECTION OF HUMAN SUBJECTS OF BIOMEDICAL AND BEHAVIORAL RESEARCH, REPORT AND RECOMMENDATIONS: PSYCHOSURGERY (1977).

[7]"Patients have a right not to be subjected to treatment procedures such as lobotomy, electro-convulsive treatment, adversive [sic] reinforcement conditioning or other unusual or hazardous treatment procedures without their express and informed consent after consultation with counsel or interested party of the patient's choice," Wyatt v. Stickney, 344 F. Supp. 373, 380 (M.D. Ala. 1972) (dealing with Bryce and Searcy Hospitals for the mentally ill). *See also* Wyatt v. Stickney, 344 F. Supp. 387, 400 (M.D. Ala. 1972) (dealing with Partlow State School and Hospital for the mentally retarded). These two cases will hereinafter be distinguished by parenthesized indication of the hospital they dealt with. *See also* the later journey of part of the litigation in Wyatt v. Aderholt, 503 F.2d 1305 (5th Cir. 1974).

[8]BANDURA, *supra* note 4, at 217–92. *See also* A. BANDURA, SOCIAL LEARNING THEORY (1977).

[9]*Cf.* McIntire, *Spare the Rod, Use Behavior Mod*, PSYCHOLOGY TODAY, Dec., 1970, at 42. Considerable controversy is, of course, generated by calls for behavioral engineering on a society-wide scale, such as is advocated in B. F. SKINNER, BEYOND FREEDOM AND DIGNITY (1971). *See, e.g.*, Ramsey, *Book Review*, 7 ISSUES IN CRIM. 131 (1972) (reviewing Skinner's book).

[10]*Cf.* BANDURA, *supra* note 4, at 249–50 (positive reinforcement as a technique for improving reading skills).

[11]*Cf. id.* at 278–79.

[12]A good introductory text on operant conditioning is J. R. MILLENSON, PRINCIPLES OF BEHAVIORAL ANALYSIS (1967). Chapters Two and Three deal with classical or Pavlovian conditioning, which is to be distinguished from operant conditioning; the latter provides the basis of the token economy. *See also* Note, *supra* note 5, at 616, 627–28 (1972).

[13]Note that the behavioral psychologist explains both normal and abnormal behavior by the same principles, in an approach which differs fundamentally from "dynamic" psychology, of which the Freudian system of psychoanalysis is probably the most familiar to laymen. The dynamic psychologists, who follow a "medical model," explain abnormal behavior as the product of "inner conflicts" and the like. For a good introduction to behavior modification and how it contrasts with traditional dynamic concepts, *see* L. ULLMANN & L. KRASNER, CASE STUDIES IN BEHAVIOR MODIFICATION 1–65 (1965). *See also* BANDURA, *supra* note 4, at 1–69. For more recent accounts of the application of behavioral psychology to clinical settings, see any recent issue of the JOURNAL OF APPLIED BEHAVIOR ANALYSIS. A recent attempt to reconcile behavior therapy and psychoanalysis appears in P. WACHTEL, PSYCHOANALYSIS AND BEHAVIOR THERAPY: TOWARD AN INTEGRATION (1977).

Technically, the term extinction is reserved for the process of reducing the frequency of a behavior by discontinuing the "reinforcing" (rewarding) consequences.

[14]Fuller, *Operant Conditioning of a Vegetative Human Organism*, 62 AM. J. PSYCHOLOGY 587 (1949). For somewhat more recent studies, *see* ULLMANN & KRASNER, *supra* note 13, and R. ULRICH,T. STACHNIK, & J. MABRY, CONTROL OF HUMAN BEHAVIOR (1966).

[15]"Shape" is a technical term used by operant psychologists to describe the process of gradually building a new behavior by rewarding closer and closer approximations to it.

[16]Ayllon & Azrin, *The Measurement and Reinforcement of Behavior of Psychotics*, 8 J. EXP. ANAL. BEHAV. 357 (1965); T. AYLLON & N. AZRIN, THE TOKEN ECONOMY: A MOTIVATIONAL SYSTEM FOR THERAPY AND REHABILITATION (1968) (hereinafter cited as TOKEN ECONOMY) (report of a project begun in 1961). In part, the flourishing is no doubt due to the fact that much behavior therapy can be conducted by psychiatric nurses, attendants, and paraprofessional personnel. *See* Ayllon & Michael, *The Psychiatric Nurse as a Behavioral Engineer*, 2 J. EXP. ANAL. BEHAV. 323 (1959). The rationale behind emphasizing the development of constructive behavior (the thrust of token economies and positive behavior control) rather than emphasizing the elimination per se of so-called "pathological" behavior appears to be that pathological traits in an otherwise well-functioning individual may well be dismissed as mere idiosyncracies and, moreover, that pathological traits may not be able to coexist with functional behavior. TOKEN ECONOMY, *supra*, at 23.

[17]These include populations of juvenile delinquents, newly admitted and chronic psychotics, mentally retarded patients, the aged, etc. TOKEN ECONOMY, *supra* note 16, at 217. For various descriptions, *see* BANDURA, *supra* note 4, at 261–82; Davison, *Appraisal of Behavior Modification Techniques with Adults in Institutional Settings*, in BEHAVIOR THERAPY: APPRAISAL AND STATUS 250 (C. Franks ed. 1969); Krasner, *Token Economy as an Illustration of Operant Conditioning Procedures with the Aged, with Youth, and with Society*, in LEARNING APPROACHES TO THERAPEUTIC BEHAVIOR CHANGE 74 (D. Levis ed. 1970); Mishara, *Geriatric Patients Who Improve in Token Economy and General Milieu Treatment Programs: A Multivariate Analysis*, 46 J. COUNSELING & CLINICAL PSYCHOLOGY 1340 (1978). *See generally* Kazdin & Bootzin, *The Token Economy: An Evaluative Review*, 5 J. APP. BEHAV. ANAL. 343 (1972). *See also* Agras, *The Token Economy*, in BEHAVIOR MODIFICATION: PRINCIPLES AND CLINICAL APPLICATIONS 64 (W. S. Agras ed. 1978).

[18]Jarvik, *The Psychopharmacological Revolution*, in READINGS IN CLINICAL PSYCHOLOGY TODAY 93 (1970).

[19]Shuman and Hawkins, *The Use of Alternatives to Institutionalization of the Mentally Ill*, 33 Sw. L. J. 1181 (1980).

[20]*E.g.*, Bruce, *Tokens for Recovery*, 66 AM. J. NURSING 1799 (1966).

[21]TOKEN ECONOMY, *supra* note 16.

[22]*See generally* E. GOFFMAN, ASYLUMS (Anchor ed. 1961).

[23]TOKEN ECONOMY, *supra* note 16, at 250.

[24]*Id.* at 134–35.

[25]*Id.* at 60. *See* Premack, *Toward Empirical Behavioral Laws: I. Positive Reinforcement*, 66 PSYCHOLOGICAL REV. 219 (1959).

[26]TOKEN ECONOMY, *supra* note 16, at 61.

[27]*Id.* at 221. *See also id.* at 64–65.

[28]*Id.* at 62–63.

[29]*Id.* at 226.

[30]*Id.* at 269.

[31]*Id.* at 188.

[32]*Id. See also id.* at 256–61.

[33]*Id.* at 239.

[34]*Id.* at 269. *But see* the remarks of Davison directed at Ayllon & Azrin's conclusion: "I believe that Ayllon and Azrin would do well to break set and at least consider the possibility that the behavior (both overt and covert) of some chronic hospital patients is regulated by processes which have little, if anything, to do with operant conditioning." Davison, *supra* note 17, at 250.

[35]*E.g.*, Atthowe & Krasner, *Preliminary Report on the Application of Contingent Reinforcement Procedures (Token Economy) on a "Chronic" Psychiatric Ward*, 73 J. ABN. PSYCH. 37 (1968).

[36]Atthowe, Ward 113 Program: Incentives and Costs—A Manual for Patients 7–8 (Veterans Ad., Palo Alto, Calif., Oct. 1, 1964).

[37]*Id.* at 4. The present author also visited a token economy where naps were available for five tokens per hour.

[38]*Id.* at 5.

[39]Lloyd & Abel, *Performance on a Token Economy Psychiatric Ward: A Two Year Summary*, 8 BEHAV. RES. & THERAPY 1, 6 (1970).

[40]Narrol, *Experimental Application of Reinforcement Principles to the Analysis and Treatment of Hospitalized Alcoholics*, 28 Q. J. STUD. ALCOHOL 105, 108 (1967).

[41]Gripp & Magaro, *A Token Economy Program Evaluation with Untreated Control Ward Comparisons*, 9 BEHAV. RES. & THERAPY 137, 141 (1971).

[42]*Id.*

[43]Glicksman, Ottomanelli, & Cutler, *The Earn-Your-Way Credit System: Use of a Token Economy in Narcotic Rehabilitation*, 6 INT'L. J. OF THE ADDICTIONS 525 (1971). *Cf.* Lloyd & Abel, *supra* note 39, at 5.

[44]*E.g.*, Schaefer, *Investigations in Operant Conditioning Procedures in a Mental Hospital*, in REINFORCEMENT THEORY IN PSYCHOLOGICAL TREATMENT—A SYMPOSIUM 25, 26 (J. Fisher & R. Harris eds. 1966) (Calif. Ment. Health Res. Monog. No. 8); Bruce, *Tokens for Recovery*, 66 AM. J. NURSING 1799, 1801 (1966); Gripp & Magaro, *supra* note 41, at 141; Lloyd & Abel, *supra* note 39 at 6.

[45]Schaefer, *supra* note 44, at 33–34. Actually, the quoted remark was made in the context of overcoming refusal-to-eat problems exhibited by some of the patients, but if the hospital is medically willing to allow those patients to miss five consecutive days of

meals, it seems reasonable to assume that the same medical standard would be applied to patients who presumably desire to eat but who have not earned a sufficient number of tokens to pay for meals.

[46]*E.g.*, Lloyd & Abel, *supra* note 39; Narrol, *supra* note 40. *Cf.* Atthowe & Krasner, *supra* note 35.

[47]Bruce, *supra* note 44, at 1799, 1802 (1966).

[48]*Id.* at 1800–01. The Patton system seems to carry to the extreme the position often advocated by behaviorists that noncontingent rewards ought to be provided at an "adequate but relatively low level," with preferred reinforcers being available "contingent upon the occurrence of desired response patterns." BANDURA, *supra* note 4, at 231. Under such an approach, therapy can be managed chiefly by positive reinforcement, without resort to punishment, and patients, the argument continues, have only themselves to blame if their privileges seem inadequate. Indeed, several programs have noted the benefits of an earn-your-way system, in notable contrast to more traditional approaches where "mandating educational or group therapy participation by threatening loss of visiting and other privileges or delayed release appeared to stimulate the social defiance and self-defeating traits of the population, and rebellion against the regulations of the institution provided an increase in prestige and enhanced status in the eyes of the peer group." Glicksman, Ottomanelli, & Cutler, *supra* note 43, at 525. Some commentators have criticized our penocorrectional system for giving inmates noncontingently whatever benefits may be available, and then denying some of the benefits as punishment for wrongful behavior—a system where "the staff members are cast in the unenviable role of punitive agents, and the [inmates] can move only in a downward direction," BANDURA, *supra* note 4, at 230. To the same effect, *see* Hindelang, *A Learning Theory Analysis of the Correctional Process,* 4 ISSUES IN CRIMINOLOGY 43, 44–45 (1969). *See also* M. Hindelang, Social Learning Theory and Social Problems: The Case of Prisons 9 (unpublished manuscript on file with author): "At the same time that a noncontingent system of rewards is operating a contingent system of punishments is attempted; the result is that inmates come to view the rewards as rights rather than privileges and when they are threatened with the denial of those rewards they become justifiably embittered." (citations omitted). It has been suggested that when contingencies are so managed, "the majority of the participants comply half-heartedly with the minimum demands of the institution in order to avoid penalties for any breach of the rules," and that, in a psychiatric setting, "patients can best maximize their rewards by merely adopting a passive patient role." BANDURA, *supra* note 4, at 230. If the legal system wishes to accept the advice of the behaviorists, the crucial question for the law, of course, will be to define, for various clinical populations, just where the line of noncontingent rewards at an "adequate but relatively low level" ought to be drawn.

[49]Narrol, *supra* note 40, at 105.

[50]As will be apparent, it also raises certain serious questions about the ethical propriety of the type of psychological research involved. *See also* Rubin, *Jokers Wild in the Lab,* PSYCHOLOGY TODAY, Dec., 1970, at 18. *See generally* DEVIANCE AND DECENCY: THE ETHICS OF RESEARCH WITH HUMAN SUBJECTS (C. Klockars & F. O'Connor eds. 1979).

[51]Narrol, *supra* note 40, at 105, 107.

[52]*Id.*

[53]*Id.* at 108. With respect to the right to treatment, the same author states: "The obligation to treat the patient need not be neglected, since purchase of all the available therapeutic services may be permitted." *Id.* at 106–07.

[54]*Id.* at 109.

[55]*Id.*

[56]*Id.* at 108. Of particular concern, from the viewpoint of the ethics of research, is that "work was made the target behavior for the purposes of simple demonstration of reinforcement technique." *Id.* at 107-08. In other words, "the project had no therapeutic purpose, but demonstrated that behavior can be controlled in a simulated economy." *Id.* at 107. The study proved simply that project patients worked 8-hour days as opposed to the 4-hour days worked by nonproject alcoholic patients. *Id.* at 109. But that is hardly a startling finding, particularly since the project was based on the Ayllon & Azrin study, which had already established the point. Indeed, the author was himself hardly surprised by the outcome: "Definite evidence of increased work output was obtained, as might be expected." *Id.*

[57]*E.g.*, Note, *Beyond the Ken of Courts: A Critique of the Judicial Refusal to Review the Complaints of Convicts*, 72 YALE L. J. 506 (1963).

[58]*E.g.*, N. KITTRIE, THE RIGHT TO BE DIFFERENT: DEVIANCE AND ENFORCED THERAPY 307-08 (1971). *Cf.* O'Donoghue v. Riggs, 73 Wash. 2d 814, 820 n.2, 440 P.2d 823, 828 n.2 (1968): "One who enters a hospital as a mentally ill person either as a voluntary or involuntary patient, impliedly consents to the use of such force as may be reasonably necessary to the proper care of the patient."

[59]Covington v. Harris, 491 F.2d 617 (D.C. Cir. 1969); Wyatt v. Stickney, 344 F. Supp. 373 (M.D. Ala. 1972) (Bryce and Searcy Hospitals).

[60]*E.g.*, CAL. WELF. & INST'NS CODE § 5325. *See* note 74 *infra.*

[61]Ironically, however, an experiment conducted by Ayllon and Azrin seems to demonstrate that "although the reinforcement for self-care was initiated to maintain a minimum standard of cleanliness and personal hygiene, changes in the reinforcement contingencies produced no appreciable difference in self-care practices." TOKEN ECONOMY, *supra* note 16, at 255.

[62]*E.g.*, Ennis, *Civil Liberties and Mental Illness*, 7 CRIM. L. BULL. 101, 122-23 (1971). At Anna State Hospital, because the token value of jobs is set by factors of supply and demand, "some jobs that were fairly demanding physically and that required about three hours through the day for completion, such as sweeping the floors, earned only about five tokens." TOKEN ECONOMY, *supra* note 16, at 204.

[63]*Id.* at 201.

[64]*Id.* at 188.

[65]*Id.* at 201-02.

[66]*Id.* at 210.

[67]Jobson v. Henne, 355 F.2d 129, 132 n.3 (2d Cir. 1966). The court also noted that if concededly involuntary labor is nontherapeutic, even compensation for the work will not necessarily satisfy Thirteenth Amendment requirements, for "the mere payment of a compensation, unless the receipt of the compensation induces consent to the performance of the work, cannot serve to justify forced labor." *Id.*

[68]Ennis, *supra* note 62, at 101, 123 (1971) (emphasis in original).

[69]Wyatt v. Stickney, 344 F. Supp. 373 (M.D. Ala. 1972) (Bryce and Searcy Hospitals).

[70]*Id.* at 381. The minimum wage law is the Fair Labor Standards Act, 29 U.S.C. § 206. Judge Johnson, in *Wyatt*, further ordered that payment to patients for such work shall not be applied to offset hospitalization costs. *Id.* at 13. For a discussion of constitutional difficulties in applying federal wage requirements to employees and patients of state facilities, see note 109 *infra.*

[71]344 F. Supp. at 381.

[72]Under *Wyatt*, the only type of work that can seemingly be "required," and the only type

of work exempt from minimum wage coverage, is therapeutic work unrelated to hospital functioning. Further, according to *Wyatt*, patients can also be required "to perform tasks of a personal housekeeping nature such as the making of one's bed." *Id.*

[73]The President's Commission on Mental Health has recommended that each state enact a "Bill of Rights" for mentally disabled persons. PRESIDENT'S COMMISSION ON MENTAL HEALTH, REPORT TO THE PRESIDENT 44, 72 (1978).

[74]*E.g.*, CAL. WELF. & INST'NS CODE § 5325. Several states have enacted Bills of Rights for the mentally disabled. *See Mental Health and Human Rights: Report of the Task Panel on Legal and Ethical Issues*, 20 ARIZ. L. REV. 49, 133–37 (1978).

[75]Wyatt v. Stickney, 344 F. Supp. 373, 381–82 (M.D. Ala. 1972) (Bryce and Searcy Hospitals).

[76]*Id.* at 383.

[77]*Id.* at 379. *See also* CAL. WELF. & INST'S CODE § 5325(c).

[78]344 F. Supp. at 381.

[79]*Id.* at 380. *See also* CAL. WELF. & INST'NS CODE § 5325(a).

[80]344 F. Supp. at 381.

[81]*Id.*

[82]*Id.*

[83]*Id.* at 382.

[84]419 F.2d 617 (D.C. Cir. 1969).

[85]Wyatt v. Stickney, 344 F. Supp. 373, 379 (M.D. Ala. 1972) (Bryce and Searcy Hospitals). The "least restrictive alternative" or "less drastic means" rationale was first applied in the mental health law area in Lake v. Cameron, 364 F.2d 657 (D.C. Cir. 1966), an opinion authored by Judge Bazelon, which held that commitment itself should be ordered only if no suitable but less drastic alternatives to commitment could be located. For a discussion of the constitutional doctrine of "less drastic means" in the commitment context, *see* Chambers, *Alternatives to Civil Commitment of the Mentally Ill: Practical Guides and Constitutional Imperatives*, 70 MICH. L. REV. 1107 (1972). For an application of the principle, *see* Chapter 6. In Covington v. Harris, 419 F.2d 617 (D.C. Cir. 1969), Judge Bazelon simply extended the doctrine to life within the confines of the hospital environment. *See also* Wexler, *Of Rights and Reinforcers*, 11 SAN DIEGO L. REV. 957, 962–63 n.8 (1974).

[86]Schaefer, *supra* note 44, at 29.

[87]A similar problem seems to be present in the token economy system of State Hospital North, Orofino, Idaho, as described in Lloyd & Abel, *supra* note 39, at 1. In addition to using tokens for "standard" reinforcers, the State Hospital North program has a phase system which requires the accumulation of tokens for phase promotion. Group C, for example, is a closed ward, and promotion to Group B, which has ground privileges, requires earning 2,000 tokens in a three week period. Further, failure to earn substantial tokens while in Group B or A may result in demotion to Group C. *Id.* at 5. To the extent that certain Group C patients could clinically manage ground privileges—which, given the system, seems almost beyond doubt—this program, and many others devised along similar patterns, seems to offend the "less drastic means" test of *Covington* and *Wyatt*.

[88]TOKEN ECONOMY, *supra* note 16, at 226. Ayllon and Azrin do not specify the percentage of patients on their ward clinically capable of exercising ground privileges, but Atthowe and Krasner, in their report on a token economy for chronic psychotics at the Palo Alto Veterans Administration Hospital, estimate that fully 40% of their patients could, without difficulty, leave the ward unescorted. Atthowe & Krasner, *supra* note 35, at 37, 38. Any scheme that required such patients to purchase ground privileges would presumably run afoul of *Covington* and *Wyatt*. For more on this, *see* Wexler, *supra* note 85, at 962–63 n.8.

[89]A token economy program in New York which involves civilly committed narcotic addicts presumably hinges release—or at least eligibility for release consideration—on the accumulation of 936 points. Glicksman, Ottomanelli, & Cutler, *supra* note 43, at 525–27. To the extent that the point accumulation system does not mesh squarely with statutory or clinical criteria for release, such a system presents serious questions regarding the unwarranted deprivation of liberty. The only saving grace for the described program seems to be that its patients are released after an average stay of 4 months, whereas committed addicts not on the earn-your-way token system are confined for an average of 7.5 months. *Id.* at 528. *See also* Atthowe, *supra* note 36, at 5, 10 (before patient can be eligible for 90-day trial visit, must be in Group A for 30 days, and it costs 120 tokens to enter Group A, assuming there is an opening).

[90]Wyatt v. Stickney, 344 F. Supp. 373, 375–76 (M.D. Ala. 1972) (Bryce and Searcy Hospitals).

[91]Another, somewhat less precise, legal problem facing token economies may exist in the confusion between activities that constitute target responses and those that constitute reinforcers. More specifically, different token economies may classify the same activity differently. For example, chronic patients at the Palo Alto Veterans Administration Hospital *earned* tokens for attending group activities, recreational events, and movies (which were viewed as target behaviors), whereas Anna State Hospital patients had to *expend* tokens to attend similar activities (which were viewed as reinforcers). *Compare* Atthowe, *supra* note 36, at 7, *with* TOKEN ECONOMY, *supra* note 16, at 226. In view of the emerging constitutional right to treatment [*see* Wyatt v. Stickney, 325 F. Supp. 781 (M.D. Ala. 1971)], it seems problematic at best to *charge* for psychotherapy sessions, as at Anna State Hospital and Richmond State Hospital, particularly when so few patients seem willing to expend tokens to attend such sessions. *E.g.*, TOKEN ECONOMY, *supra* note 16, at 66–67, 226, 234; Narrol, *supra* note 40, at 108–09. Indeed, even the previously mentioned activities (such as recreational events and movies) may have significant therapeutic value (and may fall within the scope of the right to treatment) in reducing boredom, increasing interaction, and, in the case of movies, in providing a vicarious experience for learning or modeling appropriate social behavior. *See* BANDURA, *supra* note 4, at 179–82.

It can easily be contended, therefore, that therapy sessions, recreational events, movies, writing materials (to increase contact with the world outside), and other items and events ought to be provided, as part and parcel of the right to treatment, on an absolute, noncontingent basis. *Cf.* Covington v. Harris, 419 F.2d 617, 625–26 (D.C. Cir. 1969). Interestingly, however, even the noncontingent ready availability of such therapeutic items and events may be insufficient to arouse interest in them on the part of a highly apathetic patient population. A possible solution is to convert important therapeutic activities into token-earning target responses, as Atthowe did in Palo Alto. In psychological terms, such a course of action requires "considering the selection of a reinforcer as a response to be strengthened." Ayllon & Azrin, *Reinforcer Sampling: A Technique for Increasing the Behavior of Mental Patients*, 1 J. APP. BEHAV. ANAL. 13, 14 (1968). In legal terms, we seem to have developed a new category of "reinforced rights."

Those with Hohfeldian hangups might wish to construct a spectrum of patient rights—and correlative hospital obligations—along the line of privileges (dispensed or withheld by hospital discretion), contingent rights (legitimate primary reinforcers mandatorily available by token purchase), rights (available absolutely and noncontingently), and reinforced rights (target responses which can be engaged in as a matter of right and which will be reinforced by tokens)!

[92]*E.g.*, Ennis, *supra* note 62, at 101 (1971). *See* CAL. WELF. & INST'NS CODE § 5325. The

legislative developments occasionally cover ground not touched by *Wyatt*. The California statute, for example, gives patients the right "to have ready access to letter writing materials, including stamps ." CAL. WELF. & INST'NS CODE § 5325(e). Indeed, the failure of these detailed statutes to cover some of the more basic rights (such as food and beds) must be attributed to an assumption on behalf of the draftsmen that such rights were beyond dispute or beyond denial in practice.

[93]Ennis, *supra* note 62, at 101, 123.

[94]*E.g.*, TOKEN ECONOMY, *supra* note 16, at 54; BANDURA, *supra* note 4, at 278. *See also* Lloyd & Abel, *supra* note 39, at 1, 8; Spiegler, The Use of a School Model and Contingency Management in a Day Treatment Program for Psychiatric Outpatients 6 (paper presented at Rocky Mountain Psychological Association Convention, Denver, Colorado, May, 1971).

[95]*E.g.*, G. FAIRWEATHER, D. SANDERS, H. MAYNARD, D. CRESSLER, & D. BLECK, COMMUNITY LIFE FOR THE MENTALLY ILL: AN ALTERNATIVE TO INSTITUTIONAL CARE 207 (1969) [hereinafter cited as COMMUNITY LIFE]. Indeed, the relapse rate for released chronics is so high and employment prospects are so dim that some commentators have questioned hospital release as an appropriate therapeutic goal. *See* Lloyd & Abel, *supra* note 39, at 8.

[96]TOKEN ECONOMY, *supra* note 16, at 54.

[97]Spiegler, *supra* note 94, at 4.

[98]COMMUNITY LIFE, *supra* note 95. *Cf.* B. PASAMANICK, F. SCARPITTI, & S. DINITZ, SCHIZOPHRENICS IN THE COMMUNITY: AN EXPERIMENTAL STUDY IN THE PREVENTION OF HOSPITALIZATION (1967).

[99]COMMUNITY LIFE, *supra* note 95, at 46.

[100]*Id.* at 5.

[101]*Id.* at 50–51, 54.

[102]*Id.* at 332. That cost-saving and therapeutic labor are not necessarily mutually exclusive concepts was recognized in Jobson v. Henne, 355 F.2d 129 (2d Cir. 1966). Note that the therapeutic or nontherapeutic nature of particular institutional work assignments may well vary among clinical groups. Just as those tasks may be therapeutic from the perspective of public hospital chronic patients but not for private hospital patients, *see* text accompanying note 97 *supra*, so too the work may be therapeutic for chronic state hospital patients but not necessarily for prisoners or, particularly, for juvenile delinquents—who seemingly need academic proficiency to achieve vocational success in their long lives ahead far more than they need training in janitorial work. *Cf.* BANDURA, *supra* note 4, at 278. In fact, the entire legal analysis of token economies should probably vary with different clinical populations. For instance, the law would probably view the privacy claim that a room-divider screen ought to be provided as an absolute right (rather than merely be available as a contingent reinforcer) far differently in the context of dormitory-style living for the adult mentally ill than in the context of a juvenile institution. *But see* Wyatt v. Stickney, 344 F. Supp. 387, 404 (M.D. Ala. 1972) (Partlow Hospital) (screens or curtains mandated in an institution for mentally retarded children and adults). Further, resort to certain reinforcers may be arguably necessary to encourage appropriate behavior among one clinical group, but be unnecessary to induce the target behavior among a different clinical category. Consider, in that connection, the Richmond State Hospital scheme of treating nonpsychotic alcoholics in a manner very similar to the way other token economy programs treat chronic psychotics.

[103]*Cf.* COMMUNITY LIFE, *supra* note 95, at 337. In view of the traditional astounding speedy relapse rates for the great majority of discharged chronic patients, BANDURA, *supra* note

4, at 269, marginality in the outside community seems, at least for the near future, to be an acceptable goal.

[104]TOKEN ECONOMY, *supra* note 16, at 202.

[105]*Id.* at 201.

[106]*Id.*

[107]Truly voluntary work would assume, of course, that no basic rights—food, beds, ground privileges, privacy—were made contingent on performance.

[108]Activities are less therapeutic if the skills they teach are not marketable in the outside community. There is no point in using the hospital setting to build up socially adaptive behavior if one can expect that the environment the patient is placed in after release does not also reward that behavior. *See generally,* TOKEN ECONOMY, *supra* note 16, at 49–54.

[109]A constitutional problem of sorts also lurks. Souder v. Brennan, 367 F.Supp. 808 (D.D.C. 1973) held the minimum wage provisions of the federal Fair Labor Standards Act applicable to employees, including patient employees, of state institutions. *Souder* was largely undercut, however, by the Supreme Court's decision in National League of Cities v. Usery, 426 U.S. 833 (1976), which held that federal minimum wage requirements were an unconstitutional encroachment on state sovereignty. After *Usery,* though, the federal minimum wage can be restored to state-hospital-patient employees through revenue sharing agreements or through employment discrimination regulations promulgated under the Rehabilitation Act of 1973. *See generally Mental Health and Human Rights: Report of the Task Panel on Legal and Ethical Issues,* 20 ARIZ. L. REV. 49, 69–72 (1978). And despite *Usery,* the *Wyatt* requirement of a federal minimum wage may well survive (or a minimum wage at least closely comparable to the federally mandated one may well survive) as part and parcel of the constitutionally based right to treatment.

Another possible difficulty with mandating a minimum wage is that it imposes an external force on the token economy and could upset the system's delicate economic balance, its incentive system, and so forth. Winkler, who has studied the economics of token economies, has concluded that token systems constitute subtle and intricate economic models which parallel remarkably the economic system of the outside world. Winkler, *The Relevance of Economic Theory and Technology to Token Reinforcement Systems,* 9 BEHAV. RES. & THERAPY 81 (1971). In the Ayllon and Azrin token economy, for example, the token values of the various positions were set by concepts of supply and demand. TOKEN ECONOMY, *supra* note 16, at 204. A minimum wage reinforcer for all hospital positions, even if appended to a token system with different numbers of tokens available for different assignments, would surely have a profound influence on the preexisting incentive system. *See also* Kagel & Winkler, *Behavioral Economics: Areas of Cooperative Research between Economics and Applied Behavioral Analysis,* 5 APP. BEHAV. ANAL. 335 (1972).

[110]Such as the impact of a minimum wage requirement on the economic incentive system of the hospital. *See* discussion in note 109 *supra.*

[111]*See* B. F. SKINNER, *supra* note 9.

[112]*E.g.,* BANDURA, *supra* note 4, at 227; TOKEN ECONOMY, *supra* note 16, at 269. A published case study of a patient at the Nevada State Hospital nicely illustrates the asserted psycholegal dilemma. LM was a 33-year-old extremely obese woman who had been hospitalized for the third time for a severe psychotic depressive reaction. It was apparent both to LM and to her therapists that her obesity was the major factor contributing to her self-concept of extreme worthlessness and to her poor relationships with other

persons. Yet, she had never been able to maintain an effective diet, and traditional therapies had proven fruitless in reversing her depression or her obesity. Finally, six months into her third hospitalization, she and her therapist decided to try to motivate her dieting through a token economy system. It was agreed that the target behavior of weight reduction would be rewarded by tokens which could be expended only for the rental of a private hospital room. According to the therapist, the availability of a private room as a reinforcer

> proved crucial to the target behavior plan since LM had several times confided to staff members that the most excruciating moment of her day came in the evening when she was obliged to undress for bed in the bare six-patient dormitory to which she had been assigned. At that time she was forced to expose her obesity in all its abject ugliness to the disapproving eyes of the five other women who shared her sleeping quarters.

McQueen, *The Token Economy and a Target Behavior*, 32 PSYCHOL. REP. 599, 601 (1973). As expected by the therapist, the contingent availability of a private room did indeed operate as a powerful dietary motivator, and LM achieved a dramatic and permanent weight loss, accompanied by a remission of her depression, and is now functioning well beyond the walls of the institution. The crucial point to keep in mind for the purpose of the present discussion, however, is that, under *Wyatt*, LM would be entitled as a matter of right to the privacy provided by a room divider or curtain, and hence would, in her therapist's view, presumably not be as motivated to secure a private room as she would be in the absence of the rights provided by *Wyatt*.

[113]At first blush, the behaviorist position seems to clash with the data provided by J. K. Wing, who found that the clinical states of schizophrenic patients at three different hospitals correlated closely, and positively, with the respective hospital policies on patient rights and liberty. Wing, *Evaluating Community Care for Schizophrenic Patients in the United Kingdom*, in COMMUNITY PSYCHIATRY 138, 147–157 (Anchor ed. L. Roberts, S. Halleck, & M. Loeb eds. 1969). Wing's analysis, however, might possibly be reconciled with the behaviorist contention. First, it is not entirely clear from Wing's study that patients were assigned to the three hospitals on a random basis, and if they were not, a causal connection between patient rights and clinical states could not conclusively be inferred. And even if it could, the connection could well be limited to instances where contingency management systems are absent. In other words, it may be that it is far more therapeutic to provide patients with certain privileges absolutely than it is to deny them those privileges absolutely, but that it is better still to provide the privileges on a contingent basis.

[114]*See, e.g.*, Gripp & Magaro, *supra* note 41, at 137 (summarizing results achieved by other researchers).

[115]TOKEN ECONOMY, *supra* note 16, at 269. *See also* Lloyd & Abel, *supra* note 39, at 1, 7 (at least 10 of 52 patients remained predominantly in the lowest group, which was a closed ward, throughout the course of the study).

[116]Even the drastic deprivations at Patton State did not produce spectacular results. Schaefer, *supra* note 44, at 32. Schaefer did, however, claim some spectacular results in an *individualized* positive reinforcement program, where a behavior modification plan is tailored to each patient's particular problems. *Id.* at 33–36. Individualization will be discussed further in text *infra*.

[117]Schaefer & Martin, *Behavioral Therapy for "Apathy" of Hospitalized Schizophrenics*, 19 PSYCHOL. REP. 1147 (1966).

[118]Gripp & Magaro, *supra* note 41.

[119]Atthowe & Krasner, *supra* note 35, at 37, 40.

[120]"Results based on follow-up studies disclose that approximately 70% of chronic patients

who are discharged from mental hospitals return within 18 months regardless of the type of treatment received during the period of hospitalization." BANDURA, *supra* note 4, at 269.

121In fact, token economy programs differ considerably among themselves with regard to the nature of deprivations and contingent reinforcers resorted to. For instance, food and beds were subject to purchase at Patton State Hospital but were noncontingently available at Anna State Hospital. Further, patients in certain programs are able to earn tokens for engaging in activities which would cost tokens in other programs. *See* discussion in note 91, *supra*. Unfortunately, however, because reports of token economy programs are often inadequate in their description of reinforcers, and because they often measure success according to different criteria, inferences of comparative efficacy are difficult to draw, leaving our knowledge rather incomplete with respect to the therapeutic necessity of resorting to the more drastic reinforcers.

122The technique is "impure" because, unlike the Premack principle, it relies on verbal expressions of intention to ascertain preferred behavior, and the match is not always a perfect one. Ayllon and Azrin resorted to the technique to a limited extend. TOKEN ECONOMY, *supra* note 16, at 67–72. To help insure that a patient will refrain from requesting items that he does not in fact deeply desire, a down payment of a specified number of tokens can be required at the time of the request. *Id.* at 71–72.

123TOKEN ECONOMY, *supra* note 16, at 69.

124*Id.* at 68.

125Atthowe & Krasner, *supra* note 35, at 38.

126*E.g.*, Schaefer, *supra* note 44, at 33–36 (Patton State Hospital individualized behavior modification program far more spectacular than its general token economy program); Spiegler, *supra* note 94.

127In the Patton State Hospital program, individualized problem areas included eating problems, grooming habits, and hallucinatory behavior. Schaefer, *supra* note 44, at 33–36. Note that under an individualized program, it would not be unusual to have "some people paying while others are paid to play table games." Spiegler, *supra* note 94, at 8. Such an individualized approach may solve the legal problem posed by the fact that some token economies treat as reinforcers activities which others treat as target responses. *See* discussion of the problem in note 91 *supra*. *Cf.* TOKEN ECONOMY, *supra* note 16, at 10–11 (visitors, ground privileges, recreational activities not desired by certain chronic patients).

128Wyatt v. Stickney, 344 F. Supp. 373, 384 (M.D. Ala. 1972) (Bryce and Searcy Hospitals).

129*E.g.*, Birnbaum, *The Right to Treatment*, 46 A.B.A.J. 499 (1960); Rouse v. Cameron, 373 F.2d 451 (D.C. Cir. 1966).

130*See* Davison, *supra* note 17, at 257; Atthowe & Krasner, *supra* note 35, at 41.

131The empirical evidence is convincing. *See* COMMUNITY LIFE, *supra* note 95; SOCIAL PSYCHOLOGY IN TREATING MENTAL ILLNESS: AN EXPERIMENTAL APPROACH (G. Fairweather ed. 1964) [hereinafter cited as SOCIAL PSYCHOLOGY].

132*See* references in note 131 *supra*.

133*E.g.*, BANDURA, *supra* note 4, at 269–71, 275–78.

134In this connection, Bandura cites an interesting unpublished report where the researchers "studied the amount of disruptive classroom behavior displayed by a child in the absence of any special reinforcement and during subsequent periods when either she alone earned five points, or she and her immediate peers each earned one point for her commendable behavior. It is interesting to note that the child's activities were more effectively controlled under the peer contingency even though it produced only one-fifth of the amount of reinforcement provided on the individual basis. Apparently, through the group reward, change agents were able to enlist the peers' aid in modifying the behavior of their companion." BANDURA, *supra* note 4, at 281. *See also* Fleetwood & Parish, *Relationship between Moral Development Test Scores of Juvenile Delinquents and Their Inclusion in a Moral Dilemma Discussion Group,* 39 PSYCH. REP. 1075 (1976); Rekev & Meissner, *Life Skills in a Canadian Federal Penitentiary: An Experimental Evaluation,* 19 CANADIAN J. CRIMINOLOGY 292 (1977).

[135]SOCIAL PSYCHOLOGY, *supra* note 131, at 30. Fairweather's project was conducted at a Veterans Administration Hospital, and the patients were presumably drawing psychiatric disability benefits, which is where the monetary rewards utilized in the experiment came from. Note, however, that even if this money were provided by the hospital, rather than from the patients' own sources, the total expenditure would probably be far less than if the patient labor were mandatorily compensated by the minimum wage. For comments on the possible disincentives to recovery provided by disability compensation—surely a fruitful topic for psycholegal investigation—*see* Spiegler, *supra* note 94, at 6; Davison, *supra* note 17, at 257.

[136]SOCIAL PSYCHOLOGY, *supra* note 131, at 40–41. The staff committee could of course amend or reject the suggestions. *Id.*

[137]*Id.* at 173.

[138]*Id.* at 189.

[139]*Id.* at 181, 283. The patients in Fairweather's study constituted a heterogeneous population and varied considerably in degree of chronicity, but the various task groups surely had their share of chronic psychotics. *Id.* at 33. And Fairweather's follow-up community adjustment project involved almost exclusively chronic patients. COMMUNITY LIFE, *supra* note 95, at 32, 238. It seems, then, that a comment made by Davison—that Fairweather's study did not involve chronic psychotics—is simply erroneous. Davison, *supra* note 17, at 257. As an aside, it should be noted that Fairweather's study of heterogeneous groups yielded fascinating findings regarding the ideal clinical mixture required in small groups to produce first-rate decision making. SOCIAL PSYCHOLOGY, *supra* note 131, at 193, 209.

[140]SOCIAL PSYCHOLOGY, *supra* note 131, at 61.

[141]*Id.* at 70, 283.

[142]*Id.* at 89.

[143]*Id.* at 168.

[144]COMMUNITY LIFE, *supra* note 95. When accompanied by a cohesive-group aftercare arrangement, however, chronic patients who had participated in the small group program prior to discharge had a high relapse rate, as do chronics generally. SOCIAL PSYCHOLOGY, *supra* note 131, at 168.

[145]SOCIAL PSYCHOLOGY, *supra* note 131, at 32.

[146]*Id.* at 46.

[147]*Id.* at 153. It is not clear whether Fairweather's patients were provided with such items as screens or personal lockers, but it is clear that those items were either available or unavailable *noncontingently;* that is, it is not the case, as was true at Anna State Hospital, that they were available only to those able to purchase them. Because Fairweather did not employ those items as reinforcers, his therapeutic system would seemingly be unaffected by a requirement, such as enunciated in *Wyatt,* that all patients be given those items as a matter of absolute right.

[148]*E.g.,* Bruce, *supra* note 20, at 1799, 1802 (discussing conditions for the "middle group" at Patton State Hospital); Lloyd & Abel, *supra* note 39, at 1, 5 (discussing conditions for "Group B" at Idaho's State Hospital North); Narrol, *supra* note 40, at 105, 108 (discuss-

ing steps 3 and 4 at Richmond State Hospital). *See also* text accompanying notes 52–54 *supra*.

[149]Fairweather's contingent pass device may pose a question in light of the requirement of Covington v. Harris, 419 F.2d 617 (D.C. Cir. 1969), that patients be provided with as much liberty as is clinically appropriate. But the fact that even lowest level patients are entitled in the Fairweather system to one day pass per week may alleviate *Covington* objections, especially if the contingent availability of passes above and beyond one per week are shown empirically to constitute powerful motivators. But whatever *Covington* problem may exist could, of course, be vitiated entirely if monetary rewards alone were found to be sufficient reinforcers, as future research might indeed show.

[150]Social Psychology, *supra* note 131, at 9. Group homes for the mentally disabled are now flourishing, though they often encounter resistance from the community. *See Mental Health and Human Rights: Report of the Task Panel on Legal and Ethical Issues*, 20 Ariz. L. Rev. 49, 72–74 (1978). On group homes for delinquents, *see* Wolf, Phillips, Fixsen, *et al.*, *Achievement Place: The Teaching-Family Model*, 5 Child Care Quarterly 92 (1976).

[151]One possible exception is the most extremely regressed cases who fail under all other techniques. Even under Fairweather's system, for example, it is probably true, as he admits, Social Psychology, *supra* note 131, at 172, that some patients may be unresponsive, and it is certainly possible that, for those patients, idiosyncratic reinforcers will be undiscoverable or unworkable. For them, the fields of law and psychology must face the issue whether, in the hopes of therapeutic success, basic and primitive items and activities should be used as reinforcers. If the answer is affirmative, certain safeguards should be built into the legal structure to insure that decisions to invoke the traditional token economy model are made only after full consideration and only in rare instances. For example, demonstrated ineffectivness of the Fairweather and idiosyncratic systems could be a legal prerequisite to reliance on the traditional token technique. Such an approach, which may create an additional incentive for patients to succeed within the Fairweather scheme and accordingly avoid the more distasteful ordeal of a standard token system, would insure that basic rights are not converted to contingent reinforcers for the bulk of chronic psychotics for whom that appears unnecessary and, *a fortiori*, for other clinical categories, such as juvenile delinquents and nonpsychotic alcoholics, who presumably can be motivated by nonprimitive reinforcers which fall without the prohibitions of *Wyatt* and related legal mandates. In effect, if reliance on reinforcers falling below the *Wyatt*-type baseline are to be resorted to, such a drastic scheme of positive token reinforcement should be properly deemed "aversive" for legal purposes and should follow, as closely as possible, emerging legal restrictions on aversive therapy. Hopefully, one such restriction will be the "less drastic means" rationale. *Cf.* Bandura, *supra* note 4, at 551 (complaining that "exceedingly noxious procedures are occasionally employed even though they produce no greater changes than stimuli in much weaker intensities"); Schwitzgebel, *supra* note 5, at 279 (alcoholics have been treated with drastic drugs causing respiratory arrest, even though "[t]he results . . . are not clearly better than with emetics.") A requirement of informed consent is also emerging in the aversive therapy area, [*e.g.*, Wyatt v. Stickney, 344 F. Supp. 373 (M.D. Ala. 1972) (Bryce and Searcy Hospital)], but that requirement may have an awkward application in the token economy area: it is easy to imagine homosexual or alcoholic patients consenting to aversive techniques in hopes of securing desired behavioral improvement, but it is far more difficult to imagine an apathetic long-term patient, almost by definition unconcerned about his clinical state and his future, voluntarily consenting to

forego the standard benefits of hospital life in favor of treatment under which those benefits would be available only by purchase. Surely, even if informed consent were given by such a patient, it might soon be revoked. Cf. Ex parte Lloyd, 13 F. Supp. 1005 (E.D. Ky. 1936) (addict who volunteered for treatment and contracted to remain in hospital for specified time period but later changed his mind could not be compelled to remain hospitalized for the specified period); contra, Ortega v. Rasor, 291 F. Supp. 748 (S.D. Fla. 1968). For more on the revocability of consent in this context, see Wexler, Reflections on the Legal Regulation of Behavior Modification in Institutional Settings, 17 ARIZ. L. REV. 132, 138–40 (1975). Arguably, informed consent in a token economy setting could be replaced by an alternative protective device, such as the informed approval of a judicially selected human rights committee chosen from outside the hospital. See, e.g., Wyatt v. Stickney, 344 F. Supp. 387, 400 (M.D. Ala. 1972) (Partlow Hospital) (require-ment that aversive behavior modification programs involving the mentally retarded "shall be reviewed and approved by the institution's Human Rights Committee and shall be conducted only with the express and informed consent of the affected resident, if the resident is able to give such consent, and of his guardian or next of kin, after opportunities for consultation with independent specialists and with legal counsel"). See generally Wexler, supra and Chapter 10. Further, a time limit should probably be set on the length of time the token procedure could be invoked, with provision for a return to the noncontingent availability of basic benefits for patients seemingly unresponsive to even the token system. But clear-cut answers on the extent to which traditional token economies should be treated legally as an aversive technique must await further de-velopment in the law of aversive therapy itself—an area which, as noted in the introduc-tion to this chapter, is receiving an ever-increasing amount of attention from the courts and the commentators. The use of aversive techniques raises squarely one of the peren-nial problems of law and research: society will obviously want to forbid aversive prac-tices unless they have been demonstrated to be efficacious, but research, rather than legal prohibition, is needed to demonstrate whether the practices are in fact efficacious. To the extent that many aversive therapies are obviously experimental in nature, the emerging legal and ethical restrictions regarding experimentation with human subjects ought to be pertinent in devising a balanced but protective regulatory framework for their application. See generally DEVIANCE AND DECENCY: THE ETHICS OF RESEARCH WITH HUMAN SUBJECTS (C. Klockars & F. O'Connor eds. 1979).

[152]The desirability of such studies has been repeatedly noted. See, e.g., BANDURA, supra note 4, at 274.

[153]For additional thoughts on matters raised in this chapter, see Chapter 10, as well as Wexler, supra note 85, at 957; Wexler, supra note 151, at 132. See especially id. at 138–40, where I discuss "absolute" and "contingent" rights and elaborate further on my thesis that Wyatt-type rights are arguably absolute. Paul Friedman has written a fine com-prehensive piece on behavior modification in mental hospitals and prisons. See Fried-man, Legal Regulation of Applied Behavior Analysis in Mental Institutions and Prisons, 17 ARIZ. L. REV. 39 (1975). See also the wide-ranging discussion in Singer, Consent of the Unfree: Medical Experimentation and Behavior Modification in the Closed Institution, 1 L. & HUMAN BEH. 1 (Pt. I) & 101 (Pt. II) (1977). An extensive bibliography appears in A. BROOKS, LAW, PSYCHIATRY AND THE MENTAL HEALTH SYSTEM 258–264 (Supp. 1980).

10

One Proposed Legal Mechanism for Regulating Behavior Control

INTRODUCTION

As the culminating chapter in the "law and therapy" section of this book, the present chapter will review briefly certain key concerns in the area, will introduce a few new ones, and will discuss the author's involvement in drafting a proposed administrative model for regulating behavior modification in Florida institutions for the mentally retarded. While the law relating to the mentally retarded and other developmentally disabled persons sometimes differs from the law relating to the mentally ill, the model developed here seems generally capable of being extended to other clinical populations as well as to forms of behavior control other than traditional behavior modification. Thus, the proposed administrative model is an appropriate vehicle for our discussion in this chapter.

In order properly to regulate behavior control, we need ultimately to grapple in rather concrete terms with concepts, already partially considered in Chapters 8 and 9, regarding the right to receive and to refuse treatment, the notion of informed consent, and related matters. After discussing these concepts, this chapter will explain the extent to which, under the proposed Florida scheme, competent clients can give informed consent to certain therapies (the right to treatment) and the extent to which competent clients can refuse certain therapies (the right to refuse treatment). Further, with regard to incompetent clients, the chapter discusses the extent to which the proposed model balances the right to treatment and the right to refuse treatment by resorting to concepts of "best interest" and "least restrictive alternative."

LAW ON RIGHT TO REFUSE TREATMENT

Although, as evidenced by the ongoing litigation in *Rennie* v. *Klein*,[1] the right to refuse psychotropic medication appears likely to consume much judicial energy and to break new ground, the law regarding the right to refuse treatment generally, when measured by judicial decisions rather than by articles in legal journals, still remains rather sparse. Not surprisingly, the "traditional" right to refuse treatment cases have involved particularly bizarre incidents. One such instance is *Mackey* v. *Procunier*,[2] which challenged "anectine therapy" in the California correctional system. Anectine is a relaxant which induces paralysis and respiratory arrest. It is ordinarily used, together with anesthesia, as an adjunct to electroconvulsive therapy in order to minimize the possibility of bone fracture. Mackey, the plaintiff, was a California prisoner-patient who claimed that, with his consent, he had been transferred from Folsom to Vacaville for the purpose of receiving electroconvulsive therapy. Once at Vacaville, however, he was apparently administered anectine not in conjunction with electroconvulsive therapy but instead in connection with a program of "aversive treatment," without his consent and while he was fully awake. In other words, Mackey claimed that, at Vacaville, anectine was administered to him contingent on his engaging in inappropriate behavior. Persons who have experienced the effects of anectine while fully conscious describe the sensation as one of suffocating, drowning, or dying. The Ninth Circuit ruled that proof of Mackey's allegations could raise "serious Constitutional questions respecting cruel and unusual punishment" under the Eighth Amendment or of "impermissible tinkering with the mental processes," presumably in violation of the First Amendment.

An opportunity to take more decisive action was offered to (and accepted by) the Eighth Circuit in *Knecht* v. *Gillman*,[3] a December, 1973 decision which sharply curtailed a so-called aversive treatment program at the Iowa Security Medical Facility. *Knecht*, like *Mackey*, dealt with the use of a drug for conditioning purposes. The drug in *Knecht*, however, was not the "suffocation" drug anectine but was instead the vomit-inducing drug apomorphine. Armed with blanket orders from physicians, nurses at the Iowa Security Medical Facility (an institution for the "criminally insane") apparently administered the drug whenever they determined—either first-hand or through hearsay remarks of other inmates—that institutional rules had been transgressed. Under the Iowa scheme, an incident of swearing could trigger an injection of apomorphine.

On those facts, the Eighth Circuit ruled squarely that the administration of apomorphine without the informed consent of a patient contravenes the constitutional proscription against cruel and unusual punishment. The *Knecht* court held, however, that the drug could be constitutionally administered to *consenting* patients, so long as each injection was authorized by a physician and, to increase the integrity of the fact-finding mechanism, so long as the rule violation was witnessed personally by a staff member.

Perhaps the best known of the behavior control cases is *Kaimowitz v. Department of Mental Health,* the subject of Chapter 8, in which a three-judge Michigan trial court disallowed the performance of experimental psychosurgery on involuntarily confined patients. The *Kaimowitz* court began with the premise that psychosurgery that was *coercive* or that was otherwise accomplished without a patient's informed consent would contravene constitutional commands relating to the First Amendment freedom of expression and to the constitutional right to privacy. The court ultimately concluded that psychosurgery would similarly offend the Constitution even if performed on a committed patient who ostensibly *consented* to the procedure. That result was made possible by the court's holding that involuntarily confined patients could not, as a matter of law, give legally adequate consent to experimental psychosurgery.

It will be recalled that legally adequate consent consists of three conjunctive elements: Competency, knowledge, and voluntariness. The *Kaimowitz* court found none of them to be satisfied. Competence was missing because the court viewed confined patients as being too affected by the "institutionalization syndrome" to competently make the serious and complex decision to undergo psychosurgery. Knowledge—the "informed" portion of the informed consent formula—was wanting because the outcome of the proposed operation was profoundly uncertain. And voluntariness was absent because the court viewed the lure of possible release from the institution to be so powerful that it would coerce patients into consenting. In Chapter 8, I was severely critical of the court's reasoning on each of those points, though, as a matter of policy, not of the result reached.

Certainly, few would quarrel with the proposition that drastic, punitive, and sometimes irreversible therapies are worthy of legal attention and regulation. Some would argue, however, that the above incidents, though serious, are mere therapeutic aberrations, and, moreover, that the gist of behavior change and behavior modification today consists of *positive* control—of rewarding appropriate behavior rather than of punishing inappropriate behavior. Thus, some would question the necessity of stringent legal regulation of such seemingly benign therapeutic efforts.

Such a noninterventionist argument can, however, be easily answered. First, even assuming for the purpose of argument that positive reinforcement schemes do not involve offensive *means* in their attempt to shape behavior, scrutiny is nonetheless essential to insure that behavior-shaping *goals* comport with satisfactory legal and ethical standards. Just as one can properly question the propriety of eliminating adult swearing behavior at the above-described Iowa facility, one can similarly question the propriety of shaping (even by the benign means of dispensing refreshments) exceedingly docile classroom behavior in schoolchildren and of encouraging the performance of institutional labor by mental patients, alcoholics, and juvenile delinquents.

Second, as was documented in Chapter 9, clinical endeavors in applying positive reinforcement to build desired behavior have, in practice, often involved *means* as alarming as some of the aversive techniques. Thus, "token economies," where patients earn tokens for appropriate behavior and are then permitted to cash the tokens in to purchase desired items or events, and "tier systems," where privileges increase hierarchically and patients are promoted or elevated to higher tiers on engaging in appropriate behavior, often involve severe states of *deprivation*, which in effect force patients to earn their way to improved living conditions. Thus, many very basic items and events are employed in institutional settings as reinforcers: meals, beds, ground privileges, privacy, attendance at religious services, and others.

No cases have yet squarely condemned token economies and tier systems for their fast-and-loose reliance on severe states of deprivation, but such a constitutional condemnation seems only around the corner. Judicial decisions not involving behavior modification, but extending to patients certain rights as part-and-parcel of a constitutionally required "humane environment" (according patients a right to nutritious meals, a comfortable bed, privacy, the right to attend religious services, etc.) may be interpreted as removing certain basic items and events from the arsenal of legally available reinforcers or of at least greatly restricting their legal availability.

Not long ago, a U.S. Bureau of Prisons "tier" program at the Medical Center for Federal Prisoners at Springfield, Missouri, known as the START program (an acronym for Special Treatment and Rehabilitative Training), was subject to challenge in a federal lawsuit. Among other claims, the inmate plaintiffs contended that the deprivations which they were involuntarily required to endure at the first level of the program (such as visitation rights, exercise opportunities, and reading materials) amounted to a constitutional violation. In response, the government argued that it was necessary, at the initial stage, to deprive the inmates of those rights so that those items and events might be used as reinforcers. Moreover, the government continued, the fact that the inmates deemed the denial of the rights significant enough to challenge actually established the psychological effectiveness of those reinforcers as behavioral motivators. Note that the government's argument comes close to creating a legal Catch 22: If you complain of the denial of certain rights, you are not entitled to them; you are entitled only to those rights the denial of which you do not challenge![4]

While the lawsuit was pending, the Bureau of Prisons decided to terminate the START program, though the Bureau's director testified in congressional hearings that such "positive-reinforcement" approaches would in all likelihood be employed in future correctional efforts. Because of the START termination, however, the federal court found the suit to be moot, except with respect to certain procedural aspects, and accordingly did not address the merits of the deprivation issue.

In light of the foregoing examples, the case for the legal regulation of behavior modification, both positive and aversive, and other behavior-change technologies seems to be clear. Regulation, however, does not mean outright prohibition. Blanket prohibition would, under the label of paternalism, infringe on notions of personal autonomy and privacy as much as would practices endorsing unscrutinized therapeutic techniques carte blanche.

To preserve the above-mentioned notion of autonomy while simultaneously hoping to prevent therapeutic excesses, the courts and commentators have relied on the concept of informed consent. The emerging view, at least with respect to intrusive procedures, seems to be that if a person is capable of giving informed consent to a proposed therapeutic procedure (and most prisoners and many mental patients are so capable), and if such a person in fact consents to it, the institution ought to be permitted to proceed with it, but that if consent is refused, the state lacks a sufficient interest to thrust an intrusive behavioral procedure on an unwilling competent person.

RIGHT TO TREATMENT AND PERSONAL AUTONOMY

The problem is somewhat more complex with respect to persons incapable of giving informed consent (such as certain mental patients and many residents of mental retardation facilities), but the prevailing view seems to be that the patient's supposed desire is not conclusive. He or she can be subjected to certain procedures if it is determined (the means of determination is now a matter of great dispute[5]) that less onerous alternative therapies are or have been unsuitable and that, in an anticipated cost-benefit sense, the proposed procedure is in the best interest of the patient or client.[6]

A rather recently enacted California statute[7] generally follows the above model. The statute seeks to regulate, in correctional settings, what it refers to as "organic" therapies, which exclude psychotherapy and apparently chemotherapy but include psychosurgery, electronic stimulation of the brain, electroconvulsive and insulin shock therapy, and aversive therapy involving shocks, physical pain, and drugs as part of a conditioning effort. The California scheme (1) permits the use of all those therapies when consent is obtained from competent patients; (2) disallows them if refused by competent patients; and (3) with the exception of psychosurgery, permits their use with incompetent patients if the "best interest" and "least restrictive alternative" tests are satisfied. The crucial facts regarding questions of competence, cost-benefit analysis, and less drastic therapeutic alternatives are to be found by a superior court. In other words, under the California model, the organic therapies are permissible only in accordance with a court order, which is obtainable only after a judicial hearing at which the patient is entitled to appointed counsel and to an independent medical expert.

In order for regulatory schemes that hinge on the notion of informed consent to work—and in order to preserve as best we can the right to treatment (see Chapter 8) and the value of autonomy—it is necessary to pierce through the rhetoric, fueled by the *Kaimowitz* case, that institutions are inherently coercive and that voluntary consent is unobtainable in an institutional setting because the lure of release is so overpowering. As was noted in Chapter 8, if the "inherent coercion" formula is accepted, the logical result would be that *all* therapy on involuntarily institutionalized persons would, despite their expressed desires to submit to therapy, be deemed coerced and therefore prohibited. Thus, the lure of institutional release per se ought not to be deemed legal coercion. Instead, the concept of coercion should be employed as a normative concept to condemn choices regarded as *unfair* or *unreasonable*. The normative notion of coercion is in obvious need of further refinement (to which some philosophers are now addressing their attention), but its mere recognition as such is an important assistance to the development of the law.

The remainder of this chapter will seek to apply the previously discussed concepts to the administrative model proposed for Florida. To best understand the origins of the Florida model, however, it is necessary to review general efforts to regulate behavior modification and the forces behind the marshalling of such efforts in Florida.

REFORM EFFORTS: FLORIDA GUIDELINES

Largely because of the public outcry over behavior control technologies and because that outcry is beginning to find its way into legislative and judicial forums, many mental health professionals are now scurrying to draft guidelines and to put their therapeutic houses in order. By far the greatest effort has come from professionals in behavior modification (principally persons who apply clinically the psychological theories of learning) rather than from persons who practice other forms of behavior change or behavior control. A task force commissioned by the Florida Division of Retardation has already drafted proposed standards for the use of behavioral procedures in state programs for the retarded, and an American Psychological Association Commission on Behavior Modification has published a work addressing pertinent questions in an extensive range of settings.[8]

The concentration of reform efforts among behavior modifiers, rather than among other behavior-change professionals, seems partly explainable by the greater organizational cohesion of the former group. It may, however, also be partly attributable to an accident of semantics: the public and the press do not employ the term "behavior modification" in its limited scientific "conditioning" sense; instead, they employ it nontechnically to refer to *all* forms of behavior control and behavior influence. The public's outcry, then, against such procedures as psychosurgery is expressed as a concern about "behavior modification," which has, in turn, put the purebred behavior modifiers on the defensive and has encouraged them to review and explain their techniques and safeguards with the hope of gaining public support or of at least avoiding the wrath inflicted on the psychosurgeons.[9]

The effort of the Florida Task Force was sparked not only by the above factors, but also by a full-blown scandal (extensively aired by the local press) at one of the state's retardation training centers. The problem arose at a training-center cottage which operated under a token economy and tier system and which housed retarded boys who were also delinquent or emotionally disturbed.

The abuses reported by the press (and confirmed by a Resident Abuse Investigating Committee) included, among many other things, forced public masturbation and forced public homosexual acts as punishment for engaging in proscribed sexual behavior; beatings with a wooden panel for running away; and washing the mouth with soap for lying, for abusive or vulgar language, or sometimes for speaking at all. Further, food, sleep, and visitation privileges were withheld as punishment; incontinence was punished by requiring residents to lie in soiled sheets and to hold soiled underwear to their noses; a resident accused of theft was addressed by staff and residents as "The Thief" and was required to wear a sign so designating him; and one boy was required to walk around publicly clothed only in female underpants. [10]

Even more remarkable, perhaps, is that those abuses were not isolated incidents but were parading under the banner of behavior modification as part of what the Investigating Committee found to be a system of "programmed abuse." The incidents were carried out by staff members, who recorded them in great detail in well-kept records, with the encouragement, or at least the acquiescence, of the chief psychologist (who held a Ph.D. degree, though not in psychology). Moreover, the Committee believed the participants to be generally well-meaning and hard-working and attributed the problem generally to an unscrutinized and unsupervised system run by poorly trained personnel.

The principal pitfall, according to the Committee, was the structure of the token economy and tier system, which made the system highly vulnerable to rampant abuse. At Phase I of the structure, the boys were able to earn tokens for appropriate behavior but were not allowed to exchange them for primary reinforcers (refreshments, etc.) until they had accumulated a sufficient number of tokens to be elevated to Phase II. To deal with disruptive and problem behavior, the staff members were instructed to emphasize the natural consequences of behavior, to devise their own remedies to fit the situation, and to follow through on every promise or threat.

According to the Committee's psychological evaluation of the program, the structure was faulty in several respects. For instance, the token and tier system was "upside-down." During Phase I, where behavior problems should typically be more difficult to control and strong and *immediate* reinforcement is apparently essential to bring behavior under control, tokens were not redeemable and the token reinforcers were accordingly not meaningful. (Curiously, tokens were redeemable only in Phase II, where ideally the reinforcement schedule should be thinned out and replaced by such natural reinforcers as social praise.) The system, therefore, was bound to result in a high incidence of disruptive behavior. With positive reinforcement being unavailable, the staff members were left to devise their own responses. Being untrained, they relied on familiar "home remedies," such as washing mouths with soap. As their control efforts became frustrated, they simply resorted, out of increasing frustration, to increasingly punitive methods.

As a result of the Investigating Committee's report, many of the institution's employees were discharged. But in the wake of the incident, behavior modification was itself indicted as the responsible agent. A staff morale problem developed statewide. Staff members, fearful of losing their jobs, refused to become involved in even well-recognized behavior-modification procedures, often leaving highly inappropriate resident behavior to proceed without intervention. Put another way, a highly abusive program was replaced by a virtual therapeutic paralysis.

These crises of polar extremes led to the formation of the Florida Task Force. A group of behavioral psychologists and lawyers were called to Tallahassee and were virtually sequestered in a hotel for a four-day period to draft a set of psychological and legal principles for the appropriate use of behavioral procedures in state facilities for the retarded. The psychologists prepared a manual of recognized techniques, emphasizing throughout that if "milder" procedures are ineffective, more intrusive ones should not be resorted to before ascertaining whether the milder procedures failed because of an insufficiently stimulating environment, because of improper staff training, or other reasons. The legal members of the Task Force drafted procedures of advice, review, and consent for the use of intrusive procedures.

Though the proposed legal guidelines were strict, officials and staff members of the Division of Retardation indicated that they could live with them. From their perspective of paralysis, perhaps even strict guidelines were viewed as a freeing agent, informing the staff that they could, with a sense of security, employ at least *some* procedures under *some* circumstances.

Constitutionally, the proposed Florida guidelines conform to the analysis addressed earlier. Concepts of competence, informed consent, and the least restrictive alternative are built into the scheme. But the Florida approach relies heavily on an "administrative model" to resolve issues of efficacy, fact-finding, approval of therapeutic goals, and selection of therapeutic techniques.

The guidelines contemplate the creation of one statewide Peer Review Committee (PRC) composed of highly regarded professionals trained in applied behavior analysis. A lay review committee would be created for each region of the Division of Retardation. Designated as the Committee on Legal and Ethical Protection (CLEP), it would consist of, among others, a behavioral scientist, a lawyer with experience in representing the handicapped or versed in matters of civil liberties, and a parent of a retarded person. The legal members of the Task Force urged that the members of PRC and the CLEPs be wholly unaffiliated with the Division and be appointed by the governor from a list of names submitted by the Florida Association for Retarded Citizens, an active organization of concerned citizens.

PRC and CLEP have roles to play both when behavioral procedures are proposed for initial use in Division facilities and when certain intrusive procedures are sought to be employed in particular cases. With regard to the introduction of new techniques, PRC approval is required on questions of acceptability and efficacy of the procedures and CLEP approval is also required, based on its judgment regarding the appropriateness of the behavior proposed to be strengthened or weakened and on the ethical propriety of the means to be employed to achieve the behavior change.

The heart of the Florida scheme, however, deals with the knotty questions of when particular procedures can be employed to modify particular behaviors of particular patients—questions which, before the necessity of legal intervention was recognized, used to go by default to therapists and staff members. Here, the Florida Task Force, aware that these are largely ethical questions and desirous of avoiding accusations of elitism, engaged in arguably legitimate buck-passing. Rather than deciding those important public matters itself, the Task Force proposed instead a mechanism for fairly resolving those issues. The CLEPs, presumably meeting on a statewide basis, are to classify behavioral procedures and behaviors to be modified (strengthened or weakened) according to a three-tiered scheme of escalating safeguards:

1. *Specified behavior to be modified by specified behavioral procedures regarded as standard, reasonable, and conventional.* Examples of behavior that might be specified as appropriate for strengthening could include mobility, self-help, and language acquisition. Self-stimulation or temper tantrums might be examples of behavior deemed appropriate for weakening. Behavioral procedures that might be listed under this first tier could include extinction as well as positive reinforcement employing nonbasic reinforcers. Following initial CLEP specification of these behaviors and procedures,[11] this first-level activity can be carried out, in accordance with proper professional standards, in individual cases without CLEP notification or approval.

2. *Somewhat more "intrusive" behavioral procedures regarded as sometimes necessary and as relatively standard, reasonable, and conventional, used to modify level-one specified behavior.* Examples might be brief time-out or the use of educational fines to weaken temper tantrums or assaultive behavior against other residents. Subject to initial CLEP approval, these

procedures can be employed without case-by-case prior approval of CLEP, so long as CLEP and PRC are *notified* of the use of the procedures within a reasonable time (no longer than seven days) after their use. After-the-fact notification is required so that CLEP and PRC can *monitor* the reports for possible excessive, unnecessary, vindictive, or ineffective use of the tier-two procedures.

3. *Behavioral procedures not specified in tier-one or tier-two, or the strengthening or weakening of behavior not specified as being reasonable and conventional.* This third-tier residual category, providing for the greatest protective procedures, would include the most drastic techniques and the most controversial behavior. Procedures would probably include the use of electric shock to eliminate severe self-mutilating behavior and the use of basic reinforcers for the purpose of acquiring language skills. The modification of controversial behavior patterns (such as certain sexual activity) would similarly be subject to scrutiny under this section. The third-tier protections require *prior, case-by-case* CLEP approval, and require that CLEP find that PRC has approved the use of the procedure and that the client, if competent, has consented to the proposed modification of behavior and to the use of the procedure. If the client is found by CLEP to be incompetent, CLEP cannot approve the proposal unless it finds that less restrictive alternatives have been exhausted without success or that they would be clearly ineffective. It must also find that the proposed treatment would, in a cost-benefit sense geared to normal developmental and educational goals, be in the best interest of the client. Ideally, clients should have the right to representation by appointed counsel or a legal paraprofessional in tier-three proceedings before CLEP.

With respect to the least restrictive alternative notion, an interesting provision of the proposed legal guidelines specifies that "if, in rendering a decision under [the section relating to third-level procedures] the CLEP finds that a less restrictive alternative is insufficient only because of the lack of staff or funds, it shall in each such case immediately notify the Director of the Division, the Governor, the Secretary of the Department of Health and Rehabilitative Services, the Attorney General, the Chairman of the House and Senate [Health and Rehabilitative Services] Legislative Committees, and the Chairman of the House and Senate Appropriations Committees."

The Florida guidelines follow an "administrative model" both in their method of proposed promulgation and in their contemplated function of adjudicating and approving the use of certain behavioral procedures in particular cases. There are, it seems, several advantages to this administrative approach.

In terms of promulgation by administrative regulation, rather than by legislation, there is an obvious advantage in having the package prepared by specialists and in avoiding legislative "markup" and rewrite sessions. Administrative enactment will expectedly also be swifter than legislative enactment. Of course, some of the advantages of the administrative route can be abused. For example, although administrative rule-making power derives theoretically from legislative delegation, the legislature is in practice often totally unaware of administrative action taken pursuant to delegated authority. In Florida, for example, a rather recently enacted statute will bring the administrative rule-making process out into the open. A *Miami Herald* article[12] quotes a state senator as stating that the origin of the statute can be traced to the period after the 1973 legislative session. At that session, many controversial bills were defeated, "but within 90 days we found out that the laws that failed were put into effect by agencies as rules."

That sort of legislative circumvention is unwise, particularly if legislative budgetary action would be helpful or essential to support the activities created by administrative regulation. But the principal advantage of administrative promulgation (an advantage that ought to be understood in legislative halls) is that administrative rules and regulations can be enacted, modified, and superseded more easily than can statutes, and that, in a field as new and as rapidly changing as the regulation of behavior control, the ease and flexibility of administrative action, as opposed to the "freezing" effect of legislative action, cannot be overestimated.

Equally important is the adoption by the Florida guidelines of an administrative, rather than a judicial, approach to adjudicating the propriety of resorting in individual cases to intrusive behavioral procedures. In this respect, the Florida guidelines differ considerably from the previously discussed California scheme of court-approved behavior control. Again, there seem to be several advantages to the administrative model. If the analogue of the judicial handling of civil commitment hearings for the mentally ill is relevant, there is every indication that the courts will not be eager to involve themselves in the day-to-day business of behavior control. Empirical studies firmly conclude that courts have permitted—indeed, encouraged—remarkably perfunctory procedures in civil commitment hearings and that they effortlessly and routinely rubber-stamp the recommendations of testifying psychiatrists (see Chapter 4).

A lay body such as a Committee on Legal and Ethical Protection, on the other hand, has at least a genuine potential for bringing together a broad-based group of persons carefully selected on the basis of concern and other factors and giving them a chance to develop know-how so that they might perform with skill and vigor. The acquisition of know-how is greatly facilitated in the Florida guidelines by several techniques that could not appropriately be performed by courts: The CLEP is required to conduct periodic visitations to inspect Division facilities to insure its continued familiarity with the operations. Also, the CLEP and PRC are required to monitor reports of second-level procedures for possible excessive, unnecessary, vindictive, or ineffective use of those procedures, and they are required to conduct periodic random sampling of current cases to insure that each client has an individual treatment plan and to ascertain whether CLEP notification and approval is in fact being observed in required instances.[13]

The proposed Florida guidelines[14] are, of course, far from perfect. They do, however, at least represent an important effort in grappling with the major issues posed in behavior modification and other behavior control procedures, and thus deserve to be seriously scrutinized in several settings.

NOTES

[1]462 F. Supp. 1131 (D.N.J. 1978) and 476 F. Supp. 1294 (D.N.J. 1979). *See also* Rogers v. Okin, 478 F. Supp. 1342 (D. Mass. 1979).

[2]477 F.2d 877 (9th Cir. 1973).

[3]488 F.2d 1136 (8th Cir. 1973).

> [I]t is obvious that the overall incentive to the participant to be returned to open population as the basic reinforcer is valid, as all Petitioners desire such relief herein.
>
> Further, as stated by Dr. Levinson and in essence by Dr. Menninger, . . . a reduction of any privileges which [the petitioners] may have had in such units on admission to the START Program was necessary to provide a basis from which incentives or reinforcers could be provided, and obviously, if Petitioners complain of their loss, then these privileges must be incentives.

Respondent's Memorandum of Points and Authorities in Opposition to the Petitions for Habeas Corpus Relief, Sanchez v. Ciccone, No. 20, 182–4 (W.E. Mo.), at 2.

[5]Wexler, *Reflections on the Legal Regulation of Behavior Modification in Institutional Settings,* 17 ARIZ. L. REV. 132, 135–38 (1975). *Compare* Rennie v. Klein, *supra* note 1. *See generally* the sources cited in A. BROOKS, LAW, PSYCHIATRY AND THE MENTAL HEALTH SYSTEM 258–64 (Supp. 1980).

[6]*See generally* Shapiro, *Legislating the Control of Behavior Control: Autonomy and the Coercive Use of Organic Therapies,* 47 SO. CAL. L. REV. 237 (1974).

[7]Cal. Penal Code 2670 *et seq.*

[8]S. STOLZ *et al.,* ETHICAL ISSUES IN BEHAVIOR MODIFICATION (1978).

[9]An excellent example of the semantic confusion is in the Law Enforcement Assistance Administration's (LEAA) termination of funding of so-called behavior modification programs. After the ban, LEAA received an inquiry about the funding of a token economy and tier program at a penal institution. LEAA officials responded that the questioned program did not involve drugs or electric shock—the sort of procedures that sparked its behavior modification guidelines—and that the prohibition was not clearly directed at

token systems and systems involving the graduated acquisition of privileges. (APA MONITOR, Aug., 1974, at 7, col. 1.) In other words, the clarification illustrates that the LEAA behavior modification funding prohibition was directed at programs which fall without or on the periphery of behavior modification, properly defined, but not at programs which constitute its core!

[10]*Report of Resident Abuse Investigating Committee* 10–11 (unpublished, undated); May, *Ethical and Legal Contingencies in and Upon Behavior Modification Programs* (unpublished, 1974).

[11]Although the Task Force did not do so, perhaps it should have itself specified the *minimal* placement of behaviors and procedures in the three-tiered protective hierarchy. That would enable the CLEPs to *approve* the placement or to *elevate* the protection deemed necessary with regard to certain behaviors and techniques, but would prevent the CLEPs from *lowering* the required safeguards to levels where constitutional problems might arise. It is hoped, however, that the CLEPs will be strict and responsible in their protective classification efforts.

[12]MIAMI HERALD, Jan. 4, 1975, at 18A, col. 1.

[13]An additional advantage of the Florida guidelines, not present in the California statute, is the former's explicit dealing with the problem of therapeutic *goals*, rather than merely with the question of therapeutic *means*.

[14]The final version of the guidelines were published in monograph form by the National Association for Retarded Citizens. *See* J. MAY, T. RISLEY, S. TWARDOSZ, P. FRIEDMAN, S. BIJOU, D. WEXLER, *et al.*, GUIDELINES FOR THE USE OF BEHAVIORAL PROCEDURES IN STATE PROGRAMS FOR RETARDED PERSONS (1975). For guidelines heavily influenced by the Florida experience, *see* Friedman, *Legal Regulation of Applied Behavior Analysis in Mental Institutions and Prisons*, 17 ARIZ. L. REV. 39 (1975).

11

Afterword

Thus far, the major mental health law issues have centered on the commitment process and on matters relating to law and therapy. That emphasis is reflected in the two-part structure of the present book.

Because of scholarship and advocacy leading to substantial mental health law development and reform in the seventies, certain new—or "second generation"—legal issues are now beginning to emerge. Because of stricter commitment standards, procedures, and durational limits, for example, fewer persons are being committed, and for shorter periods of time, than in the past.

The resulting process of "deinstitutionalization" has raised a host of legal issues relating to community life for the mentally disabled. One of the main problems, for example, is how to accomplish genuine, planned, effective deinstitutionalization and to avoid merely "dumping" patients into substandard boarding homes. Increased attention must now also be paid to upgrading, and enforcing, standards of nursing homes and of board-and-care facilities. Relatedly, questions are now arising regarding zoning laws that seek to exclude group homes of the mentally disabled from certain areas and to concentrate those group homes in social service ghettoes, far removed from the mainstream of community life. If the deinstitutionalized mentally ill are to attain a more mainstream community existence, attention must also be paid, of course, to practices of discrimination in housing, education, and employment. Furthermore, to the extent that the mentally disabled are, for whatever reasons, not well integrated into the community, they may, if commitment remains difficult, increasingly confront the criminal justice system. If they do, new twists will obviously arise in the criminal commitment system discussed in Chapters 5 and 6.

While those, and many other, second generation issues are exciting and worthy of the attention of scholars, advocates, and policy-makers, it is important to remember that the "first generation" issues remain very much alive. Many important landmark decisions, won over the past decade, will constitute mere paper victories unless creative (and even monotonous) monitoring and implementation efforts are continually undertaken. Further, virtually none of the first generation issues have yet been resolved by the Supreme Court. In the courts and in the legislative halls, lively debate continues, for example, over much of the subject matter of Chapter 2: the propriety (and practicality) of a dangerousness criterion of commitment versus a paternalistic criterion of commitment. And the right-to-refuse-treatment question (see Chapters 8–10) is raging in lower federal courts.[1] Indeed, even procedural requisites for commitment remain very much up in the air. Although, as noted in Chapter 3, the Court in *Addington* required a fairly stringent standard of proof in commitment cases, much of the language of the decision indicated that the case was in no sense to be regarded as a wholehearted rejection of the "medical model" of commitment decision making. Moreover, on June 20, 1979, less than two months after its *Addington* decision, the Court, in *Parham* v. *J.R.*,[2] held that due process does not require a judicial hearing for the commitment of juveniles being "volunteered" for admission by their parents or guardians. Due process would be complied with, the Court held, so long as a so-called neutral fact finder (who may even be a staff physician) conducts an inquiry into the propriety of admission, reviews the commitment periodically, and has the ability to refuse admission to a child who does not satisfy the medical standards for admission. Though the *Parham* Court confined its decision to the context of juvenile commitments, the Court's broad language expressing deference to medical and psychiatric diagnosis has led some mental-patient advocates, suffering from "post-*Parham* depression," to wonder privately whether the bare-bones *Parham* protections will ultimately be held sufficient even with respect to the commitment of adults. It may be, for example, that, coupled with a few other minimal safeguards, a "two-physician certificate," rather than a judicial hearing, may eventually be held to satisfy baseline federal constitutional standards for the commitment of adults.

Whether or not those suffering from post-*Parham* depression are wholly out of touch with legal reality, it does seem evident that the Supreme Court as currently composed is unwilling to launch a mental health law revolution resembling in any fashion the criminal law revolution spawned by the Warren Court. Nonetheless, much work remains for scholars, policy-makers, advocates, and administrators. A staff report submitted in September, 1979 to the Juvenile Justice Committee of the Arizona State Legislature concluded, for example, that juvenile courts in Arizona, when they act to commit wards of the state to mental health facilities, are routinely out of compliance with even the minimal protections mandated by *Parham*.[3] The report notes that juvenile courts often commit juveniles before the juveniles have been adjudicated neglected or dependent. Further, they do so without a hearing, without a psychiatric examination, and on the mere recommendation of a social worker. Finally, they often order the state hospital to retain the minor for a specified *minimum* period of time.[4]

That report ought to inspire advocates to take action to insure that *Parham* is being fully implemented, and it may inspire the legislature to act—and perhaps to provide protections in excess of those specified in *Parham*. Indeed, the report ought to inspire even the state hospital and *its* advocates to take action. Advocacy, and the delivery of legal services for the mentally disabled, should prove to be a major concern of the 1980s, as evidenced by the birth in 1979 of *Advocacy Now: The Journal of Patient Rights and Mental Health Advocacy*. As part of the advocacy effort, progressive administrators of mental health facilities, and progressive attorneys employed by those facilities, should ascertain areas where there is a confluence of interest between mental patients and facilities. In those areas, the *state* should see whether *it* could act to serve both its own interests and the interests of its patients. Such a course of action will be evidence of state concern for the rights of patients, will help to provide representation to a severely underrepresented group, and will serve as well to vindicate some of the state's interests. One example may be the previously described situation of insufficient compliance by juvenile courts with *Parham* protections. If, in the *Parham* context, the state has an interest in not having thrust on it patients who are not in need of state hospitalization, then the state itself might seek to challenge a court order mandating that a minor be kept and treated at the hospital for a specified minimum time period.[5] Importantly, given the helplessness and the general unavailability of advocacy services, it is helpful to recognize that such a challenge, if not brought by the hospital, will probably not be brought at all. Such a hospital-initiated challenge, incidentally, would likely help to quiet complaints that hospitals, for bureaucratic and budgetary reasons, actually have an interest in retaining a *high* patient population and thus, in retaining even patients who do not need hospital services.

Although, as noted earlier, it now seems unlikely that the Supreme Court will, through constitutional construction, mandate major changes in mental health law, those changes may nonetheless very well occur even without constitutional command. In the area of criminal procedure, for example, after the Burger Court began backing off from and diluting decisions announced by the Warren Court, a number of state courts began to interpret state law and *state* constitutional provisions as requiring protections *greater than* the minimal protections required by Burger Court interpretations of the *federal* consititution.[6] In mental health law, where public and judicial sentiment for rights may outstrip the sentiment for rights of criminal suspects and prisoners, state court decisions may, by the force of their own constitutional provisions, require results in excess of what the Supreme Court would mandate as a national norm. If so, state court rulings may resemble the rulings rendered by many lower federal courts (*Lessard, Wyatt,* etc.) before the Burger Court indicated its reluctance to read the U.S. Constitution expansively in the field of mental health law.

Even more probable, major changes in mental health law—above and beyond changes required by federal constitutional command—are likely to emanate from state legislative halls. To date, many state legislatures (Arizona is a good example) have, on their own initiative (and without prodding from court cases in their jurisdiction), enacted progressive mental health statutes.

Such legislative reforms (as well as reforms mandated by state court cases) are likely to come about, however, only if the decision makers are informed of actual practices, abuses, and potential alternative courses of action. Many mechanisms are available for collecting and disseminating information regarding the actual administration of mental health law. Test-case litigation, for example, is thought to be useful not simply in setting precedents in successful cases, but also in raising the consciousness of the public, the press, and the legislature about essential policies, practices, and conflicts. If a legislature senses the existence of a troublesome area, it may, through the process of legislative hearings, muster the type of material (and the sentiment) necessary to achieve effective law reform.

Moreover, policy makers are perhaps most likely to become informed of actual practices and of workable alternatives by mental health law scholars and students who undertake empirical investigations of mental health law in operation and who compare and contrast the workings of one system with the workings of alternative systems in operation elsewhere. In fact, the empirical study on the administration of psychiatric justice in Arizona (the subject matter of Chapter 4) led to widespread legislative and administrative reform. It led, in short, to a major revamping of the state's civil commitment system,[7] and seems as well to have been of use in other jurisdictions. Many of the issues raised in this book, both "first generation" and "second generation" issues,[8] seem to be equally amenable to empirical and doctrinal examination. It may be, then, that the future of mental health law will be largely dependent on the future of mental health law scholarship.

NOTES

[1]Rennie v. Klein, 462 F. Supp. 1131 (D.N.J. 1978) and 476 F. Supp. 1294 (D.N.J. 1979); Rogers v. Okin, 478 F. Supp. 1342 (D. Mass. 1979). *See also* A. BROOKS, LAW, PSYCHIATRY AND THE MENTAL HEALTH SYSTEM 258–259 (Supp. 1980).

[2]99 S.Ct. 2493 (1979).

[3]Mental Health Commitments of Children in Custody (September, 1979) (unpublished).

[4]*Id.*

[5]In a letter to the legislature commenting on the report cited in note 3, I noted that some solutions to the *Parham*-type problems could be achieved through litigation initiated by the state hospital. The state hospital agreed and brought an action resulting in the clarification of several major juvenile commitment questions. State *ex rel.* Dandoy v. Super. Ct., No. 14743–PR (Ariz. Sup. Ct., 6/4/80).

[6]*See generally* Wilkes, *The New Federalism in Criminal Procedure: State Court Evasion of the Burger Court*, 62 KY. L.J. 421 (1974): Wilkes, *More on the New Federalism in Criminal Procedure*, 63 KY. L.J. 873 (1975).

[7]Shuman, Hegland, & Wexler, *Arizona's Mental Health Services Act: An Overview and an Analysis of Proposed Amendments*, 19 ARIZ. L. REV. 313 (1978) (the Act was a result of the 1970–71 study; the proposed amendments, an outgrowth of a later study, were also enacted—in a form rather similar to the form in which they were proposed). For another example of the persistent interrelationship between scholarship and law reform in the area of mental health law, *see* Contemporary Studies Project, *Involuntary Hospitalization of the Mentally Ill in Iowa: The Failure of the 1975 Legislation*, 64 IOWA L. REV. 1284 (1979).

[8]For more on "second generation" issues, *see Mental Health and Human Rights: Report of the Task Panel on Legal and Ethical Issues*, 20 ARIZ. L. REV. 49 (1978).

Index